T0314250

THE ASCENT OF
MARKET EFFICIENCY

THE ASCENT OF MARKET EFFICIENCY

Finance That Cannot Be Proven

Simone Polillo

CORNELL UNIVERSITY PRESS   ITHACA AND LONDON

First published 2020 by Cornell University Press

Library of Congress Cataloging-in-Publication Data

Names: Polillo, Simone, 1978- author.
Title: The ascent of market efficiency : finance that cannot be proven /
    Simone Polillo.
Description: Ithaca [New York] : Cornell University Press, 2020. |
    Includes bibliographical references and index.
Identifiers: LCCN 2019050409 (print) | LCCN 2019050410 (ebook) |
    ISBN 9781501750373 (hardcover) | ISBN 9781501750380 (epub) |
    ISBN 9781501750397 (pdf)
Subjects: LCSH: Efficient market theory. | Economics—Sociological aspects. |
    Knowledge, Sociology of.
Classification: LCC HG101 .P656 2020 (print) | LCC HG101 (ebook) |
    DDC 332—dc23
LC record available at https://lccn.loc.gov/2019050409
LC ebook record available at https://lccn.loc.gov/2019050410

Contents

THE ASCENT OF
MARKET EFFICIENCY

INTRODUCTION

The Data-Method-Theory Triad,
or Why Finance Cannot Be Proven

Over the past half century, in the United States and many other countries, finance
has become deeply enmeshed in, and consequential for, everyday life. Virtually
ubiquitous and all-powerful, financial markets now play a fundamental role in
determining the life chances of individuals, serving as indispensable sources of
funding both for everyday necessities, as testified by the expansion of credit card–
fueled expenses, and for lifelong savings strategies—witness the proliferation of
long-term, heftier investments, from retirement portfolios to car loans and home
mortgages.

There are many complex reasons behind the rise of financial markets, ranging
from the emergence of institutional investors (i.e., nonfinancial institutions whose
budgets rely on substantial trades in financial securities) to the political support
national governments and international financial institutions have lent to the financial sector over this multidecade period; from the move of mass production
away from developed countries, and its replacement by financial activities, to the
rise of globalization. Each of these dimensions has drawn substantial scholarly
interest. We know less about how financial markets have gained *intellectual credibility*: how financial economists successfully defend financial markets and make
a case for their fundamental and positive role in the economy when they have
failed to provide an analytically sound and theoretically robust framework to explain how markets behave. This puzzle is the focus of this book.

In the 1950s, financial markets became the object of analysis of a new
discipline—financial economics—and have shaped its evolution ever since. It
would not be an exaggeration to say that the new discipline of financial economics

was made possible by a certain way of theorizing, collecting data about, and analyzing markets. Central to this new approach to modeling market behavior is what came to be known as the *efficient-market hypothesis*. The hypothesis entered the canon of financial economics and went on to shape its trajectory for years to come. In the process, it changed the professional status of financial analysts: self-professed "new finance men," armed with this new analytical toolkit, with its new methods, mathematical models, and data, could now claim that their work was scientific rather than merely technical, systematic rather than impressionistic, and based on rigorous empirical evidence rather than on anecdote.

How did the efficient-market hypothesis allow financial economists to recast their work in scientific terms? According to the hypothesis, markets are efficient when individuals can make financial decisions on the basis of all relevant information. No theory can fully or even satisfactorily explain why they make these decisions, and a theory will certainly not predict *what* specific decisions individuals will make. Some investors may want to hold an asset as a form of long-term saving; others may want to hold an asset on a bet that its price will go up in the very short term. Some may feel intimidated by the risky nature of an investment; others may be drawn to it precisely because of the risk.

None of these contingencies matters, though, because when financial markets operate free from outside interference, they price assets such that all relevant information is incorporated within them. Therefore, it becomes impossible to predict how prices will change over time. The moment that new information becomes available, prices change to reflect it. The theory of efficient markets is therefore a theory of unpredictable markets.

This foundation of unpredictability is surprising for several reasons, both political and intellectual. Why should unpredictable markets be entrusted with the central role they now play in modern economies? In the period leading up to the Great Depression, and then again after the end of World War II, there was renewed faith in attempts to theorize what scholars thought were the underlying driving forces operating behind markets; and inchoate theories about the possibility of predicting the behavior of financial assets, and of the markets in which they were traded, started gaining traction. Financial analysts understood that past economic behavior influenced the future; so, in the hope of learning useful lessons they could apply to their own economic situation, they began to look back at economic history, considering it a source of knowledge about markets.

But the perspective of unpredictable markets, based on the idea that the market makes such exercises in prediction futile, and the analyses of individual strategies they encourage a foolish waste of time, vanquished this conflicting view once and seemingly for all. By the 1960s, it was becoming common sense that, through the workings of the market itself, the moment new information about assets traded in the market became available, the prices were updated accordingly. No other arrangement could accomplish such a feat: as long as the market set prices in such a way that they would reflect all available information, rational investors were better off trusting the market. Those financial analysts who claimed to be able to beat the market were thus seen as charlatans and hypocrites; rational investors should ignore them. Because market prices were the best evaluations of the value of an asset, they held no secrets. Rational economic decisions could, and should, be made on the basis of market prices alone.

The idea that markets are unpredictable and therefore *better* at allocating resources than the recommendations and plans devised by specialists was partly an attack on the investment management profession. It also became the core idea of a broader movement—some call it neoliberalism (see, for instance, Slobodian 2018), others market fundamentalism (Block and Somers 2016)—whose central ideological message was that markets were superior to any other sort of economic intervention. According to this view, financial markets, and by extension all markets, can allocate claims to ownership over valued resources efficiently when they are freed from the interference of noneconomic actors, like governments in their capacity as regulators. It is, in fact, precisely when markets are infused with personal contacts, collusions, and counterproductive outside regulation that they stop working efficiently. Impersonality and unpredictability, by contrast, go hand in hand with efficiency. Let the market serve as the ultimate arbiter of value, and the economy will flourish.

Even when we take into account the broader political context, the intellectual puzzle of how financial economists came to associate efficiency with unpredictability remains unsolved. Early scholarly investigations into market behavior may have looked like predictive failure, or at least a potential deficiency in explanation. Some of these early studies of the behavior of financial securities did indeed uncover anomalous patterns, and not always small ones, which could have made market efficiency seem like nothing more than an inability to understand the nature and causes of these patterns in complex data. More important is that the efficient-market *hypothesis* (and this is perhaps the reason why financial scholars keep referring to it as a hypothesis rather than a theory), because it theorizes on the basis of *absence of evidence, cannot be* proved. Testing the theory empirically requires making additional assumptions about the behavior of markets: only if those assumptions are correct can the failure to detect patterns be construed as the *absence* of patterns. Financial economists recognized almost immediately the severity of the problem posed by the "joint hypothesis": understanding how markets behave and whether markets behave efficiently are two sides of the same coin. Yet financial economists invested their energies on efficiency, bracketing off anomalies or treating them as additional factors that, once they were accounted for, helped preserved the notion of efficiency. Financial economists then used the efficient-market hypothesis to back up a broader claim that their research was based on science: that they were not engaging in the impressionistic and therefore inexact analysis of financial markets. The joint hypothesis was treated, de facto, as a unitary hypothesis, shifting with the context of the specific study at hand, with efficiency serving as the foundational framework that gave the hypothesis meaning, and with empirical tests proving not efficiency per se but the myriad (and often changing) assumptions necessary for efficiency to be operationalized.

By the early 1980s, as a result, market efficiency was widely recognized as financial economists' main explanatory achievement, indeed as a resounding success. Alternative perspectives lost out and were forgotten. By accepting that financial markets priced assets rationally, in the sense that investors and traders always used all available and relevant information as they assessed the value of financial assets, such that no systematic patterns could be uncovered after their intervention had been properly taken into account, financial economists moved away from the kinds of questions that were initially quite central to their emerging field. These questions would return with a vengeance later in the wake of the financial crisis, especially after 2007: Why do markets expand and then crash? How can markets be structured to encourage certain kinds of behaviors and discourage others? To be sure, as a result, the efficient-market hypothesis is no longer as dominant today as it was in the 1980s, as investigations into the irrational behavior of markets have begun to make an impact. But proponents of efficient markets continue to stand their ground.

Understanding the rise and persistence of market efficiency as a theory of market behavior, I argue, requires a focus on processes that are, ironically, quite personal, filled with trust and emotion, contingent but not unpredictable, or at least amenable to historical reconstruction. These are the processes that gave rise to scholarly networks, specifically to the intellectual relationships that financial economists established with one another. Accordingly, this book focuses on the people who gave us the fullest elaboration of this perspective: those US-based scholars of finance, such as Eugene Fama and Richard Roll, who played a crucial role in granting coherence and credibility to the idea that markets are unpredictable. These financial economists argued, with increasing success over time, that it was not possible to anticipate the future movement of stock prices, because any relevant information was already incorporated into present prices. Financial economists argued that unpredictability is a signal of markets processing information efficiently rather than a symptom of underlying problems or of explanatory deficiencies in the model itself.

Zeroing in on how financial economists collaborated, provided mentorship to new scholars, and developed distinctive ideas about the kind of work they considered to fall under the purview of financial economics will reveal the social processes and social practices that allowed market efficiency to flourish as a theory of market behavior. Financial economists, I argue, built their discipline through a new interplay of *theory*, *methods*, and *data*: they recombined theory, method, and data so that data analysis would drive the development of the discipline. In general, theory, data, and methods form a triad in social research: they can each provide the focus of attention of distinctive networks, and disciplines crystallize through the combination of any of these networks in different ways. In the case of financial economics, networks of data analysts provided the original, creative impetus; theory and methods developed around data analysis. This particular combination gave financial economics a distinctive *affect*: as a social structure of collaboration and coauthorship, financial economics came to be held together by a common appreciation of distinctive scholarly virtues, through which financial scholars increased trust in one another, made their work credible, and built a self-sustaining network pursuing research on efficient markets.

Centered on Eugene Fama, financial economists developed collective understandings of what counted as knowledge and what made a scholar trustworthy. In both respects, data analysis became the primary driver of research that financial economists came to consider creative. Cutting-edge financial research analyzed data; as data analysis climbed to the apex of the theory-data-method triad, theory descended to the bottom. Over time, consensus grew about the virtues that should characterize sound scholarship in finance, and this allowed the structure of the network to expand and reproduce itself. Understanding how this network emerged, why it took the specific shape it did, and why it proved to be durable and resistant to critique for so long is the first set of goals of this book. Using the theory-method-data triad as a lens, and showing how it can yield a sharper focus on the dynamics of social knowledge, is the second and more general goal.

Is Efficiency an Objective Property of Markets?

Finding evidence for the configuration of data, theory, and methods that steered the network of financial economics toward market efficiency, and understanding its contours and significance, will take us on a journey through many different sociological theories. But before we embark on this journey, some potential objections should be addressed straightaway. A financial economist might suggest an easier and more straightforward answer to the puzzle of unpredictable markets: that the theory of market efficiency prevailed because it worked, and that it worked because it captured fundamental aspects of market behavior that other models, theories, or hypotheses simply did not. A sociologist of professions might say that the research program underlying market efficiency was made possible by the particular configuration of institutional resources and professional opportunities open to financial economists in the post–World War II period, and that understanding group dynamics comes with the risk of missing the forest for the proverbial trees. What if market efficiency is simply based on comprehensive data on financial markets, making it not a subjective theory based on experience but a systematic, scientific investigation of market processes? Let us begin with our hypothetical economist.

This economist would have a strong ally on her side: the committee that, in 2013, awarded Eugene Fama the Sveriges Riksbank Prize in Economic Sciences in Memory of Alfred Nobel. This is the brief justification motivating the award: "In the 1960s, Eugene Fama demonstrated that stock price movements are impossible to predict in the short-term and that new information affects prices almost immediately, which means that the market is efficient" (NobelPrize.org 2013). That it took the committee more than fifty years to recognize the importance of Eugene Fama—one of the founding fathers of financial economics, and its most steadfast proponent of the efficient-market hypothesis—can be construed as a testament to the rigor of the scientific process behind his work. It was only after sufficient evidence in support of the hypothesis had accumulated that Fama's hypothesis would receive such an important recognition. But there are at least two reasons to be doubtful about this account. One has to do with the kind of theory the efficient-market hypothesis is; the second, with the limits data play in proving, or disproving, such a theory.

First, as efficient-market theorists would themselves recognize, efficiency is, and has always been, less a factual representation of markets than an idealized model that nevertheless shapes the behavior of market agents (and often market regulators and policymakers as well). Economic theory is an intervention *into* the economic world that constitutes the practices through which that world is then constructed. Over the past two decades, scholars who have paid attention to this relationship between economic models and their object of analysis have described it as a process of mutual influence: put in the stronger language of MacKenzie (2006), one of the most sophisticated proponents of this approach, economic theory "performs" the economy. The approach has given rise to a school of thought labeled *social studies of finance*, whose proponents are concerned with the consequential linkages between the economy and economic theory. They say, for instance, that market efficiency becomes a powerful theory because it has practical consequences for the financial world, such as the creation of index funds, financial portfolios whose composition replicates the risk profile of the market as a whole, thereby directly incorporating fundamental insights from the efficient-market hypothesis. Scholars in this tradition would suggest that as index funds become more popular and widespread, the market starts behaving in the ways hypothesized by the theory behind these financial instruments.

The social studies of finance's claim that economic models are not neutral representations of some objective economic reality but rather "constitute" and "perform" that reality is crucial to our understanding of the power of economic theory. However, I argue that there is still theoretical work to be done to explain the successful rise of a theory of efficient markets. For one, as also argued by MacKenzie (2006), the simple adoption of a model by authoritative sources, either scholarly communities or broader groups of practitioners, and its subsequent dissemination do not imply that the model will affect the economy. Rather, the model has to produce some relatively stable outcome as well, which means that, for instance, it cannot be based on mathematical mistakes or produce results that others armed with better models may find easy to exploit to their own advantage. The properties of the model itself increase the likelihood of the model affecting the economy.

Does this mean that the model has to *work* before it can be *put to work*? The problem, I believe, is a larger one. Market efficiency is an abstract and general concept; it is only weakly related to the many and more specific models that scholars have shown to be amenable to practical use by market operators. It may well be that the success of these more specific models reinforces the theory. Yet, if we examine the historical trajectory of the theory and the details in the research process that led to its articulation, we will immediately see that the path to market efficiency was riddled with stumbling blocks and multiple forks in the road, and that choosing a route other than the one actually taken would have created different kinds of hypotheses about the nature of markets. As a distinct though related tradition in the sociology of knowledge and culture broadly termed the *strong program* informs us, a sociologist must treat any of the alternative paths not taken in the same way she or he would treat research deemed successful. Truthfulness is accomplished through social processes (Barnes 1986; Bloor 1991). It is therefore important to find out what theories, models, and hypotheses emerged as potential contenders to the efficient-market hypothesis, and understand their demise without resorting to the power of hindsight. I pursue this line of inquiry throughout the book.

More important, it also follows from this argument that there is no single test that can prove or disprove a general theory like market efficiency. This is the second reason we should be skeptical of the efficient-market hypothesis: even more complex tests are ultimately vulnerable to critiques of the adequacy of their own assumptions and the quality of the data on which they are based. "Underdetermination" is the core point of the Duhem-Quine thesis in the sociology of science:[1] theories are tested with data that may be flawed or incomplete; working assumptions, necessary to operationalize key constructs, make it impossible to directly test the central predictions of a theory (MacKenzie 2006, 23). For this reason, theories often survive a long time after they have allegedly been disproved. A field like financial economics, where data represent human activities and therefore cannot be controlled, manipulated, and experimented with in the ways data about *natural* objects can, is no exception (see, e.g., Hacking 1983).

One might even say that a theory like efficient markets is always, to some degree, underdetermined because its empirical content can be evaluated only by making additional hypotheses, which are themselves not tested. Eugene Fama (1970, 413–14) recognized as much: "The theory only has empirical content . . . within the context of a more specific model of market equilibrium, that is, a model that specifies the nature of the market 'equilibrium' when prices 'fully reflect available information.'" But the theory did not specify what this model of market equilibrium should look like; one had to make an assumption in this regard. As Richard Roll (1977, 145), a student of Fama, would later add: "There lies the trouble with joint hypotheses. One never knows what to conclude. Indeed, it would be possible to construct a joint hypothesis to reconcile any individual hypothesis to any empirical observation."

As a consequence, the success of market efficiency cannot be attributed exclusively either to some objective quality of the market itself or to its success in generating models that shape market behavior, because there is no direct, unmediated connection between the theory and the market, and the theory and the specific models employed in the market. Tests of market efficiency are always, also, tests of additional hypotheses about markets. While this flexibility has been generative of a vibrant research tradition, it forces us to rethink the possibility of a direct relationship between the efficient-market hypothesis and specific financial practices. By the same token, market behavior is shaped by academic theory, to be sure; but it responds to other forces as well. And so does financial economics as a discipline. It might be informed and shaped by developments in real financial markets, but this is not the whole story.

One might then argue that understanding market efficiency is not so much a matter of assessing the accuracy of the model but more a matter of understanding how the discipline that produced the model became more powerful. And, to be sure, between 1950 and 1980, financial economics underwent a process of mathematization, formalism, and abstraction, mimicking the path followed by financial economists' more powerful disciplinary counterparts, the economists, in their quest for scientific authority. As shown by scholars who emphasize the cultural and political foundations of expertise, working under the umbrella of the *sociology of professions and expertise*, US economists tend to understand themselves as autonomous professionals for hire as private consultants ("merchant professionals," as Marion Fourcade calls them): formalism allows them to claim that their expertise is based on technical skills, the development of which takes years of specialized training (Fourcade 2009; Steinmetz 2005; Whitley 1986a).

Perhaps, then, it is complex mathematics, embedded in a disciplinary framework capable of accumulating increasing amounts of resources for research, that gave us the theory of efficient markets? Pragmatically, recasting financial economics in a mathematical language allowed financial economists to distance themselves from financial analysts, the kinds of practitioners they accused of pseudo-scientism (in an early period in the discipline, for instance, financial economists would openly deride "chartalists," the practitioners who claimed to be able to predict the future value of stock prices based on their analysis of past stock price behavior). Mathematization also served to make financial economics look more legitimate in the eyes of economists, opening up funding opportunities as well as institutional venues within which financial economics could thrive (especially the business school).

Yet, the rise of mathematics in financial economics is not quite the same as the rise of the theory of efficient markets. Mathematics is a language, and this term implies that more than one theory of market behavior can be articulated in it; indeed, more than one theory was. In fact, as we shall see, market efficiency was less the result of investigations formalizing market behavior in new ways than it was the result of empirical studies of market data. For similar reasons, attributing the rise of the efficient-market hypothesis to the rise of neoliberalism is useful but insufficient. Friedrich Hayek, the intellectual father and tireless promoter of neoliberal thought, whose role in making Chicago a neoliberal stronghold has been widely recognized (Overtveldt 2009), had returned to Europe by the time the efficient-market hypothesis was taking shape, and it is difficult to draw a direct line between his scholarship and financial economics. To be sure, without the political savvy of academic entrepreneurs and scholars such as Aaron Director and Milton Friedman—themselves very successful at building neoliberal institutions at the University of Chicago—it would be difficult to explain why financial economics became so receptive to arguments about the superiority of markets (Mirowski and Plehwe 2009). However, explaining why a specific theory prevailed as a model for the behavior of markets—how the joint hypothesis was swiftly reframed as allowing for empirical tests of market efficiency—forces us to dig deeper. We must extend our analysis to the research process itself if we want to reconstruct the emergence of this powerful and consequential theory; especially if we believe the idea to be enmeshed in the broader politics of the neoliberal movement, it is imperative to flesh out the specific mechanisms by which the ideology acquired academic currency. And to do so, it is helpful to pay attention to the intellectual strategies and research practices through which scholars of financial markets kept the theory open ended while making it resistant to critique: how they turned it into a springboard for new innovations and creative inquiries rather than treating it as a mere hypothesis to be tested.

In sum, how financial economists made unpredictable markets look like desirable social arrangements is, to some degree, a puzzle in the sociology of ideas. Current perspectives on the rise of financial economics give us important building blocks and empirical material to work with, but they cannot solve this puzzle. If, on the other hand, we take the perspective of those who worked multiple decades to make the theory credible and inspirational for future work, a solution is possible. Their work, as I will show, involved building trust across a community—a *network*—of data analysts rather than coming up with complex mathematics, testable hypotheses, or new methods. They certainly engaged in those activities too, but they did so with the goal of building the network. Market efficiency came into being not because it was theoretically strong but rather because relevant data were assembled to make it look reasonable and valid.

The problem of underdetermination, that there may be several theories that explain the given data, extends to data as well. No individual dataset can disprove a theory as a whole, and this applies to financial economists, as it does to any other scientist (social or natural). Data do not have intrinsic power or self-evident properties. They are never complete and free of error, so when data fail to verify theory, it may be as much a problem with the data as it is with the theory itself (Gitelman 2013). Moreover, whenever the tendency to quantify prevails over other approaches, it necessarily leaves out potentially important areas of inquiry where quantification is more difficult (Espeland and Stevens 1998). Quantification changes the kinds of questions a field is able to pursue. When numbers become central to a discipline, then, it is because a network of scholars orients itself toward producing knowledge in a certain way: their intellectual strategies develop in a broader context, and without an understanding of this context, we cannot make sense of the centrality data take to the kind of research carried out in the network.

Empirical research came to mean something quite specific in the context of financial economics, and only when financial economists settled the question of what data could do for their theoretical and methodological purposes, and what theory should look like as a result, did they turn data analysis into a driver of innovative financial knowledge rather than a means of verifying theory. Financial economists confronted particularly thorny questions along the way: What should count as empirical research, or specifically, what would it take to understand and reach a working agreement on what constituted empirical verification and data? What methods should financial economists consider appropriate, and how should they arrive at an understanding of the limits of those methods? What about theory? Since theory was not understood as prediction, what, then, was it? How did these three aspects of financial research—theory, methods, and data analysis—intersect? Just as scholars of knowledge argue that underdetermination is overcome depending on complex factors that researchers cannot assume to operate a priori, understanding how the idea of efficient markets became crucial to the way financial economists model markets means looking at this accomplishment as a practical solution to the challenges of doing financial research.

This book draws from a long tradition in the sociology of knowledge springing from the strong program (e.g., Bloor 1991) and finds answers to these questions by examining alternative arguments, disagreements, and pathways that were not followed. Financial economists, I argue, built their discipline on new ways of manipulating data. In the 1950s, for the first time, they developed the capacity to muster data with ease, in formats that permitted endless manipulations. And as a result, they began to use those data as truthful representations of markets. Rather than framing data as foundations for new theoretical advances, financial economists now used them to produce empirical patterns to which they could give economic meaning. In the case of market efficiency, they articulated the notion of unpredictability of future prices from the data rather than from theory. And later, after much struggle and opposition, they retrofitted unpredictability into a theoretical property of markets. An important reason for their success is that, with efficient markets, they could construct a divide between financial economics and financial experts, which gave the theory a populist connotation. The unpredictability of security prices became a tool financial economists could rely on to promote the creation of financial instruments that would help expand participation in financial markets. An individual investor, equipped with the right instruments, could trade financial assets of his or her own accord without having to seek the (expensive) advice of investment managers. Thanks to their data practices, financial economists could frame the market as open and democratic, rather than subject to manipulation by insiders.

What I add to this well-known story is that the settlement of controversy around market efficiency depended on a particular configuration of networks, which in turn produced durable, affect-laden values as it shifted the balance away from the pursuit of theoretical goals and toward the analysis of data as a way to build theory. Innovation in data practices intervened at a point where financial economists understood theory, methods, and data differently than they do now, precisely because there was not a clear line dividing academically oriented scholars and professionals like portfolio managers. This shift contributed to a general perception of finance as a low-status, vocational, applied field, one in which practical orientations prevailed over scholarly concerns. An important reason was that information about stock prices—the most important data for financial analysis concerned with market behavior and investment—was publicly available, but it was not easy to process: it was reported inconsistently and was therefore difficult to analyze. Consider, for instance, how the economist Alfred Cowles opens his 1960 rebuttal to a critique the econometrician Holbrook Working had just published of his earlier work, by pointing to the difficulty of establishing the nature of the data on which that work was based: "The Cowles-Jones 1937 *Econometrica* paper makes no reference to whether the data employed in the analyses there reported in Table 1 and Figure 1 were averages of time units or closing quotations. No statement is made, for example, as to whether the unit of one month was an average of daily, weekly, or high and low stock prices for the month, or whether it was an average of end-of-the-month prices. Our work sheets of 23 years ago have not been preserved and today I have no clear recollection as to details regarding the data employed" (Cowles 1960, 910). The problems highlighted by Cowles characterized other studies as well. In general, whether security prices were reliably recorded at the daily close of the stock market, or were averages of daily quotation, or were computed in an altogether different way were questions defying easy answers. Uncertainty around what the numbers meant made it particularly difficult to build time-series data. That computers and electronic databases were only beginning to make an appearance added to the problem of consistent manipulation of data for the purpose of analysis, which remained difficult and was often outright impossible. Market analysis was therefore the purview of financial analysts, professionals who made a living from giving financial advice and were, as a result, less than transparent about the foundations on which such advice was built.

For the market to become available as an object of analysis, then, at a minimum, reliable and openly accessible data on the market were needed first (Fisher and Lorie 1964; Lorie 1966). Yet, even as the advance of computers was opening new avenues for sophisticated financial analysis, a number of issues, with no clear technological solutions, remained to be settled for the market to be understood as possessing certain qualities. What data should be used? How should data be handled? One paradox here was that the more data availability increased, the more it became unclear whether it was appropriate to test the theory with data. When should data collection stop? Should researchers build their theories in one dataset and then test them on a different dataset? Or should financial economists limit themselves to using the best available data and not refrain from claiming that their results were generalizable? There are no technical solutions to these problems, but as I show in chapter 2, what technique cannot achieve may be accomplished through other pathways.

The main path through which financial scholars came to see data as legitimate foundations for their analysis of markets is through the articulation of a new style of research that, instead of highlighting the revolutionary nature of what they were doing, emphasized the continuity that data analysis afforded the field. Data analysis allowed financial economists to claim that they were providing reasonable tests of theoretical perspectives. When they experienced opposition from colleagues, financial economists opted for a strategy of letting the data "speak for themselves." If the analysis of data on security prices yielded no pattern, they saw no point in building more elaborate models, importing new analytical methods from other disciplines, or developing new techniques altogether. Those financial economists who did make a case for new methodological tools acquired a reputation for innovative but idiosyncratic work: they did not become the leaders of the field. Fischer Black, the researcher renowned for his work on the pricing of options and on the Capital Asset Pricing Model, is the most illustrious example of a scholar whose innovative work was impactful but did not generate a research group and long-term trajectory.

This is not to say that the practices and patterned interactions that made market efficiency possible were arbitrarily selected or, worse, were picked when other—better—practices were available. It is rather to say that the extent to which research practices were appropriate for the study of markets could not be known a priori, and that the object and practices evolved together. We can reconstruct the path that financial economists took in developing their theory of financial markets.

A focus on financial economics as a constellation of practices anchored to innovation in data-processing networks also yields a number of more general insights. It introduces a new dimension to our understanding of the ways knowledge advances: theory, data, and methods can each provide the focus of attention of distinctive networks, and different disciplines can crystallize these networks in different ways. The focus shifts from the general notion that collaborative networks motivate the production of knowledge, to the more specific idea that collaborative networks developing around the pursuit of different perspectives on knowledge set themselves a range of tasks depending on the kind of innovation they are pursuing. In other words, there are patterns in the ways knowledge is produced, depending on the extent to which different network configurations are assembled in the pursuit of such knowledge.

How Understanding Financial Economics Helps Us Build a Theory of Creative Knowledge

Theory, data, and methods are the three arenas—the triad—I focus on to understand how financial economics developed. The insights these concepts afford into the rise of the theory of efficient markets would be lost from different perspectives. But characterizing market efficiency as an innovation in data analysis giving rise to a particular kind of network, I believe, also advances our more general understanding of how knowledge is made, especially in the human and social sciences. Financial economics embodies a constellation of practices with respect to theory, data, and methods that can be found in other disciplines. Therefore, in this book I focus on how financial economics works and unfolds, with an eye to what the development of financial economics can teach us about the more general problem of knowledge production in the human sciences.[2] There are both empirical and theoretical reasons for choosing to focus on financial economics, and for highlighting theory, methods, and data as three dimensions of knowledge production. Having summarized the empirical and historical reasons behind the use of this framework, I now expand on the theory and then return to why financial economics constitutes a particularly useful case.

A more traditional perspective in the sociology of knowledge would find it sufficient to draw a distinction between theory and observation, or theoretical and empirical perspectives, and then take a position on the nature of this distinction. Since Karl Popper's seminal intervention, much ink has been spilled on the question of the extent to which theory should be falsified by data. Therefore, I need to justify the usefulness of drawing a more fine-grained distinction among theory, methods, and data. Aren't data and methods, after all, part of the more general process of empirical verification?

The idea that there is a neat and unbridgeable separation between theory and data has been most successfully debunked by Bruno Latour (esp. 1987), who proposes that theory and observation lie on a continuum by contextualizing this continuum within chains of "inscriptions," or "visual displays" that "translate" and "represent" richer information flowing into the nodes of the network where the "device" producing the inscription is located. At the core of the network of inscriptions, Latour argues, lies a "center of calculation," where traces of more localized knowledge are processed in such a way that they can be stabilized and made portable so that they can travel further up the chain, all the while remaining faithful to the traces they subsume (Latour 1987, 215–57). For instance, the Census Bureau might collect information on the total number of births for a given year; this number is obviously not the same as the crying babies it represents, quips Latour, but it allows for a degree of manipulation and control that would not be possible if the number could not be communicated across different departments in the bureau and beyond, or if the number kept changing, or if it was simply wrong (1987, 234–35). Moreover, the number of births in, say, 2017 can be combined with numbers from other years, thereby generating a series that allows for other calculations (e.g., trends in births), or with other indicators, so that one can compute, say, birthrates. As the traces of crying babies travel up the networks that make up the centers of calculation, the representations become more abstract and theoretical, and their properties can be increasingly manipulated without regard to the underlying traces they represent and translate: birthrates formally resemble mortality rates by virtue of similar inscription practices (they can both be treated as rates, that is).

In Latour's understanding of science, then, empirical observation and theory are activities connected through concrete, empirically observable (though complex) links. Theory increases as one moves toward the core of a center of calculation, where experts manipulate more formalized traces than the experts operating at an order of abstraction below.

Latour's understanding of theory and observation in terms of a network pushing information up and down its constitutive chains, in a format that makes it usable for the purposes of the level it reaches, highlights the importance of paying attention to both the methods (or practices) whereby information is transmitted across a network and the nature of information itself. This expansive picture of what a science might look like is the picture of a successful science. Thus, whether a center of calculation is firmly in place, and whether it centralizes information flows to facilitate control from the top, are empirical matters and matters of degree. Latour's broader point (in line with the constructivist approach to knowledge that he spearheaded) is that a successful science tends to create a boundary between its accumulated knowledge, the validity of which is surrounded by consensus, and the scientific frontier ("science in the making"), where disagreement and conflict generate a creative push for innovation. But not all sciences accomplish this feat, nor would all sciences consider it within reach.

In some sciences, controversies are never settled. As Panofsky (2014) shows for the case of behavior genetics, some scientific disciplines are simply unable to generate a stable framework that allows them to tell the good, scientifically sound claims from the less scientific ones. In other sciences, like financial economics, controversies are not so much settled as they are reframed through interlocking debates about methods and data. The problem in such a case is twofold: How is stability achieved in a science where the settlement of conflicts about proper ways of understanding and representing data poses limits to what theoretical and methodological advances are possible? And, on the flip side, how is the research frontier constituted when settlement of controversies relies on acceptance of established ways of handling data?

To understand how a science, and especially a science of human processes and phenomena like financial economics, defines what counts as innovative knowledge, it is important to remind ourselves that science, whether narrowly or broadly construed, cannot be characterized as a unitary endeavor, reduced to a method, or neatly depicted as privileging one approach over others. This is true for the hard sciences as well. As Peter Galison argues with respect to scientific inquiry in physics, theory and observation (e.g., experiments) should be understood as potentially autonomous strata. In the context of physics, for instance, he submits:

> At least since the early twentieth century, physicists have themselves recognized the split between theorists and experimentalists. The two groups are frequently considered separately as they apply to graduate school; in graduate school they take different courses; subsequently they enter upon markedly different apprenticeships as they develop their research. Techniques and practices shared among experimentalists form their own, partially autonomous, traditions not necessarily coincident with theoretical traditions. Thus any model that we adopt, even a provisional one, ought to leave room not only for theoretical traditions, with breaks and continuities, but for experimental traditions with their own, equally complex set of internal dynamics. (Galison 1988, 208)

In other words, science (even hard science) emerges from the work of different communities of inquiry, trained in the mastery of different skill sets, focused on different questions, and organized around different styles of research and communication—even when they work within the same discipline. The communities are not entirely separate, but they are partially autonomous, at least to the extent that their members are selected through different criteria and rewarded according to different standards.

Whether a model of inquiry that works in the hard sciences, as posited by Galison (1988), can be applied to the human sciences as well is, of course, a difficult question. Mirowski (1995) suggests that recognizing the potential divide between theory and experiment sheds light on the development of econometrics, and especially the ways in which econometricians reach agreement on, or validate, empirical results: empirical researchers produce results they consider valid and credible, he suggests, not simply because they use appropriate econometric tools. Rather, empirical results are validated through complex interactions between theorists (both in econometrics and in economics as a whole) and applied econometricians. What to Galison, focused on the established discipline of physics, looks like a two-sided community becomes in Mirowski's more specialized case a multinested community.

I find it useful to introduce a further distinction as I generalize this model: in the humanities and social sciences, while experiments have become important methods of inquiry for certain disciplines, it is less a matter of theorists and "experimentalists" than it is a matter of theory, methods, and data coming together and intersecting in contingent ways that cannot always be encompassed through the language of experiments alone. Even Latour's centers of calculation, which specialize in making information more abstract the more it nears the core of the network, achieve this outcome when both the methods and the data themselves have been stabilized and turned into research practices by the specific networks that produce knowledge through them. One important reason for distinguishing among theory, data, and methods is that, as Zald (1995; see also Zald and Reed in Swedberg 2014) argues, *cumulation* is not the same thing as *progress*, in particular in the social and human sciences: the systematic storage and organization of knowledge do not go hand in hand with the achievement of new breakthroughs or new and creative ways of looking at the world.

This is the case, I would argue, in part because the scholarly networks focused on the organization and storage of data are often autonomous from those focused on the formal properties of knowledge (theory) and from those focused on the mechanics of identifying social scientific phenomena (methods). Distinguishing among theory, data, and methods helps show that advances in data collection, data processing, and data manipulation may not necessarily have the same implications for knowledge as do methodological advances: it is a matter that can be adjudicated only in the context of specific configurations.

At the same time, it is also important to remember that when we use the language of communities of inquiry, the language is not meant to be metaphorical. We are talking about concrete networks of relationships scholars create in order to advance knowledge in whatever guise they deem most important. My analysis of financial economics rests on these premises in order to focus on the communities of inquiry that build on theory, methods, and data, so that they will make innovative moves that shape a discipline. Theory, methods, and data serve to "focalize" the attention of a community of inquiry, much as Merton (1973, 452–53) argued that prominent, individual scientists serve to sharpen the focus of attention of a more diffused group. Understanding how communities of inquiry combine (or separate) theory, data, and methods allows us to say something about the quality of the research activities and the outcomes of these activities taking place in such communities. But, more specifically, understanding research as a constellation of practices—as patterns of activities focused on one or more modalities of producing knowledge, or as recombinations of the theory-method-data triad—also means understanding the qualities, or kinds, of social relations that underlie those practices. The term "community" is not precise, and I will soon replace it with the term "network." But it does have one advantage: it suggests the importance of trust and so serves to highlight two important issues. First, what happens to research when the communities that produce knowledge trust their members and/or trust outsiders? By contrast, what happens when members of a community of inquiry do not trust one another and/or face skeptical audiences? Second, what implications does the presence or lack of trust have on the kinds of creative constellations possible? Under what conditions do data networks take control of the innovative process?

Trust and Credibility: Building Scholarly Networks with Affect

Knowledge requires recognition, in the sense that individual producers of knowledge must impress on their expert peers the truthfulness of their discoveries—their contribution to knowledge must be recognized. Relevant outside communities must also be enlisted in the validation, certification, diffusion, and further refinement of knowledge claims (see esp. Bourdieu 1993). How scientific ideas gain credibility in the face of skeptical and potentially noncooperative or even hostile audiences is therefore a difficult problem, one that has implications for how we think about the role of trust in the production of knowledge.

Theodore Porter's work on numbers provides an important perspective. Porter (1995) approaches the problem of credibility from the point of view of quantification, and specifically the extent to which producers of a body of knowledge are secure enough to base their claims on their own expertise, or must resort to numbers in order to bolster their claims through more means that appear to be more objective. In this way, Porter thus argues that sciences (including both the physical and the social/human sciences) develop different "cultures of objectivity": when a discipline is strong and secure, its claim to knowledge through expertise, with all the tacit assumptions that make it possible, meets little criticism. For instance, Porter draws from Traweek's (2009) research on the world of high-energy physics to show how even a highly technical field can rely on very informal means to produce new knowledge: high-energy physicists do not rely on published work as much as they do on personal communication and personal networks. It is not that they do not publish but that publications are not the arena where innovative knowledge is disseminated.

When, by contrast, a discipline is weak and must face skeptical audiences unwilling to accept its expertise at face value, it resorts to quantification (from standardized metrics to statistics) to justify its claims. Quantification, in other words, is often a symptom of scientific weakness and uncertainty, not in the sense that powerful disciplines do not use numbers but in the sense that strong disciplines do not have faith in the belief that numbers can act as a substitute for expert knowledge. Quantification is a "weapon of the weak" (Scott 1990), as the quantified and standardized style in which knowledge is communicated derives from the inability of the discipline to exercise its professional authority uncontested: it is a form of "disciplinary" or "mechanical" objectivity (Megill 1994, 5–7; Porter 1995, 4–7) that tries to mask as much as possible the intervention and opinion of the expert.

Yet, this expansive view of how trust facilitates communication with outsiders needs some refinement when turned inward. Quantification and standardization can originate in different parts of a discipline, at different stages, and with different purposes, and it is not necessarily the presence or absence of skeptical external audiences that determines whether quantification will be a recognized and accepted strategy. Put differently, quantification may be intended to provide verification, contestation, or critique; it may also be a tool for the production of new knowledge. Often, knowledge producers will use quantification in both ways, so the two processes will occur simultaneously. Or, as in some of the cases discussed by Porter (1995), quantification may be resorted to in order to explain and justify claims that were originally made in a different language or that did not depend on strong faith in the objectivity of numbers.

It is easier to understand the range of possible scenarios if one starts with the idea that quantification is the work of specific networks. These networks face more or less skeptical audiences not only outside but also within the discipline and domain of knowledge they consider their home. What they experience is not so much a trade-off between expert knowledge and quantification. Quantification itself is a form of expertise, and whether networks make claims to discovery based on numbers, methods, theory, or a combination of any of these three practices depends on the degree to which they trust these practices and, conversely, the degree to which these practices are met with skepticism.

Trust and distrust are central ingredients of what Lorraine Daston (1995, 3–4) calls the "moral economy" of science, the broad web of "affect-saturated values" that members of a given community of inquiry weave together to develop common understandings of what constitutes good work and, just as important, what qualities a good scholar must possess. What questions are worth pursuing, suggests Daston, is partly a function of the qualities (even moral character) the practitioners of a given science strive to develop (see also Shapin 1994). Is a science successful when it produces precise measurements? Or should accuracy be privileged? Any of the several objectives a science sets out for itself may become a "virtue" worth pursuing for its own good. For instance, quantification can go hand in hand with theory, in what Whitley (2000) calls "conceptually integrated bureaucracies" like post-1945 physics: these cases correspond to Porter's strong, quantitative disciplines that can combine numbers with expert, even subjective, interpretation. But decrease the extent to which there is consensus over what technical approaches are best suited to produce analytically valid results, and you get what Whitley calls "partitioned bureaucracies," or scientific fields where there is a gap between analytical knowledge and empirical knowledge (as in economics).

The point is, if we understand theory, methods, and data as a triad—in terms of different practices enacted by different, though potentially overlapping, networks of inquiry—we can turn the trade-off between expert knowledge and quantification into a continuum. Numbers, for instance, may produce mechanical objectivity when disciplines interact with inquisitive publics, but their objectivity may not be accepted in quite the same way in conflicts within a given discipline with other like-minded scholars. Or numbers may generate trust both inside and outside. It is not that Porter does not recognize this; it is just that his focus is on the political regime within which expertise unfolds. What from the bird's-eye view of Porter looks like disciplines taking up strategies of quantification and standardization to protect themselves, upon closer inspection appear as networks within a discipline mobilizing symbolic and material resources to shape the development of knowledge.

Trust and Creativity

An approach to numbers in which the numbers constitute a solution to problems of distrust and skepticism may turn out to be more than a function of interactions between a discipline and an outside audience. It may also be a matter of how intradisciplinary networks hang together. If so, how can we reconceptualize trust and its relationship to knowledge, especially creative knowledge, in a more nuanced yet parsimonious way? Two reframings may be necessary. First, we need to shift our focus from the dissemination to the production of knowledge, and also to the role data are understood to play in this process. More specifically, as we have just seen, the extent to which data are framed as self-explanatory, objective, or conducive to new theoretical breakthroughs varies empirically not only as a function of the difficulties a discipline faces in having its results accepted but also in terms of how the development of knowledge itself unfolds. Data and methods are not just about testing or providing evidence. They are not just about making credible claims. Data and methods must be understood from the point of view of credibility and creativity, simultaneously, for under certain conditions, they can become the primary site of creative discoveries rather than being relegated to a more accessory or subordinate role.[3]

Second, attention to theory, data, and methods as a triad of potentially autonomous networks taking the lead in the production of innovative knowledge means understanding knowledge production dynamically, in particular through a lens that is attentive to both continuity and disruption. Continuity, as argued by scholars of creativity, is the background condition for the development of expertise in a domain. Disruption, by contrast, is the process by which a recombination of existing knowledge leads to new outcomes (Sawyer 2012). This second aspect of the creative process is intuitive: we tend to associate creativity with innovative, unexpected moves rather than with the interplay between training/familiarity and discontinuity/disruption. But it is precisely when disruption takes place within a well-defined domain that creativity becomes possible.[4]

Scholars who have looked at the process by which knowledge is creatively disrupted tend to emphasize micro- and macrolevel sources of disruption: from concrete networks of apprenticeship and collaboration, and specifically how they provide opportunities for innovators to exploit, to the role of technology (especially with respect to the hard sciences), to broader institutional transformations. A focus on numbers, quantification, and more generally data allows us to identify new potential sources of continuity and disruption, especially if we understand data not in contrast with expertise but in terms of moves data analysis affords a given community of inquiry. By breaking down science into its constituent networks, we gain appreciation of the multiple sources of innovation as well as the multiple potential obstacles in its path. Theory, data, and methods can fall within the purview of separate networks; whether any of these networks pursues traditional approaches, or welcomes innovative ones, is an empirical question.

None of this implies that theory, methods, or data refer to fixed entities: in sociology alone, Abend (2008) differentiates among seven ways of characterizing theory; methodological practices range from qualitative to quantitative and are often seen in opposition to each other; and data are similarly contested not just in terms of their validity or appropriateness but even in regard to their ontological status (e.g., Heritage 1984). And if the complexity of fixing the meaning of these terms in sociology makes the project quite daunting, attempts to define any of them in terms of fixed essences across several disciplines would ultimately be guaranteed to fail. Nevertheless, we do not need to rely on a priori definitions. Instead of searching for a common essence, we can take the perspective of the networks of scholars that, within a given discipline, or in interdisciplinary contexts, define themselves as theorists, methodologists, data analysts, or any combination of the three. We can observe how they base their arguments on practices they define as theoretical, methodological, or data centered. To the extent that networks of inquiry refer to their concerns as theoretical, methodological, or data oriented, this self-characterization gives us a sufficiently strong foundation to build on.

Continuity and disruption then become a matter of degree: networks of inquiry specializing in different kinds of practices (theoretical, methodological, data-focused) can come together to generate new puzzles and new solutions, producing new affect-laden values in the process. Theory, data, and method networks combine thanks to the development of particular affective orientations. In the following chapters I present an empirical characterization of affect-laden networks in the context of financial economics. Other disciplines will generate different affective dispositions, and my analysis of financial economics will provide at least a set of sensitizing concepts with which to identify these dispositions.

For now, it should suffice to make a few tentative points. Networks of inquiry centered on theory, data, or methods are sometimes encompassed within disciplines, where they develop distinctive approaches to their subject matter, different traditions, and different styles of thought. Thus, for instance, economic theory is different from sociological theory or political philosophy; social statistics as practiced in sociology is different from the kind of statistics practiced by political scientists or by econometrics (see Camic and Xie 1994 for the historical origins of these differences). Also, just as important, the management of social data is handled differently than the management of economic data, and the role and meaning of data vary as a function of discipline as well.

A disciplinary home affords a network the ability to develop its own distinctive forums, journals, and sometimes even conferences. Disciplines can therefore also provide the context for innovation, when they supply the networks with resources or allow for these networks to crisscross. A combination of networks happens when, say, scholars active in a theory-oriented network propose a theoretical advance along with a new method, or when scholars active in a method-oriented network introduce a new method uniquely suited to handle new kinds of data. The theory-data-method triad can be rearranged in different ways. Whether cross-network relationships are characterized by trust determines the extent to which innovation can take place in each of these networks simultaneously: Do specialists in the analysis of data recognize the importance of the tools devised by the methodologists? Do methodological experts favor an alliance with theorists in the pursuit of a new idea? Under certain circumstances, moreover, the networks can become more autonomous from their home discipline and open themselves up to borrowing and innovations from networks located in other disciplines. Thus, economics and sociology can be joined theoretically under the umbrella of rational choice theory. Or psychology and economics can be brought together through cognitive science–based experiments. These network-based recombinations of knowledge are possible to the extent that networks find sympathetic allies across disciplinary boundaries. In other words, theory, data, methods, or any combination of them, within or across disciplines, can be mobilized in the making of innovative knowledge to the extent that there are networks open to such moves. Shifting the triad by turning to previously underplayed research strategies can provide a springboard for creativity.

There is a dynamic of innovation and tradition that can play out in multiple networks simultaneously but can also take place differentially. My focus on networks and the theory-method-data triad they assemble is a way of translating Kuhn's classic discussion of the essential tension between tradition and innovation in science into a meso-level set of potential openings and opportunities. For instance, Camic and Xie (1994) show that statistics at the turn of the twentieth century drew much admiration from scholars: to them, it represented a new method that promised to put the social sciences on a new, scientific foundation. Yet the way disciplines like sociology, psychology, economics, and anthropology incorporated statistics into their frameworks varied dramatically, because each discipline sought simultaneously to conform to statistical standards of knowledge and differentiate itself from neighboring disciplines. This is an example of how even an allegedly monolithic and standardized discipline like statistics can have very different research implications once it interacts with different networks. Statistics allowed social science disciplines to pursue both innovation and tradition, to be both cutting-edge in terms of methods of inquiry and traditionalist in terms of how the methods were conceptualized and concretely applied.

Another contribution to the sociology of knowledge that emerges from my argument lies in an elaboration of this point. Each network—theory, methods, data—develops practices of research that may or may not be amenable to cross-pollination, or exchange with other networks. One network may be more collaborative than others, it may have different expectations as to how research should be communicated, and so on. Whether a certain configuration is desirable is often a function of how disciplines are perceived with respect to broader hierarchies: as Simonton (2004) shows, sciences can be ranked in terms of as many as seven dimensions, ranging from whether a discipline thinks of its discoveries as laws or theories to whether researchers within a discipline have a consensual understanding of their subject matter. More consensual, harder disciplines draw more prestige than more fragmented, softer ones. One could therefore hypothesize that disciplines positioned on the low end of this hierarchy are more likely to borrow from above disciplines than vice versa: sociology will borrow from economics, but not the other way around.

But if we break down disciplines into networks, this may not always be the case. To the extent that data do not simply validate knowledge but underlie data expertise and therefore constitute a domain within which creative moves can be made, whether data drive creative knowledge is a function of how data networks interact with method- and theory-oriented networks in ways that do not necessarily, or neatly, map onto disciplinary hierarchies. One potential scenario is that the networks come together in a way that carves out an opportunity space for innovative moves in one network, backed up by a reinforcement of tradition in others. This, as I argue, is the case of financial economics, where already-existing theories of markets and already-existing methodological approaches to the study of markets were reinforced just as financial economists were proposing new ways of handling data.

One suggestive, more contemporary example that displays a similar logic is big data, a diffuse intellectual movement that calls for theory to be abandoned in favor of letting the data speak for themselves. With big data, any theory-driven explanation becomes suspect. Like financial economics, big data fashions itself as an innovation in the management and manipulation of data. Also, like financial economics (especially in its early stages), big data does not rely on sophisticated statistical methods. Just as financial economists abandoned theoretical innovation so as to mitigate resistance from more powerful theoretical networks in economics, and adopted well-understood statistical techniques to assuage the fears of methodological traditionalists, so too big-data proponents do not focus on theory or methods but on data management techniques themselves. To be sure, unlike financial economists, big-data analysts tend to be scornful of theory and methods; perhaps this is a symptom of the increased prominence, legitimacy, and resource-rich role of datasets in modern society. But if my argument is correct, avoidance of theory and methodological innovation is also a sign of distrust in the networks through which such innovative moves could be made. Because they trust data and data analysis alone, the affect of big-data scientists is different from the affect of financial economists. We will return to this comparison in the concluding chapter.

Innovative knowledge, in short, can involve work originating with networks active in one or more of these arenas: intellectual creativity takes different forms depending on what creative moves are made within what network, ranging from purist to more hybrid approaches. Put in perhaps too simplistic a way: let theory drive innovation, and you get intellectual positions that emphasize the centrality of ideas, and debates around how ideas should be manipulated, synthesized, rendered more abstract or more concrete, and so on; let methods drive innovation, and you get debates about the importance of removing the point of view of the analyst from the study, and debates about replicability becoming central; let data drive innovation, and you get debates about the representativeness of data taking center stage. Combinations of innovative moves originating in different networks lead to different styles of doing research. Each network develops different modes of adjudicating what it considers important and worth focusing on, and what pathways are dead ends. Each network develops a distinctive affective disposition.

The triad of theory, methods, and data (with one or more practices at the apex, in any combination) defines the goals scholarly networks in the human sciences set for themselves. Financial economics allows us to see the formation of such a triad (a data-method-theory triad, since data and methods take the leading, creative edge) with great clarity. But this is not the only field where such a triad pushed the research frontier forward on the grounds of new empirical knowledge rather than through new theoretical or methodological approaches. Data-driven triads can emerge in any discipline, or they can recombine to embrace goals that may have little to do with data or quantification. The kinds of intersections that generate these networks, the meanings that circulate within them, and the combinations they propose all vary, constituting fascinating empirical material for the analyst, as well as important resources for the scholars themselves. Thus the very terms "theory," "data," and "methods" do not have a fixed meaning, and they may intersect in various ways in any given discipline. This flexibility gives academics opportunities to generate scholarly collaborations on multiple grounds. Such individuals may combine theory and methods in innovative ways, assemble new datasets, offer new methodologies, and so on. Different alignments of networks of research provide the ingredients for intellectual creativity in the human sciences. Elaborating and generalizing this point serves as the main theoretical contribution offered by this book.

Plan of the Book

Chapter 2 focuses on two debates from an early stage of financial economics, separated by ten years, and uses this comparison to highlight how stylistic changes, and in particular the emergence of a standard of reasonability, helped settle conflicts within the discipline and turn data analysis into the apex of what became the data-method-theory triad. Financial economists developed this mode of constructing credible arguments where data analysis played a new role by the late 1970s: data analysis should be reasonable rather than exact or objective, and these methods should be simple and easily derived from the existing analytical toolkit of statistics. Reasonableness and simplicity became affect-laden value orientations for financial economists. These affective dispositions helped financial research crystallize around an approach to data where current practices of manipulating and analyzing data were made legitimate.

Being reasonable and simple meant developing a set of agreed-upon practices that regulated data analysis and helped scholars differentiate between claims that were warranted and claims that were not. Therefore, reasonableness and simplicity were not simply cognitive categories; they were affect-laden values. Chapter 3 presents quantitative data on the development of collaboration in financial economics, and its relationship with success in the field, thereby reconstructing the structure of the network that reasonableness and simplicity helped bring together.

I show that financial economists tended to collaborate with the same people, repeatedly. They worked in small groups and, as a result, participated in an economy of affect, to repurpose a term from Lorraine Daston (1995), that privileged the communicability and interdependence of their findings rather than their precision or accuracy, as the centrality of data to what they did might suggest. The network of financial economics came to value communicability and interdependence along with reasonableness. I use a dataset of prizewinning papers as well as bibliometric and network data to present systematic, quantitative evidence about the kind of social structure that sustained these affective dispositions.

Chapter 4 zeroes in on the conflict between the exponents of two different and incompatible ways of conducting financial research (Fischer Black and Eugene Fama), and shows why one approach won the battle. I contrast the trajectory of the efficient-market hypothesis with that of the Capital Asset Pricing Model (CAPM). Financial economists ultimately relegated CAPM to the status of one among many competing (and, allegedly, more empirically accurate) methods of portfolio selection. Market practitioners continue using it to make quick, back-of-the-envelope calculations; academic scholars, however, have largely abandoned it as a theoretical framework (but see Dempsey 2013). While recognized as a "centerpiece of modern financial economics," CAPM is now mainly discussed in terms of historical significance, practical implications, and empirical shortcomings.

What accounts for the contrasting fortunes of these two models? The heart of the matter is that CAPM could be framed as one of the auxiliary assumptions that tests of the joint hypothesis of market efficiency relied on, but the reverse was true as well. Attending to the question of what theories could be falsified by what tests, I submit, requires investigation of the sociocultural and affective processes and practices through which economic knowledge was codified and disseminated. It requires an understanding of how the models were incorporated into scholarly networks that privileged data, and then methods, over theory.

Financial economists built a case that their discipline was scientific on the basis of their technical proficiency and access to new data, and the success of the efficient-market hypothesis helped them gain legitimacy for such a view. But there is much at stake in attempts to define financial economics as a science, especially if, as critics have charged, this term does not capture the nature of financial knowledge, and financial economists appropriate it simply to secure prestige. Such debates were common in the formative periods of the discipline as well, when calls for financial economics to become a positive science were met by resistance from institutionalists, who believed the discipline to be much closer to history and political economy than to statistics and mathematics.

In chapter 5, I turn the question about the scientific status of the discipline into two empirical questions concerning the degree to which finance is scientific, and the kind of science financial economists pursue. Focusing on articles published in the *Journal of Finance* between 1950 and 2000, I investigate the forms and practices financial economists came to rely on to communicate their results to one another. I document the ways in which financial economics changed as mathematics and statistics became dominant, and how, in particular, mathematics and statistics changed the affective dispositions of financial economists. I analyze how financial scholars used specific communicative practices and *inscription devices* as a function of how they conceptualized expertise. I draw the more general lesson that techniques of quantitative analysis are no substitute for relationships of trust among knowledge producers, while pointing to the limited role numbers play in the construction of social knowledge when they are not backed by social relationships.

Finally, the concluding chapter extracts the main theoretical lessons of the book and develops a typology of creative social knowledge that emerges from the intersection of different ways of combining theory, methods, and data in social scientific scholarship and beyond. After further expanding on the concept of the theory-method-data triad—focusing in particular on how affective values or feeling-laden beliefs help the triad crystallize—the chapter then goes beyond the case of financial economics to provide a broader framework with which we can better grasp variation in the micro- and meso-level processes of knowledge production in the human sciences. Scholarly networks, I argue, emerge at the intersection of theory, data, and methods: different combinations of these three research activities lead to different affective dispositions. I offer a typology of such networks, as well as concrete examples, by specifying how, when theory, data, or methods take the lead, this changes the network's understanding of what constitutes creative work. In turn, different combinations of theory, methods, and data lead to different kinds of conflicts and different kinds of alliances. For instance, fields that grow by incorporating and standardizing data tend to fight with outsiders; questioning the data from within is destructive to the field as a whole. The conclusion also addresses similarities and differences between the theory-method-data triad and other approaches to social knowledge, specifically actor-network theory and practice theory.

As a final example, I focus on the more specific lessons that the case of financial economics holds for our understanding of big data. Big data, like financial economics, emerges from a revolution in data analysis, but it is also more radical in its rejection of non-data-driven approaches, and more aggressive in its claim that potential biases in data collection can be safely overlooked thanks to the sheer volume of data available through new algorithmic techniques and increased storage capacity. Yet it is difficult to imagine that big data will replace other approaches to social knowledge. I argue that the social structure necessary for big data to turn into long-term career opportunities for scholars and big-data experts will generate pressure toward some theoretical and methodological compromise with existing approaches.

THE RHETORIC OF MARKET EFFICIENCY

How Data Analysis Became Legitimate

In 1977, a professor of finance at the Anderson School (UCLA's business school), trained at Chicago under the "father of modern finance" Eugene Fama, and himself on his way to becoming a central figure in financial economics, wrote and published a paper that would quickly become a classic. His name was Richard Roll, and the main topic of the paper was asset-pricing theory, a burgeoning research program that strives to develop objective methods to determine how much an asset is worth. He began the paper with a decidedly nontechnical quote: "If the horn honks and the mechanic concludes that the whole electrical system is working, he is in deep trouble" (1977, 129). This tongue-in-cheek observation acted as a jab at scholars who were satisfied with superficial tests of complex models. In the paper, Roll then proceeded to offer a "broad indictment of one of the three fundamental paradigms of modern finance," quipping that it "will undoubtedly be greeted by my colleagues, as it was by me, with skepticism and consternation. The purpose of this paper is to eliminate the skepticism. (No relief is offered for the consternation.)" (1977, 130).

The three fundamental paradigms of financial economics Roll referred to are (1) corporate financing, where the two-decades-old Modigliani and Miller's (1958) classic formulation of the irrelevance of financial policy to the value of a firm constitutes the most important breakthrough; (2) the evaluation of capital assets, under the rubric of the then-dominant Capital Asset Pricing Model; and finally (3) the broader study of financial markets, where the efficiency of the market serves as a foundational hypothesis (Bernstein 1992). Dismantling current ways of measuring the value and performance of stocks (the second pillar of finance), which was Roll's objective, therefore meant attacking one of the most central undertakings of what, by the late 1970s, was still a relatively young, recently established discipline. And potentially, it also meant threatening the scientific ambitions financial economists had been so carefully cultivating over this formative period.

Relentlessly, Richard Roll provided mathematical proof for why tests of this fundamental paradigm were not just difficult but radically mistaken. He reviewed the most important contributions to asset-pricing theory to date and pointed to what made them problematic. Roll argued that the assumption at the core of this paradigm is untestable. The assumption holds that prices reflect only two parameters: the expected return and the risk of the asset. But risk, argued Roll, can be correctly computed only if one has comprehensive and complete data on the market as a whole and knows exactly its composition. "Human capital" and other nontraded assets would have to be included in that portfolio as well. No such data exist. Roll ended with a mathematical appendix on set theory (a branch of mathematics), which further cemented his critique in a solid scientific terrain.

Two indignant scholars—David Mayers, also at UCLA, and Edward Rice, at the University of Illinois, Urbana-Champaign—took up the challenge, wrote a critique of Roll's paper, and published it just two years later. They reanalyzed Roll's data and peppered their writings with astonished expressions: Roll's tests, they argued, were "severe" and "vastly overstated" (Mayers and Rice 1979, 3–4, 21).

> Roll correctly suggests that the use of a proxy variable increases the risk of type I and type II error in testing. Yet, it is almost impossible to find the "true" measure of any variable in economics. Proxies must be used constantly to test all types of economic theories. Are we to abandon studies of inflation because the change in the Consumer Price Index (CPI) is merely a proxy for the inflation rate? . . . Are we to abandon all empirical studies? (22)

Later on:

> In fact, [Roll] is certainly correct in that a *definitive* test of the theory cannot be made without solving these problems. It is also unfortunately true, however, that definite tests are nearly always impossible. We disagree with Roll in his almost total condemnation of all empirical studies to date, implying that they provide virtually *no* information at all. . . . In an ideal world, these problems would not exist—and we would certainly support the creation of such a world, were it costless—but this provides little justification for rejecting (ignoring) studies done in the world in which we now live. (22–23)

Mayers and Rice concluded with their own appendix of mathematical proofs. The final words in the conclusions are a quote from Stigler (1966): "The answer is that it takes a theory to beat a theory. If there is a theory that is right 51 percent of the time, it will be used until a better one comes along." "In the case of CAPM [the theory Roll was criticizing]," they added, "it is far from clear what the suggested alternative is" (23).

Richard Roll wrote his own rebuttal shortly thereafter, and firmly stood his ground. Mayers and Rice, he protested, "did not disagree with the basic technical aspects of my criticisms of the previous empirical work. . . . Instead, they allege falsely that I condemn 'all empirical studies to date'" (Roll 1979, 394). To their criticism that even something as uncontroversial as measuring inflation would fall under Roll's scrutiny, he replied that the consumer price index "does not have the same stringent mathematical structure as the asset pricing theory," the target of his critique (395). He added: "Even if the criticized papers had used a market proxy that everyone deemed reasonable, without further analysis we should not have accepted conclusions in support of the two-fact asset pricing theory. Those conclusions were based on data analysis with the grouping procedure, a faulty method in this particular application because of the theory's structure" (396). In other words, the mismatch among theory, methods, and data could not be ignored.

Finally, Roll questioned his critics' conclusions that no alternative theory was available. He cited four studies (two of which had him as author/coauthor) providing alternatives, and three studies providing additional critiques. In the remainder of his reply, Roll went on to explain in more detail why the analysis he proposed cast doubt on the established model of asset pricing to which Mayers and Rice professed allegiance.

Three points, when considered together, are remarkable about this exchange:

1. *Theory can be made controversial through empirical analysis.* Mayers and Rice did not have a substantive disagreement with Roll, as Roll quickly pointed out. Rather, they were concerned with the methodological implications of his critique. They were afraid that once you open the field up to Roll's critique, you lose important methodological tools for which you have no easy replacement. Moreover, they argued, this loss is unwarranted because it is theory that defeats theory, not methods and data. Roll replied that while the problems he pointed to have long been known but have not turned out to be lethal in other subfields, they are particularly thorny in the case of asset-pricing theory because of, as he put it, the "structure" of the theory. And this structure is such that new theory will not help improve the general understanding of the phenomenon at hand. It will be through better fit with the data that new, stronger

knowledge will be produced. Current theory should be revised, because it is not supported by the data in ways no one had quite realized before. And while new theory was indeed available, added Roll, it is only from the vantage point of empirical analysis that financial economists can come to understand why this new theory is necessary.

2. *Methods and data will move the field forward.* It is worth repeating Roll's argument: "Even if the criticized papers had used a market proxy that everyone deemed reasonable, without further analysis we should not have accepted conclusions in support of the two-fact asset pricing theory" because "data analysis" was based on a "faulty method in this particular application." In other words, Roll wanted the field to be more sophisticated, careful, and critical of received knowledge, especially when it concerns data analysis.

3. *Roll won the controversy.* Richard Roll published two subsequent papers that generated much debate and eventually led to the delegitimation of the asset-pricing model he criticized (not a complete demise, but definitely a downgrade from the canon). We will pick this story up in a subsequent chapter. The important point is that his methodological critique stood the test of time. And his suggestion that data, when properly analyzed, should shape theory ultimately succeeded.

On their own, these points are interesting but not necessarily surprising, and certainly not peculiar to financial research. What makes these points more remarkable is that this was not the first time that financial economists were engaged in a debate framed around the methodological challenges that would emerge from taking a new theoretical perspective. Financial economists had already looked at the costs of recognizing methodological inadequacies in econometric modeling some ten years earlier: the Roll–Mayers/Rice debate was not the first time that financial economists weighed such costs against the potential benefits of introducing new theories. In fact, the discipline itself crystallized in the wake of one such debate: the debate between Benoit Mandelbrot and his critics, in particular Paul H. Cootner and Eugene Fama.

In the mid-1960s, Mandelbrot proposed that theory should be subordinate to data, that the analysis of data required particular kinds of methodologies suitable for the task at hand, and that the strategies that seemed reasonable in other contexts should be carefully evaluated when applied to the analysis of financial data: the very same points Roll would make about a decade later. Yet Mandelbrot's call was not heeded, and his theoretical apparatus, as we shall see, was abandoned in favor of more traditional methodological and theoretical approaches. Why did Mandelbrot fail where Roll succeeded?

I answer this question, and by doing so also provide an initial answer to the rise of efficient markets in financial economics, by focusing on the stylistic changes experienced by financial economics through the late 1960s and 1970s, at the critical moment when Eugene Fama started building a network (of which Richard Roll was to become an important member) around his research program on new empirical foundations—on data. By *stylistic* changes, I mean the changes in the manner by which arguments in financial economics were conducted, with specific reference to meanings and roles financial economists attributed to the terms "theory," "methods," and "data" and to how they conceptualized the relationship among the three.

Throughout the 1960s, financial economists whose research relied on the quantitative analysis of data kept bumping up against a seemingly insurmountable running block: there was no consensus about what kinds of methodological tools were most appropriate for the analysis of financial markets. And as a consequence, the data themselves appeared suspicious.

By the late 1970s, however, this running block had been removed, and Richard Roll, as well as scholars in his larger network, could now work toward making the theoretical perspective they had built through data analysis—market efficiency—resistant to critique. Eugene Fama's efforts at developing a mode or *style* of constructing arguments, where data analysis played a different role than it did in the past, made this shift possible. Fama's mode of argument was centered on the importance of being reasonable rather than exact or objective, and of communicating one's findings in a simple and accessible manner, resorting to tried and true methods rather than advocating for new analytical tools. Being reasonable meant linking theory with data in a way that required the least amount of expert knowledge in matters of finance: an understanding of simple statistical methods would be sufficient for a reader to judge the credibility of an argument, Fama argued, such that being a financial economist meant being a data analyst rather than, say, a student of the history and evolution of financial institutions or a sophisticated mathematician. Reasonableness was not an economic, financial, or statistical criterion, of course. It was a social value Fama invoked in this tumultuous time of controversy to equip the community of scholars around him with a flexible but useful standard.

In the process of redefining what financial economists could achieve through data, other pathways closed off. Ambiguities were understood as exceptions, or "monsters," in the language of Lakatos, as further elaborated in MacKenzie (2006, 89–118): rather than spur new, innovative moves, anomalies were reclassified as secondary, or peripheral, to the main theory. And, just as important, theories for which data did not yet exist (either because the data had not been collected or because the infrastructure for collecting them was itself yet to be built) lost out to theories that could be built out of data, whether existing ones or ones within close reach. In other words, the style of reasonableness was not neutral, as it was forged through an alliance in networks of research that privileged certain approaches over others, and therefore affected research outcomes in systematic and patterned ways.

By 1976, thanks to Fama's effort at systematizing his position, market efficiency that was reasonably supported by empirical evidence had entered the canon of financial economics. As a result, by the time Richard Roll engaged in his debate with Mayers and Rice in the late 1970s, the analytical ground had shifted, and attacks against financial research like Mandelbrot's that implied potentially high costs for scholars invested in existing econometric methods no longer gave rise to "monsters." The discipline could accommodate critique because of the renewed centrality of data to its enterprise; stylistically, this was reflected in the standard of reasonableness that now allowed the field to move forward. Data ascended to the apex of what was now the data-method-theory triad as financial economists devised new social criteria for evaluating good arguments.

Mandelbrot

Benoit Mandelbrot (1924–2010) intervened into finance between 1962 and 1972, at a moment of effervescence in this emergent field. This effervescence can be captured through two simple plots, figures 2.1 and 2.2a–b, which display the citation patterns of the *Journal of Finance* and the dominant themes in the *Financial Analysts' Journal*, respectively.

The *Journal of Finance*, in print since 1946, is the official academic publication of the American Financial Association (founded in 1939) and the top journal in business and finance. Figure 2.1 shows the distribution of journals cited by papers published in the *JoF* (excluding self-citations to papers published in the *JoF* itself). In the 1940s and 1950s, the journal that was consistently cited by financial scholars was the *American Economic Review* (the flagship, general-interest journal of the American Economic Association, published since 1911). It accounted for between 5 and 10 percent of all citations. Another economic journal that financial economists publishing in the *JoF* tended to cite is the *Journal of Political Economy*. Some years saw spikes of citations to law journals (such as the *Columbia Law Review*). No broad patterns stand out: the *JoF* served as an eclectic forum dealing with a variety of issues concerning the financial system.

Contrast this with what happens from 1960 onward. During this period, citations to other journals in financial economics took off. The *Journal of Financial and Quantitative Analysis*, established in 1966, along with the *Journal of Business*,

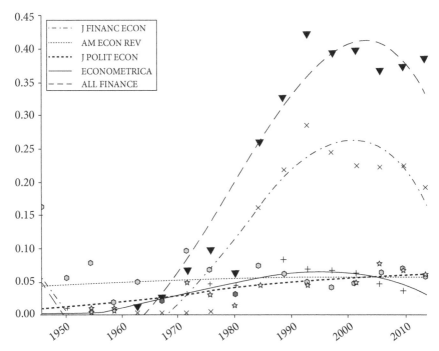

FIGURE 2.1   Citation patterns in the *Journal of Finance*. The figure is based on citation data from all articles published in the *Journal of Finance* between 1945 and 2015. Data were collected from JSTOR.

the *Review of Financial Studies*, and, later, the *Journal of Financial Economics* (established in 1974) accounted for about 40 percent of all cited journals by 1990. The *Journal of Financial Economics* alone received about 30 percent of all citations. This simple analysis demonstrates that, beginning in the 1960s, the flagship journal of financial economics started looking inward in order to produce new knowledge. The discipline of financial economics was quickly coming into its own, transitioning from "business finance" to "financial economics" (Whitley 1986b).[1]

A peek into the general themes that not only financial scholars but the experts and professionals invested in the financial sector were paying attention to over this period gives us insight into the evolving nature of financial economics. The primary outlet for these conversations is the *Financial Analysts Journal* (*FAJ*), the flagship publication of the Chartered Financial Analyst (CFA) Institute since 1945, and therefore a central practitioner journal for the investment management community. Figure 2.2a shows the relative prevalence of the themes that characterized articles published in this outlet in the 1960s: *dividends, companies, earnings*, and *investments*. These terms are all concerned with the activities of what financial

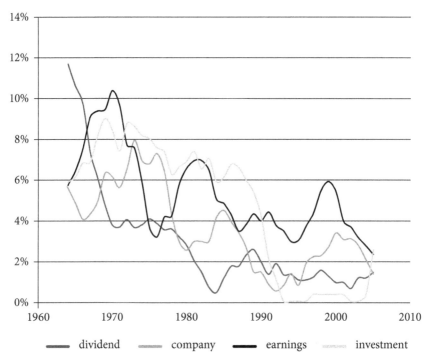

FIGURE 2.2A *Financial Analysts Journal*, analysis of keywords prevalent in 1960.

scholars considered the dominant actor of the time: the corporation (Davis 2009). Up until 1970, these themes were the focus of about 20 percent of all articles.

By the 1990s, however, themes dealing with the activities and attributes of the corporation ceased to be the focus of attention for the journal and, as shown in Figure 2.2b, were replaced by new topics: *portfolios*, *assets*, and *stocks*. These are the attributes of a different kind of actor: the *financial market*. In 1990, more than 20 percent of articles published in the *FAJ* dealt with such themes.

Scholars such as Mandelbrot contributed to the shift away from the corporation and toward the market, and from the investment strategies a focus on the corporation necessitated, to the kinds of processes one needs to understand to study stock exchanges and other arenas where financial securities are traded. At the center of this shift, in the 1960s, lay the idea that stock markets move randomly and that changes in the prices of securities cannot be predicted—the idea behind the application of "random-walk" models to financial markets.

The point of departure for the theory that stock prices are unpredictable is that information about past prices (i.e., historical data) is not useful for predicting future prices. Behind this claim was the understanding that markets are efficiently

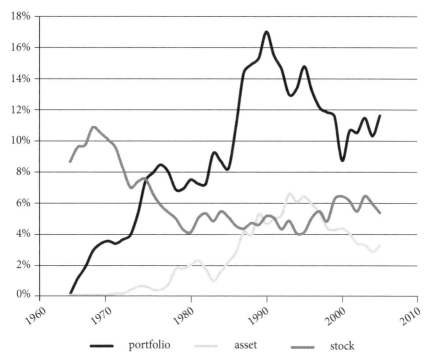

FIGURE 2.2B   *Financial Analysts Journal,* analysis of keywords prevalent in 2005.

incorporating all relevant information into prices, and that price movements are only a function of unpredictable events: more technically, they follow a random walk, with price changes just as likely to be negative as they are to be positive. The notion of independence of changes in stock prices, in turn, relies on the statistical concept of serial independence, or lack of correlation among price changes over time.

This property of stock market prices had been derived statistically more than twice already: by Paul Samuelson[2] and Maurice Kendall, and even earlier by Louis Bachelier, a French statistician writing in 1900. In 1953, the British statistician Maurice Kendall conducted a study based on British securities that helped revive the random-walk hypothesis, most importantly by piquing Samuelson's interest. The latter's contribution was to further develop the statistical properties of the model, as well as lend the prestige of his position to the hypothesis. By the time Samuelson published his work in 1965 (after spending about a decade developing his approach and lecturing about it), a small group of economists was intent on refining their economic understanding of the properties of stock prices over time along the lines of a random-walk model. This group of luminaries included, besides Paul Samuelson himself, Paul Cootner, Harry Roberts, M. F. Osborne, Arnold Moore, and Hendrik Houthakker (Fox 2011).

Benoit Mandelbrot was a late joiner of this group, and he would be the one to leave the most durable mark in the evolution of this theory. But it was a negative mark, a legacy others did not follow. Mandelbrot was first and foremost a mathematician; he would go on to engage in interdisciplinary work in fields such as physics and geology, and would become most iconically associated with the development of fractal theory. Unsurprisingly, given his eclecticism, Mandelbrot's contributions to finance originated in the 1960s with a set of idiosyncratic moves. At the time, he was employed by the IBM Research Center at Yorktown Heights in Westchester County (near New York City), but he would make frequent visits to the University of Chicago (Read 2013, 96), where others—such as Eugene Fama, then a young PhD scholar—shared his keen interest in random walks. Mandelbrot, however, saw things differently from his interlocutors in academia. Random walks, he believed, were not so much interesting in and of themselves, as many economists were increasingly convinced; rather, they were interesting as an entry point into a much larger and more significant problem that had eluded most of his colleagues: the proper understanding of economic dynamics. More specifically, he believed random walks did not move deep enough into the terrain of the temporal dynamics of prices.

Random-walk analysis assumes that price changes are distributed normally over time: because they follow a Gaussian distribution, price changes can be described through standard statistical properties, like means and standard deviations. Mandelbrot, however, believed this simple but fundamental assumption to be wrong. He insisted that the distribution of price differences over time does not behave normally. Large price movements are likely to occur—much more likely, especially, than implied by Gaussian models. Even more problematic, medium-size jumps in prices are also likely. There are moments of tranquility and moments where multiple sources of fluctuation impact prices simultaneously. Mandelbrot thus argued that one problem with economic time-series is the

> presence of extremely long range "persistence," defined as a "tendency" for large (positive or negative) values to be followed by large values of the same sign, in such a way that economic time series seem to go through a succession of "cycles," including "long cycles" whose wavelength is of the order of magnitude of the total sample size. . . . This picture of cyclical behavior is, however, complicated by the fact that the long cycles seen in different samples of the time series have different wavelengths, so that different samples do not look alike from the viewpoint of dominating cyclic behavior. (1969, 83)

One implication is that, what to Gaussian analysts look like rare events (i.e., outliers from the normal distribution) are simply too frequent, and therefore they cannot be easily accommodated within that framework. Gaussian tools, like the standard deviation, are deceiving in a context where the underlying distribution is non-Gaussian, and merely assuming the problem away and modeling the distribution of changes in prices in a way that is not consistent with systematic empirical deviations from the normal distribution means applying a framework to the data that is severely inappropriate. "It is my opinion that these facts warrant a radically new approach to the problem of price variation" (Mandelbrot 1967, 395). Eugene Fama captured these implications succinctly but effectively: "The hypothesis implies that there are a larger number of abrupt changes in the economic variables that determine equilibrium prices in speculative markets than would be the case under a Gaussian hypothesis. . . . [The] market is inherently more risky for the speculator or investor than a Gaussian market" (1963, 427).

Just as important, Mandelbrot took issue with current methodological approaches to the study of price changes. "A second symptom common in economics, especially in the time series of price changes, is that the few largest observations in a sample can be extremely large and vary greatly between samples," he writes. "Like the presence of persistence effects . . . the presence of such 'outliers' makes different samples of the same series appear different from each other. Moreover, the sample variances are enormously influenced by the precise values of the outliers; attempts to estimate 'the' population variance end in grief (1969, 84)." In other words, the violation of Gaussian assumptions not only makes the calculation of standard statistics meaningless; it also has implications for sampling theory and inference, and specifically weakens the confidence with which analysts can rely on sampled time-series data. Standard sampling strategies do not give insight into validity of the sample. It is impossible to tease apart noise from signal.

In sum, Mandelbrot saw random-walk theory as an opportunity to tackle problems he considered to be pressing, even fundamental, to economics. But random walks were only a starting point, an intuition about the complex nature of price changes that needed to be framed in a more radical understanding of economic dynamics. Mandelbrot wanted financial economics to rethink its basic assumptions and reinvent itself (Mirowski 1990a). His effort to innovate on multiple fronts simultaneously is key to our understanding of his demise, because, in spite of Mandelbrot's influence on a new generation of scholars, he was writing at a time when the networks of inquiry coming together to bolster financial research were opposed to this radical kind of creativity.

The Reaction to Mandelbrot

Random-walk models were attracting a significant amount of scholarly attention by the time Mandelbrot elaborated his critique of econometrics. Research on random walks was voluminous enough that in 1964, MIT professor Paul Cootner published an edited collection of cutting-edge work in this area. He included a very critical assessment of Mandelbrot's work in this volume. Cootner came from a different tradition than Mandelbrot's followers, who were mostly based at the University of Chicago; Cootner's tradition was less keen on the idea that markets are freely competitive arenas, and more comfortable with the notion that markets are imperfect. It was also a tradition that, by virtue of its skepticism of markets' ability to regulate themselves, tended to be favorable to some degree of government regulation. The economist Robert E. Hall crystallized this distinction in a 1976 working paper titled "Notes on the Current State of Empirical Macroeconomics" by defining the market-friendly Chicago-based approach as the "freshwater" view and that of the Cambridge-based institutions Harvard and MIT as the "saltwater" view.[3]

None of these aspects, however, informed Cootner's critique. Cootner's critique, rather, was motivated by bewilderment at the *methodological* costs Mandelbrot's strategy would inflict on economics and finance. Mandelbrot's project, as Cootner understood it, required a leap into the unknown; he found Mandelbrot's tone "messianic," which made Cootner "just a bit uncomfortable." Cootner continued (in a much-quoted passage): "Mandelbrot, like Prime Minister Churchill before him, promises us not utopia but blood, sweat, toil, and tears. If he is right, almost all of our statistical tools are obsolete—least squares, spectral analysis, workable maximum-likelihood solutions, all our established sample theory, closed distribution functions. Almost without exception, past econometric work is meaningless. Surely, before consigning centuries of work to the ash pile, we should like to have some assurance that all our work is truly useless" (1964a, 333, 337). In other words, the problem with Mandelbrot's proposal was that it would immediately relegate all empirical work up to that date to obsolescence, without providing any compelling reason or reassurance as to why such a step might be warranted.

Where was Cootner's anxiety coming from? One source was surely the threat to his overall disciplinary project represented by Mandelbrot's critique. Cootner and the financial economists working on the larger project of applying scientific tools to financial analysis were struggling to demarcate their field against professional traders. The difference hinged on the role they understood probability to play in their view of market prices. In the words of Sidney Alexander, whose work Cootner featured in his edited volume, "There is a remarkable contradiction between the concepts of behavior of speculative prices held by professional stock market analysts on the one hand and by academic statisticians and economists on the other. The professional analysts operate in the belief that there exist certain trend-generating facts, knowable today, that will guide a speculator to profit if only he can read them correctly," either as "fundamentalists," who attempt to gain knowledge on the "external factors that lie behind the price changes," or as "technicians," who leave to "others the study of the fundamental facts in the reliance that as those others act on their knowledge there will be a detectable effect on the price of the stock or commodity. The technician, accordingly, studies price movements of the immediate past to telltale indications of the movements of the immediate future" (Alexander 1961, 7).

By contrast, economists and statisticians take a probabilistic view. This view begins with the "assumption that a stock or commodity speculation is a 'fair game' with equal expectation of gain or loss or, more accurately, with an expectation of zero gain," which Alexander (1961, 7–8) characterized as the core of the random-walk model. To see why Mandelbrot's attack could appear so dangerous to this project, one need simply consider the next sentence in Alexander's paper: "But in fact, this picture of a speculative price movement is as much based on empirical findings as on theoretical predispositions." Alexander was suggesting that random-walk models beat professional analysts at their own game. They make better use of data than the analysts do, and therefore put financial research on a more solid and scientific basis not only from the point of view of theory but empirically as well. Obviously, then, weakening the methods means weakening an important tool financial economists were deliberately building up to erect a disciplinary boundary (Gieryn 1983).

But the fight against professional traders in the name of theory and methods was not the only fight Cootner was committed to, and here lies an important difference between Cootner and younger followers of Mandelbrot like Fama, as well as the second, important source of Cootner's anxiety. Cootner was specifically wedded to a mode of analyzing data that was more traditional, careful, and cumulative, in the sense of building on previous knowledge, than Mandelbrot allowed. Mandelbrot wanted to replace Gaussian statistics with what are technically called Pareto-Levy distributions, a family of statistical distributions that differ from normality in displaying "fat tails": a large number of observations that are farther from the mean than a normal distribution would allow. Both Gaussian and Pareto-Levy distributions are members of the same family, but they are radically different in terms of what statistics should be used to represent them.

The most important of such differences is that Pareto-Levy distributions, by virtue of their large number of outliers, exhibit infinite variance. Mandelbrot could adopt the strategy of calculating the variance of a number of samples of stock price data to convince his peers that, indeed, Gaussian variance is an inappropriate statistic. But, as we saw, Mandelbrot believed that inference from samples was just as problematic. Unless new sampling methods are devised, he argued, it is not possible on the basis of data to assess whether one distribution is more appropriate than the other.

Cootner found this position untenable. In his comments on Mandelbrot's work, he quipped: "I was continually reminded, as I read it, of the needling question a teacher of mine was wont to ask—What evidence would you accept in contradiction of your hypothesis? While there is a wealth of evidence presented in this lengthy paper, much of it is disturbingly casual. Much of the evidence is graphical and involves slopes of lines which are not given precise numerical values in the paper" (Cootner 1964a, 333). He continued: "At one of the few places where numbers are mentioned, some data are dismissed as 'absurdly large,' are 'corrected,' and in the new data a number, 18, is accepted as reasonably close to another number which should be somewhere between 21 and 31" (334). On what basis were such decisions made? wondered Cootner.

The main point of this critique was that, without exacting methods and robust empirical evidence, financial research will not move forward. Mandelbrot, however, did not seem to value these objectives. Further, Mandelbrot's call to innovate simultaneously on methods and modes of inference contradicted Cootner's project in that it took away the emphasis on careful empirical analysis that Cootner championed and presented as a distinctive feature of financial economics. As a result, what seemed reasonable to Mandelbrot—that, for instance, 18 worked as an approximation for a number between 21 and 31—hardly seemed reasonable to Cootner. Only on more robust empirical foundations would such approximations acquire credibility.

Cootner's position in this respect remained consistent over time, even as the field changed. As late as 1977, when random-walk models were beginning to be challenged as depictions of market behavior, Cootner reiterated how the discipline's commitment to the market as an empirically clear, transparent, and non-problematic entity underlies its success—this, in the context of making a case for inefficient markets!

> The thing that distinguishes the relative success of analytical methods in finance has been our ability to draw on the requirements of markets and equilibrium. Thus while imaginative and original application of quantitative techniques can produce a portfolio theory, an option pricing formula, or an optimal financing model, the powerful predictions of the M&M theories [Modigliani and Miller], the capital-asset-pricing model, or the Black-Scholes results depend critically on the existence of

markets and arbitrage. . . . While I suspect that other branches of business studies might similarly benefit from a more careful evaluation of the role played by markets, I might observe that some of my colleagues in those other fields probably disagree with my sermon. In their view, finance will not make *real* progress until it gives up this silly notion that markets work. Nevertheless it is clear to *me* that the success of our field has arisen from the fact that finance is largely a study of markets. Indeed, the areas within finance that have progressed more slowly are either those internal to the firm and most immune to market constraint, or those in which financial institutions' very *raison d'etre* arises from the imperfection of markets. (Cootner 1977, 553–54)

What is striking, then, is that Cootner's vision for financial economics, regardless of the specific claims financial economists would make, hinged on a concept of the market that data had made "readable." Finance is successful because it studies markets, Cootner stated, but this belief only made sense to the extent there was a market out there to be analyzed to begin with. How was this vision consolidated? How could Cootner be so sure that what financial economists saw corresponded to a real entity, especially when scholars like Mandelbrot suggested that economists' depictions of markets were outright deceptive because they relied on untested and ultimately unreasonable assumptions? For Cootner's vision to be possible, a way had to be found to make data analysis speak to theory without, however, making unrealistic demands on the data, and without calling for radical theoretical innovations even when the data seemed to push theory in a new direction.

A Critic of Market Efficiency

Understanding how financial economists came to embrace a particular view of markets means understanding the increasing interpenetration between financial knowledge and financial practices that Callon, Mackenzie, and their colleagues and followers write about (see, for instance, MacKenzie, Muniesa, and Siu 2007); it also means understanding the increasingly secure institutional footing of financial economics as a discipline, largely as a function of the increased power of the business school, where financial economists found their natural home (Fourcade and Khurana 2013). Underlying these macroscopic and institutional transformations in markets and disciplines, however, a set of microlevel changes in the ways data were handled, processed, and given legitimacy as reasonable representations of real-world phenomena was also taking place.

I focus on this set of microlevel changes because attention to this level of analysis reveals a key source of strength not only for positions within financial economics that were directly connected to market practices, but also for those that were critical of mainstream views. Changes in data practices bolstered financial economics as a whole. Consider, for instance, MIT Sloan School professor Sidney Alexander's work, included in Cootner's edited volume (Alexander 1961; reproduced in Cootner 1964b). Alexander authored a piece that was critical of market efficiency, but the specific ways he constructed his argument are informative in that they reveal the kinds of strategies analysts should follow if they want their data to be taken seriously. The chapter begins by discussing Maurice Kendall's findings from 1953 that confirmed the random-walk hypothesis. "Contrary to the general impression among traders and analysts that stock and commodity prices follow trends, Kendall found, with two or three exceptions, that knowledge of past price changes yields substantially no information about future price changes" (Alexander 1961, 9). Alexander, however, was interested in precisely those exceptions, and continued: "There was one notable exception, however, to this pattern of random behavior of price changes. That was the monthly series on cotton prices in the United States since 1816. . . . For this series there did appear to be some predictability, and Kendall felt impelled to draw the moral that it is dangerous to generalize even from fairly extensive sets of data. For, from the behavior of wheat prices and the stock prices, one might have concluded that speculative markets do not generate autocorrelated price changes—and here was cotton providing a notable exception" (9). Alexander emphasized Kendall's attention to data even when they disconfirmed his original hypothesis, but he remained critical of this move. He explicitly stated: "Alas, Kendall drew the wrong moral. The appropriate one is that if you find a single exception, look for an error." And indeed Alexander did find an error in Kendall's data,

> for the cotton price series was different from the others investigated by Kendall. Almost all others were series of observations of the price at a specified time—say, the closing price of Friday each week. Each observation of the cotton series was an average of four or five weekly observations of the corresponding month. It turns out that even if the original data—the Friday closing prices—were a random walk, with successive first differences uncorrelated, the first differences of the monthly average of four or five of these weekly observations would exhibit first-order serial correlations of about the magnitude Kendall found for cotton. So Kendall's exception vanishes, and we are left with the conclusion that at least for the series he investigated the serial correlations were not significantly different from zero. (10–11)

The larger lesson Alexander drew from this case is that the temporal framework one imposes on the analysis is crucial, and that, before data can be used to support one interpretation of market behavior as opposed to others, careful attention must be paid to the ways data are handled. Moreover, he continued, short-term fluctuations may hide a long-term, underlying, smooth movement in prices, and perhaps a week is not an appropriate period of observation if one is invested in tracing this long-term trend. Market analysts, he suspected, would likely have this point of view, and Alexander therefore tested where serial correlations appeared at different time intervals, providing a negative answer, for the most part.

In the remainder of the paper, there is an unexpected twist. Alexander turned to M. F. M. Osborne, an astrophysicist whose work was an early investigation into random walks, with a specific focus on "ensembles of price changes." Specifically, as reported by Alexander, Osborne found the distribution of changes in the logarithms of stock prices "over any period in a given market, principally the New York Stock Exchange," to be approximately normally distributed, therefore displaying random-walk behavior (Alexander 1961, 14).

A normal distribution in the changes in logarithms, however, did not mean an expectation of zero profits—the hallmark of efficiency. The reason Osborne used a logarithmic transformation was empirical. His data included a wide range of prices: thus stocks priced at ten dollars were much less likely to experience a ten-dollar increase in price than stocks priced at one hundred dollars, and a logarithmic transformation makes it possible to fit stocks of different prices in the same distribution. To account for the nonlinear relationship between prices and changes in prices, while retaining the expectation of zero gains, Alexander proposed an alternative: percentage changes. He applied this transformation to wheat prices and showed evidence in support of the random-walk hypothesis. When he applied the same transformation to the distribution of runs of Standard and Poor's monthly composite index of stock prices (1918–1956), however, the assumption of a random walk of equal probability of rise or fall was disconfirmed. A month's movement in stock prices depended on the previous month's movement. Alexander showed this to be a function of "using an average of weekly prices for each month's observation" (19). Substituting monthly averages yielded a different result.

Finally, Alexander entertained the hypothesis that trends in stock price changes are masked by "the jiggling of the market." He therefore applied a filter to the analysis, ignoring changes ("moves") that fall below a certain threshold. He found the application of small filters to yield substantial profits, and on the basis of this evidence concluded that

> there *are* trends in stock market prices, once the "move" is taken as the unit under study rather than the week or the month. . . . The many

statistical studies which have found speculative prices to resemble a random walk have dealt with changes over uniform periods of time. The filter operation, however, deals with changes of given magnitude irrespective of the length of time involved. . . . [I]n speculative markets price changes appear to follow a random walk over *time*, but a move, once initiated, tends to persist. . . . The riddle has been resolved. The statisticians' findings of a random walk over the time dimension is quite consistent with non-random trends in the move dimension. Such a trend does exist. I leave to the speculation of others the question of what would happen to the effectiveness of the filter technique if everybody believed in it and operated accordingly. (26)

This paper, in short, made two important moves simultaneously: it showed why market efficiency in terms of random-walk models does indeed characterize price movements, and it made space for the possibility (entertained by professional traders) of opportunities for profit through market speculation (or arbitrage). This is how Alexander solved the riddle of unpredictability and nonrandom trends. What makes the paper even more interesting is an additional aspect of the argument—namely, that visions of markets must be accompanied by thorough investigations of market data, and by appropriate manipulation in terms of the frequency, timing, and aggregation techniques used to process the data. The call for thoroughness in data analysis underlies Alexander's argument, and the call for the use of appropriate tools of analysis provides the foundation for a stylistic turn in financial economics, where data analysis must meet new standards of reasonableness in order to become the basis for innovative research.

Enter Fama

While Mandelbrot was busy producing new theories of markets, basing them on the intuition that price time-series exhibit unusual behavior that existing methods do not capture very well, Cootner was helping to lay the groundwork for a subtler shift in the standards of inference and practices of data analysis. This shift, unlike Mandelbrot's, enjoyed long-term success. Cootner, however, provided only the original impetus. The main author was Eugene Fama.

Fama is a towering figure in the field. Thanks to his seminal contributions to the analysis of markets, he is widely recognized as the "father of modern finance."[4] After earning a bachelor's degree at Tufts in 1960, Fama pursued an MBA and subsequently a PhD at the Chicago Graduate School of Business, joining its faculty in 1963 (a year before earning his doctorate). From the very start of his career,

Fama was invested in empirically verifying the hypothesis that markets are efficient, in the specific sense implied by random-walk models that stock price changes cannot be predicted on the basis of past prices. Importantly, his belief in the hypothesis stemmed partly from his work as an undergraduate assistant to Martin Ernst at Tufts, which he further developed at Chicago. This research entailed the analysis of daily stock price data that Fama himself had collected and cleaned. Trading strategies did not make a profit, Fama concluded after exhaustive tests (Mehrling 2005, 89).

What problems did Fama face once his conviction that markets are efficient solidified and the task of convincing others became paramount? "Are we to abandon all empirical work?" asked Mayers and Rice in their rebuttal to Roll in 1977. "Surely, before consigning centuries of work to the ash pile, we should like to have some assurance that all our work is truly useless," protested Cootner in his 1964 critique of Mandelbrot's work. More than a decade separates the two critiques, and yet the content is virtually identical: it reveals the sticky problem faced by those financial economists who favored the emergence of new approaches to financial research but were afraid that the costs of methodological and empirical innovation would outweigh the benefits of advancing theory. In other words, to financial economists who understood theory to occupy the apex of the theory-method-data triad, a recombination that put data or methods on top seemed ill advised.

To be sure, the problem is not unique to financial economics: there is, for instance, a long-standing debate in econometrics that focuses on the problems that new statistical approaches bring to the analysis of economic data, especially when they rely uncritically on rules of inference developed for data that are generated through experiments rather than observation (Leamer 1983). What is peculiar to financial economics is the response that scholars devised to the challenge posed by the mismatch between methods and data. They did not focus on the development of radically new methodologies, despite what the anxious reactions of scholars like Cootner might suggest. Rather, financial economists *changed the role and meaning of empirical work*: they turned their data into a reliable source of creative work, as they built implicit understandings of what data manipulations were necessary to test new theory, therefore introducing new practices to financial research that, rather than stir controversy, allowed for replication.

Eugene Fama's role in this development is paramount and twofold. First, as MacKenzie (2006) and Jovanovic and Schinckus (2016) emphasize, Fama was at the forefront of the computing revolution that swept through finance in the 1960s. Second, Fama provided a new analytical style through which the computing revolution could be put at the service of producing empirical work relevant to financial economics.

The computing revolution had at least two components. The first component was the computing languages and programs, which became increasingly necessary tools for the manipulation and analysis of economic data; this was especially the case in financial econometrics, where specific applications were developed to test some of the field's foundational theories (Jovanovic and Schinckus 2016, 14–15; Renfro 2009). The second component was the assemblage of new datasets on stock market prices that helped overcome the limitations of previous empirical investigations. For instance, with computerization, it became feasible to collect financial data regularly: monthly and even daily. Similarly, computers made it possible to record transactions taking place outside official markets. More complete, frequently collected, reliable, and systematic datasets were crucial to financial analysis, given the importance this field places on the detection of systematic patterns in financial time-series (Knorr-Cetina in Camic, Gross, and Lamont 2011; Jovanovic and Schinckus 2016, 15).

Fama was connected to both aspects of the computing revolution through his involvement in the Center for Research in Security Prices (CRSP). Set up by the Graduate School of Business at the University of Chicago, the CRSP is considered among the most important datasets to emerge in this formative period for the discipline of finance (Jovanovic and Schinckus 2016). Lawrence Fisher and James Lorie, along with the statistician Harry Roberts, designed CRSP in order to provide "the first comprehensive and refined measurement of the performance of stocks listed on the New York Stock Exchange for a significant number of time periods [between January 30, 1926, and December 30, 1960] under a variety of assumptions about taxes and reinvestment of dividends" (Fisher and Lorie 1968, 291; see Fischer and Lorie 1964 for the first part of the study). By 1968, the data had expanded through December 1965 and contained "all common stocks listed on the New York Stock Exchange . . . from the end of each year to the end of each subsequent period, a total of 820 time periods" (Fisher and Lorie 1968, 291). Fisher and Lorie's 1968 analysis, for instance, was performed on data for 1856 stocks (291). In 1960, then a graduate student in the Chicago School of Business, Fama worked with daily price data before the dataset made its official debut, and his inability to find systematic patterns in price movements made him an early convert to random-walk models (Mehrling 2005, 89). Fama was thus a member of the first cohort of financial scholars who began their career by investigating empirical evidence rather than working on theory or methods, or coming to finance from other areas of specialization in economics (see table 2.1 for a chronology).

That important work was being carried out with empirical evidence collected by the CRSP is worth noting for a number of reasons. Certain assumptions are always and necessarily built into the data, but two things tend to happen when research is produced on the basis of such data. First, a stream of work that uses a

TABLE 2.1. Key papers on market efficiency

AUTHOR	YEAR	AFFILIATION	TITLE AND KEY FINDINGS
M. G. Kendall	1953	Division of Research Techniques, London School of Economics	"The Analysis of Economic Time-Series-Part I: Prices." *Journal of the Royal Statistical Society. Series A (General).* Martingale model of returns on London Stock Market securities.
M. F. M. Osborne	1959	U.S. Naval Research Laboratory, Washington, DC	"Brownian Motion in the Stock Market." *Operations Research.* The logarithm of security prices is the appropriate transformation for the analysis of price movements over time.
Harry V. Roberts	1959	University of Chicago	"Stock-Market 'Patterns' and Financial Analysis: Methodological Suggestions." *Journal of Finance.* Returns on the Dow Jones Industrial Average are statistically independent.
Paul Samuelson	1965	MIT	"Proof That Properly Anticipated Prices Fluctuate Randomly." *Industrial Management Review.* After arbitrage (which eliminates profits), the remaining errors on returns follow a Gaussian distribution.
Eugene Fama	1965	University of Chicago	"Portfolio Analysis in a Stable Paretian Market." *Management Science.* Results consistent with Samuelson (above) and Mandelbrot (below), but expressed in a more general theoretical framework.
Benoit Mandelbrot	1966	Research staff member, IBM Watson Research Center, Yorktown Heights, New York, and institute lecturer, MIT	"Forecasts of Future Prices, Unbiased Markets, and 'Martingale' Models." *Journal of Business.* Like Samuelson, Mandelbrot concludes that stock returns follow a "memoryless" martingale. Random-walk models describe the distribution of returns net of fundamental analysis.
Michael Jensen (student of Fama and Scholes)	1968	University of Rochester College of Business	"The Performance of Mutual Funds in the Period 1945–1964." *Journal of Finance.* Mutual funds, on average, are not able to "predict security prices well enough to outperform a buy-the-market-and-hold policy." Individual funds do no better than what we would expect from chance.
Eugene Fama, Lawrence Fisher, Michael Jensen, and Richard Roll	1969	Graduate School of Business, University of Chicago	"The Adjustment of Stock Prices to New Information." *International Economic Review.* The analysis of how split stocks (CRSP data) are priced by the market reveals its efficiency in incorporating new information into prices.
Benoit Mandelbrot	1969	IBM	"Long-Run Linearity, Locally Gaussian Process, H-Spectra and Infinite Variances." *International Economic Review.* The paper is critical of attempts to use standard statistical techniques for the study of security price time-series. It crystallizes Mandelbrot's view and marks his departure from the field.

(continued)

TABLE 2.1.   (continued)

AUTHOR	YEAR	AFFILIATION	TITLE AND KEY FINDINGS
Eugene Fama	1970	Graduate School of Business, University of Chicago	"Efficient Capital Markets: A Review of Theory and Empirical Work." *Journal of Finance.* Building on his 1969 collaborative paper, this review posits strong-form efficiency as a limiting case, making the case for weaker forms of efficiency as accurate characterizations of market behavior. Because it incorporates insights from event studies (split-stock analysis), the review also highlights the importance of the joint hypothesis to the falsification of informational efficiency.
Eugene Fama	1976	Same as above.	*Foundations of Finance.* This book recasts the theory of market efficiency around the problem of the joint hypothesis, which it solves by pointing to simple models of price formation that produce successful joint tests of equilibrium and efficiency.

given dataset tends to relax its original focus on the validity of those assumptions and increasingly strives to accomplish what it sets out to achieve. In the specific case of finance, the more work making use of stock price data found its way to publication, the more the assumptions through which the data were generated shifted to the background, until they were effectively forgotten. Even when these assumptions are not particularly controversial, they do give the data a particular shape and format. Second, data formatted and shaped in a particular way lend themselves to certain kinds of analyses as opposed to others (Gitelman 2013). This is because, as MacKenzie (2006) perceptively points out, for all their apparent completeness and representational validity of datasets, "even something as basic as the 'cleaning' of price data to remove errors in data entry can, in a sense, involve theory" (24).

In the specific case of CRSP, as Lorie (1965) himself explained, uncertainty about units of analysis, accuracy, and procedures required "theory-driven" or expert intervention in the construction of CRSP data. Let us look at each in turn. With regard to the units of analysis, Lorie wrote: "It was our original belief that the raw prices themselves could be recorded adequately by untrained clerks. Even this hope proved unfounded. The main difficulty was in deciding what was a common stock. We generalized from the work of Gertrude Stein, who, you may recall, said that a rose is a rose is a rose. We thought that a common stock is a common stock is a common stock; but it isn't. Further, some things not called common stocks are. . . . Of our almost 400,000 price quotations, over 30,000 required more than clerical attention" (1965, 5). In other words, expert intervention was necessary even in activities as simple as identifying common stock, the basic units of analysis in the dataset.

With regard to accuracy, Lorie noted that CRSP data were assembled with the "laudable and assuredly extravagant ambition" (1965, 6) of making them more accurate than the sources they came from. This was made possible by accurately recording the data and then using a computer to "identify 'suspicious,' inconsistent, or impossible items" (6), where inconsistencies were identified as changes in prices during one month that were followed by a change in similar magnitude in the opposite direction in the following month.

Finally, there was uncertainty about the degree to which these procedures yielded satisfactory results, so other flags were identified, such as impossible fractions (e.g., a price of "$8 7/7"), discrepancies in bid/asked quotations, and missing data. In other words, CRSP data were being processed so that monthly time-series did not exhibit suspicious features. But suspicious observations were identified on a theoretical basis, not on the basis of the data themselves.

This would not be particularly controversial if scholars like Mandelbrot were not vociferously criticizing the underlying framework and models economists used to understand the time-dynamics of economic series to begin with. But in the face of Mandelbrot's indictment of the ways economists decided what counted as signal and what counted as noise, adjustments to time-series data were necessarily problematic, and work that relied on this particular way of processing data without resorting to alternative specifications and data sources was by extension problematic as well.

But there was no such alternative. The CRSP, initially commissioned by Merrill Lynch for the purpose of calculating historical returns in the New York Stock Exchange, was the only game in town, which gave its users an advantage. In fact, once CRSP had been put together, there was pressure for it to be used: Jim Lorie was "worried that no one would use the data and CRSP would lose its funding."[5] Fortunately for him, the alternative was not between CRSP and some other dataset but between CRSP and lack of similarly comprehensive data. Fama, who was in fact intrigued by Mandelbrot's theoretical arguments in favor of new statistical distributions, repeatedly highlighted the problem that there was no data infrastructure available to test whether Mandelbrot was correct (Jovanovic and Schinckus 2016, 36–41), and that, by contrast, existing data constituted useful opportunities for new research.

Fama's full participation in the computing revolution was, therefore, his first intervention into the shift in the meaning of empirical data, which opened the door for market efficiency as a theory of financial markets. His second intervention was his effort to develop a new analytical style, which, in the broader context of the computing revolution, contributed to the collective forgetting of the assumptions underlying data. This style relaxed the relationship between theory and data and, by highlighting the important but nonconclusive role evidence plays in testing theory, also naturalized the meaning of evidence. Fama's contribution in this respect was essential.

Fama shifted the emphasis of inference away from the idea that imperfections in data can lead to misleading results, and pushed it toward the idea that theories are untestable in their totality, but as long as they meet a reasonable empirical standard, they are worthy of further refinement and development. Thus, in *Foundations of Finance*, a 1976 textbook that became the canonical statement of the emerging "new" finance, Fama warned his readers:

> Remember that no null hypothesis, such as the hypothesis that the market is efficient, is a literally accurate view of the world. It is not meaningful to interpret the tests of such a hypothesis on a strict true-false basis. Rather, one is concerned with testing whether the model at hand is a reasonable approximation to the world, which can be taken as true, or at least until a better approximation comes along. What is a reasonable approximation depends on the use to which the model is to be put. For example, since traders cannot use filters to beat buy and hold, it is reasonable for them to assume that they should behave as if the market were efficient, at least for the purposes of trading on information in past prices. (1976b, 142)

Later, Fama added that empirical evidence "consistent" with the model is not the same thing as evidence "proving" the model:

> This does not say, however, that the evidence proves the assumption. Like any statistical evidence, it is at best consistent with the general model in the sense that it does not lead to rejection either of the hypothesis that the market is efficient or of the hypothesis that equilibrium expected returns are constant through time. This just means that, at least as far as the evidence from the autocorrelations is concerned, the hypotheses are reasonable models of the world. Like any models, however, they are just approximations that are useful for organizing our thinking about the phenomena of interest. They do not necessarily rule out other models which might also be reasonable and useful approximations. (149–50)

This rhetoric of reasonableness, calm, and confidence that the validity of one's work is a matter of reasonably interpreting the connection between theory and evidence might seem puzzling. Isn't financial economics supposed to become a science at exactly this time, or, put more precisely, isn't it making a claim to scientific status based on its systematic approach to empirically driven research? Fama's appeal to reasonableness is strikingly cavalier if scientism is at stake. Consider, as a contrast, Milton Friedman's rhetoric in his famous "Methodology of Positive Economics" essay. "Positive economics" deals with "what is," argued Friedman (1953, 4), "its task is to provide a system of generalizations that can be used to make correct predictions about the consequences of any change in circumstances. Its performance is to be judged by the precision, scope, and conformity with experience of the predictions it yields. In short, positive economics is, or can be, an 'objective' science, in precisely the same sense as any of the physical sciences." Friedman spoke a language of falsificationism that Fama significantly tempered down (Hands 2003).

Fama, to be sure, had a particular problem at hand: market efficiency could be tested only by way of auxiliary assumptions about how the market calculated value. One had to have some model of how markets are dealing with uncertainty with respect to basic phenomena like inflation. And so Fama was very explicit that tests of market efficiency were also, necessarily, tests of the particular method scholars used to model the ways prices are constructed. Mandelbrot's admonition lurked in the background: if economic data do not behave in the way predicted by economic models, economic analysis is near worthless. But Fama never took this step. He said, for instance:

> Thus, autocorrelations of $\tilde{R}_{jt}$ that are close to zero are consistent with a world where the market is efficient and equilibrium expected returns are constant through time. But they are also consistent with a world where the market is efficient and where equilibrium expected returns wander over time, but not sufficiently to have any important effect on the autocorrelations of $\tilde{R}_{jt}$. Since we are primarily concerned with testing market efficiency, the choice between these two models of equilibrium expected returns is that apparently they do not wander enough or in such a way as to invalidate autocorrelations as a tool for testing the hypothesis that the market is efficient, at least with respect to any information in historical returns. (1976b, 150–51)

In other words, tests need not give incontrovertible evidence in favor of one position as opposed to others. The evidence simply needs to be consistent with theory and for the purposes at hand.

Fama's *Foundations of Finance* textbook had several goals. Besides setting up reasonableness as a criterion for research and specifying the relationship between theory and data in a way that highlighted the reliability of data, Fama wanted to establish and demonstrate mathematically that the methods of finance were consistent, in fact often identical, with more broadly used statistical methods, the implication of such continuity being that finance produced results that were not only reasonable but also simple to understand. In a 2008 interview with Richard Roll, Fama went as far as saying that he wrote the textbook to convince his skeptical colleague Fischer Black that a framework for conducting cross-sectional tests of asset-pricing models needed to rely on nothing more sophisticated than ordinary least squares methods.[6]

Foundations of Finance is a highly cited text in the discipline (over twenty thousand times by December 2017, according to Google Scholar), and works that cite it are themselves highly influential, including Fama and Jensen's seminal article "Separation of Ownership and Control" (1983) and, more important for our discussion, a series of studies that purportedly critique market efficiency (e.g., Ball 1978; Banz 1981; Watts 1978).[7] With regard to such critiques, Jensen reports in a special issue of the *Journal of Finance*, "The studies viewed individually are interesting, stimulating, and puzzling. Unlike much of the 'inefficiency literature' of the past, each and every one of these studies is a carefully done scientific piece. Each of the authors displays in varying degrees a commonly held allegiance to the Efficient Market Hypothesis—witness the general reluctance to reject the notion of market efficiency" (1978, 100–101). In other words, after Fama's textbook set the methodological standards for studies that test market efficiency, it became difficult to reject the theory. Much like reasonableness, Fama's appeal to simple methods, and his demonstration that the methods worked *on the kinds of data available to financial economists at the time,* mitigated skepticism and anxiety about the kinds of innovations financial economics was taking on; and, at the same time, it constrained the freedom that future studies would have in applying different and new methods to the data at hand.[8]

The theoretical payoff of establishing reasonableness as a criterion for inference from imperfect data and simplicity in methods was a theory of market efficiency that turned out to be not only remarkably ambiguous but also remarkably flexible, and that nevertheless moved the research agenda forward because it consolidated the notion that data were driving theory. As Jovanovic and Schinkus (2016) point out, there are at least two different versions of the theory by Fama alone, separated by about ten years.[9] In the first version, elaborated in 1965, markets are ultimately about processing information. "In an efficient market," argued Fama, "competition among the many intelligent participants leads to a situation where, at any point in time, actual prices of individual securities already reflect the effects of information based both on events that have already occurred and on events which, as of now, the market expects to take place in the future. In other words, in an efficient market at any point in time the actual price of a security will be a good estimate of its intrinsic value" (1965, 56).

He continues:

> Because there is vagueness or uncertainty surrounding new information, "instantaneous adjustment" really has two implications. First, actual prices will initially overadjust to changes in intrinsic values as often as they will underadjust. Second, the lag in the complete adjustment of actual prices to successive new intrinsic values will itself be an independent, random variable with the adjustment of actual prices sometimes preceding the occurrence of the event which is the basis of the change in intrinsic values (i.e., when the event is anticipated by the market before it actually occurs) and sometimes following. This means that the "instantaneous adjustment" property of an efficient market implies that successive price changes in individual securities will be independent. A market where successive price changes in individual securities are independent is, by definition, a random walk market. (56)

In short, market efficiency consists of information being processed in such a way that changes in stock prices follow a random walk.

The second definition, which Fama developed in 1976, made the problem of the joint assumption much more central to market efficiency. As we saw, "joint assumption" refers to theories that are operationalized by making subsidiary assumptions: a test of the theory, then, is also a test of those assumptions, such that there is ambiguity as to what the test is actually falsifying. Stephen LeRoy (1976) noted that the theory of market efficiency, as operationalized by Fama, was tautological, and this prompted Fama's response. "Rather than defending the efficients [sic] market theory as presented [in the past], I shall present the model in a different way which hopefully is free of whatever is misleading or difficult to follow in the earlier approach" (Fama 1976a,143). In this new presentation of market efficiency, Fama now posited that testing market efficiency required making predictions from a theoretical model that captured the techniques employed by traders in calculating prices and returns, and then comparing those predictions with actual price and return data. This was no longer a theory of random walks. In this new definition, market efficiency was a way of representing and analyzing information in the same way that traders do. Could market efficiency be both a random-walk model of security prices over time and a model of how traders calculate prices in real life? Fama did not guide his readers through the evolution of this concept. And this was part of a more general problem: a "proliferation of theoretical developments combined with the accumulation of empirical work led to a confusing situation. Indeed, the definition of efficient markets has changed depending on the emphasis placed by each author on a particular feature," claim Jovanovic and Schinckus (2016, 21).

Jovanovic and Schinkcus (2016) nevertheless suggest that

> the efficient-market hypothesis represents an essential result for finan-
> cial economics, but one that is founded on a consensus that leads to ac-
> ceptance of the hypothesis independent of the question of its validity
> (Gillet 1999, 10). The reason is easily understood: by linking financial
> facts with economic concepts, the efficient-market hypothesis enabled
> financial economics to become a proper subfield of economics and con-
> sequently to be recognized as a scientific field. Having provided this
> link, the efficient-market hypothesis became the founding hypothesis of
> the hard core of financial economics. (20)

In other words, the hypothesis, whether or not it was valid, brought a network of
scholars together because it established a disciplinary "common sense" that allowed scholars to bracket off background expectations regarding the behavior of
markets (Garfinkel 1960, 1988).

But the answer can be further refined by paying more attention to the kinds
of networks the hypothesis mobilized. The efficient-market hypothesis was built
from data processing networks: Fama, who operated at the center of these networks, strived as much to establish the importance of efficiency as he did to build
consensus around what constituted proper financial data. Put more strongly, the
subject of analysis was not market efficiency; rather, it was the behavior of financial data as constructed through new datasets. And rather than being motivated
by a question of trust or skepticism toward market efficiency, financial research
was oriented toward finding new ways *to let the data speak*. Fama made data legitimate because he pointed to the limits of what data analysis could achieve; by
relaxing the standards tying evidence and theory, Fama's work helped others differentiate between claims that were warranted and claims that were not. In other
words, Fama introduced a "data thinking cap" to financial economics, in Hacking's
(1984) sense.

Conclusions: Efficient Markets and the Data Network

Influential social-science studies of the rise of financial economics identify the
efficient-market hypothesis as its springboard. As MacKenzie (2006, 38), among
others, puts it, the efficient-market hypothesis was one of the strands of the "move
from [a] predominantly descriptive and institutional approach to the academic
study of finance to [an] analytical, economic, and increasingly mathematical
viewpoint."

This chapter provides evidence that is broadly consistent with this thesis. I demonstrate that market efficiency, as theorized and tested by Fama and his colleagues, accomplished what alternative visions for financial economics, like Mandelbrot's, could not. The efficient-market hypothesis served as a crucible where theory, methods, and data could be melted together to produce a new crystallization that proved to be durable and influential.

What gave efficiency power, I argued in this chapter, is social structure, held together by an orientation to data that reflected social criteria. Financial analyses, after Fama's intervention, came to be judged as credible insofar as they were *simple*—that is, making clear, incremental, supportive contributions to the body of knowledge developed in this field through quantitative analysis. This constituted a major break with then-current traditions that emphasized the institutional complexity of financial processes, as we will see in greater depth in chapter 5. Simplicity went hand in hand with a preference for statistical analysis, even though its standard assumptions were known to be problematic for the study of financial data.

Financial economists also emphasized the *reasonableness* of one's results as a marker of good scholarship: as long as data had a reasonable fit with existing theory, the analysis would be considered an important stepping-stone for future research. Emphasis on this virtue was distinctive to financial economists. Unlike their counterparts in economics, financial scholars relied closely on the empirical analysis of data. Instead of invoking new theories or building complex mathematical models, financial scholars assessed the credibility of knowledge by invoking reasonableness of fit with data.

Fama's invocation of reasonableness and simplicity in methods was not based on financial or economic theory. Instead, it was more of a rhetorical strategy, intended to rally a new network of scholars around the notion of market efficiency. And by emphasizing shared values, toward which scholars could orient themselves, Fama gave this network a particular kind of affect. Reasonableness and simplicity seem to connote lack of passion; a research strategy that values such criteria, it was implied, would not be affected by the idiosyncratic preferences of any individual analyst but rather would be "objective" (Megill 1994). Yet it would be a mistake to take the rhetoric at face value and to ignore the context within which the rhetoric was employed. The context was one of initial skepticism against data (from powerful people like Mandelbrot), and of shocked, passionate reaction from other prominent scholars, like Paul Cootner. Reasonableness and simplicity made sense to the financial scholars who embraced Fama's agenda in that it allowed them to stay as close to the data as possible.

Fama, to be sure, was no relativist. He believed in objectivity, and he was renowned for the care with which he approached new datasets. But he was also a firm believer that the emphasis on reasonable and simple arguments that could be understood by a broad audience constituted the market of good scholarship. Being reasonable came to mean relying on a set of agreed-upon practices around data analysis, so that scholars could differentiate between claims that were warranted and claims that were not. Value was attached to such criteria, in the sense that scholars who pursued reasonable research strategies could be expected to be perceived as reasonable themselves: the criteria helped scholars build consistent reputations. Richard Roll himself, in the passage at the beginning of the chapter, protested against using "reasonable" criteria when they were based on an erroneous understanding of the data and how they fit the structure of the theory. To make data legitimate, scholars had to first learn to show appreciation of the limits of data and the constraints data impose on analysis, without thereby calling for more radical deviations from the emerging canon.

In an important analysis of the different meanings two international groups of physicists give data, Harry Collins (1998) introduces the concept of "evidential culture," which, he argues, reflects the institutional setting in which research takes place. An evidential culture embodies specific assumptions about the role of the individual, as opposed to the collectivity, in assessing the validity and meaning of scientific results; assumptions about how significant a result should be before it can be reported; and the evidentiary threshold a result must pass. Unlike Collins, I focused in this chapter on a network of scholars situated in the same institutional setting; nevertheless, I captured the emergence of a new evidential culture coming together as scholars reached consensus about what research in financial economics should look like. Emphasizing the networks that were assembled to make the theory stronger, and the cultural work necessary for the networks to work together so as to provide working solutions to ongoing controversy, revealed that financial economists considered data and methods incomplete. Observations could be removed to generate trends that would not otherwise exist. More fundamentally, differences in basic assumption about the kinds of statistical distributions involved in testing could lead to very different results. Yet to the potentially paralyzing challenges posed by these problems, moving research agendas in the field found ways to provide working solutions. Whether those solutions were adequate did not matter as long as they helped scholars produce more research over time. Put differently, whether the results were true was not a useful criterion, precisely because there was debate about the adequacy of data and tests in adjudicating truthfulness; and only once those debates were silenced could the question of truthfulness be handled, though with flexible criteria.

The driving virtues of reasonableness and simplicity are not peculiar to financial economics; in the social sciences, scholars who struggle to frame their research as more scientific than that of their opponents often invoke qualities of this kind. But what I think is specific to financial economists is that these qualities of research were leveraged in fights with rivals who were just as invested in turning financial economics into a science. Mandelbrot, for instance, as he pursued a vision for financial economics that called for a radical break with current methodologies, including econometrics, was not interested in reasonableness and simplicity; it was Fama who paved the way for the discipline to embrace these values. Moreover, reasonableness and simplicity served as much to characterize scholarship as they served to characterize the scholars themselves (see esp. Shapin 1994). We will see this convergence in assessment between research and scholar again in chapter 4. The point I want to make here is that, rather than to erect a boundary between proper, scientific financial scholars and their misguided, less scientifically sound opponents, these virtues were mobilized to cement alliances across networks to ensure that financial research would no longer raise the kinds of concerns that Cootner had voiced against Mandelbrot.

Among the many reasons, then, behind the success of market efficiency, our analysis reveals that market efficiency provided a crystallization of positions that *minimized conflict among networks*. These positions—standard statistical methods, a flexible theory of efficiency broadly consistent with economics, and keen attention to data—went together well, and what gave the controlling notion of reasonableness coherence and power is that it allowed for networks to repeatedly come together and generate new research without getting blocked by unrealistic demands on theory or data. Achieving consensus over data and methods led to repetition, consolidating consensus in theory. Reasonable results would mark the scholars themselves as reasonable. The harnessing of data and methods to perfect competition and efficiency generated enthusiasm through a shifting of standards of evaluation and what was reasonable given the state of knowledge shifted in favor of one particular position, that of efficiency.

A focus on the development of reasonableness as an affect-laden value circulating within new networks of financial scholars raises a set of questions about the shape of these networks, the collaborative structure that financial economics adopt, and the more specific character of Fama's network. We will now turn to explore these questions.

COLLABORATIONS AND MARKET EFFICIENCY

The Network of Financial Economics

By the end of the 1950s, rapid advances in computer technology were making data manipulation faster, cheaper, and more effective. This development was stimulating for younger faculty members though troublesome for their older colleagues. Economist Eugene Fama . . . recalls those days with a gleam in his eye. The IBM 709, which he characterizes as "the first serious machine," had just become available. Fama claims that for a long time he and a member of the physics department were the only people at the university who knew how to use it. "We could just pop the data in," he told me. "We were kids in a candy store."

—Peter Bernstein, *Capital Ideas: The Improbable Origins of Modern Wall Street*

By 1979, the basic structure of "orthodox" modern finance theory was essentially complete. At the start of the 1960s, Eugene Fama had felt like "a kid in a candy store." A decade later, Stephen Ross still felt the same sense of intellectual opportunity: "It was a good time. You just knew you would pick up nuggets of gold."

—Donald MacKenzie, *An Engine, Not a Camera*

As Eugene Fama and Stephen Ross—two central figures in financial economics—recalled their first encounter with the new technologies and datasets that would soon become central to the "basic structure of orthodox modern finance theory," they painted a picture of thrilling excitement and buoyant expectation. To Fama, it felt like being "a kid in a candy store," an analogy that hints at both the joyful abundance of data now awaiting him ("nuggets of gold," as Stephen Ross called them) and his own newness to the discipline. Although he possessed unique technical skills for operating the computers, skills that others were still far from mastering, Fama seemed to think of himself not as an expert capable of exercising "trained judgment" (Galison, in Galison and Jones 2014) but rather as an excitable novice eager to soak up, and be shaped by, new knowledge (perhaps, to take his analogy to a kid seriously, even at the cost of indigestion).

Understanding how scholars recast expertise in the language of being open to discovery, and how they experience a sense of wonder as they examine data from the point of view of a novice, even a child, may seem frivolous. In light of social science traditions developed around the problem of how knowledge is constructed, it would seem a better idea to focus on how researchers develop skills to carefully assess evidence in relation to the accumulated knowledge of their field, rather than on how analysts *feel* toward their data. Knowledge is about organization, interests, and power, not about feelings, the skeptical social scientist would say, adding that attention to feeling and affect is, as a matter of fact, anachronistic. It would make sense only to those who are still indebted to the old, Romantic tradition that used to celebrate the genius-like qualities of the scientist. Rather than attempt to explain how science is made, this tradition would point to ethereal factors like inspiration or paint scientists as a lone eccentrics, so ahead of their time that their contributions to knowledge would likely remain unrecognized (Garber 2002; Sawyer 2012).

Organization, interests, and power certainly become even more central to modern-day knowledge, as scholars increasingly rely on machines—the computers that generated so much enthusiasm in Fama and his students—and data analysis turns into a driver of knowledge production. In what I am calling the theory-method-data triad—the range of research practices scholars can recombine to open up new creative venues—the ascent of data to its apex should coincide with a depersonalization of expert work. While machines, to be sure, invite collaboration and a division of labor, a focus on teamwork and on the social processes emerging around new knowledge-making technologies would not necessarily justify renewed attention to affect: collaborations can also become routinized and instrumental, and attention to how scholars divide their intellectual labor up could even reinforce our original resistance to considering affect as nothing but secondary and superficial. When data analysis becomes central to a discipline, we would likely confront rational and systematic collaborative work; such work may even be characterized, perhaps, by massive, fleeting collaborations of the type implicit in the rhetoric of data analysis, where individual expertise matters only insofar as it grants quicker access to patterns in data, because "we can throw the numbers into the biggest computing clusters the world has ever seen and let statistical algorithms find patterns where science cannot" (Anderson 2008).

Or, this is what research on collaborations might lead us to expect. *Theory-driven* innovations can fragment a field of inquiry because scholars active in theoretical research tend to collaborate less than those who pursue methodologically or data-driven research (Moody 2004). But shift the triad so that data analysis drives research in a field, and collaboration should flourish. As more scholars acquire the appropriate programming skills, one would expect to see specialization, team-based research, and the development of particular kinds of technical expertise allowing scholars to participate in multiple, more complex projects that none of them would be able to conduct on their own.[1] Thus, as quantitative analyses become more complex, scholars would be more likely to rely on colleagues with the analytical skills necessary to get the job done, therefore increasing the occurrence of coauthored work (see also Hudson 1996). Scholarly expertise can be easily combined because contributors to a project know exactly what they are bringing and how their contribution can be evaluated.

In short, if we take Fama's view of financial research as the manipulation of financial data at face value, a paradox emerges. Once data become increasingly standardized, well understood, and accessible, and more and more scholars acquire the appropriate skills to manipulate such data, we should expect financial research to become less centered on the work of individual scholars and more open to collaboration—something like an assembly line, the quintessential technology of Fordism, the social regime that has an elective affinity with big datasets and large collaborations (Steinmetz 2005). In the process, we should also expect financial collaborations to be driven by a rational search for complementary skill sets. The childlike feeling of spontaneous wonder and boundless excitement at the availability of new data would be quickly replaced by a utilitarian, colder, more measured approach.[2]

If we accepted this hyper-rationalized vision of the research process, we would be surprised to hear Stephen Ross talk about "gold nuggets" still hiding in datasets a decade after Fama had used the same language to describe his relationship to data. We would perhaps attribute Ross's discoveries to underdeveloped technologies or complexities in datasets not fully understood yet. But we would be especially puzzled if, after Stephen Ross, financial economics never developed opportunistic, assembly-line-like collaborations aimed at maximizing the benefits of specialization. We would consider such lack of opportunistic collaborations detrimental to the progress of the field. It would indeed be perplexing to see team-based research not leverage the skills of the broader network.

Yet, finance scholars never quite adopted this rational strategy of specialization, in spite of the opportunities offered by data analysis. This chapter solves the paradox. Using coauthorship and other bibliometric data as my primary source of evidence (turning data analysis onto itself, so to speak), I demonstrate that financial economists did not form collaborations in ways that would depend on the expertise of each participant through the recombination of teams. As new data became available, financial economists did not branch out into new topics. Rather, those who produced innovative financial research did so through small, steady collaborations they built up over long periods of time, often entire careers: financial economists developed a preference for repeated collaborations with the same people. And by working in small groups, financial economists participated in an economy of affect, to repurpose a term from Lorraine Daston (1995): they valued the communicability and interdependence of their findings rather than precision or accuracy; further, their vision of financial knowledge painted it as cumulative.

As the discipline established itself, the most successful groups in financial economics tended to be dyads, pairs of coauthors who collaborated repeatedly over many years on similar but nonoverlapping topics, contributing to the expansion of financial knowledge in the name of developing theories that had a reasonable fit with the data. These small groups specialized in topic areas that had little overlap with the research conducted by others in the field; therefore, getting others to trust one's findings and results could pose particularly thorny challenges. Whose measurements should be trusted? What did financial economists need to know about the authors of new research before they could grasp the significance of their contribution, as well as confirm the validity of their results? And finally, what were the ramifications of accepting a particular finding or result?

Affect—a particular set of affective dispositions that, in this field, came to be oriented toward simple results that could be communicated to others and presented as cumulative—helped the development of financial economics because of the way financial research came to be socially organized. Financial economists, as I suggested in chapter 2, learned to make affective judgments based on the extent to which they perceived others to be reasonable in the specific sense of having a flexible understanding of the relationship between theory and data. Here I add that reasonability became morally compelling through affect as it linked up with social structure: in this way, reasonability, as it allowed scholars to communicate and build on existing knowledge, helped financial scholars increasingly trust one another. Collaborative pairs emerged as financial economists carved a middle ground between conducting research that reflected the idiosyncratic preferences and intuitions of its authors and conducting research that was collectively distributed to such an extent that its authorship no longer mattered.

Market Efficiency as Data: Can Machines Study the Market?

One of the most important outcomes of collaborative work in financial economics is the establishment of the efficient-market hypothesis. As we have seen, the hypothesis states that traders cannot repeatedly do better than the market. The market incorporates information into the prices of securities as soon as that information becomes available. As a result, traders cannot hope to make consistent profits on the basis of superior access to knowledge.

How did financial scholars prove the existence of efficient markets? First, they had to construct markets themselves as objects of knowledge, ready for tests of the validity of the efficient-market hypothesis, through data analysis. "Financial economics has a simple beginning: it is basically the coming of the first computer," says Fama in a 2008 interview with Richard Roll.[3] Therefore, questions about trust in measurements, trust in scholars, and trust in particular findings were intimately connected, from the very beginning, to the question of what markets *were*. Financial economists had to reach working consensus on what the term "market" *meant*, so that this understanding could go on to inform how they would study the market, how they would turn it into an object of analysis. While the issues of trust in measurements, trust in the scholars making those measurements, and trust that the object of analysis (the market) was properly delineated can be fleshed out analytically, in practice the three interpenetrated quite deeply.

As the architect of the efficient-market hypothesis, Fama introduced an approach to data that became fundamental to the development of this canonical understanding of markets. Markets came to be defined *empirically* in terms of the financial instruments that are traded within them, and the recorded transactions of these trades (Preda 2002). But consider Fama's elaboration in his 1976 foundational textbook, which elevates the *statistical* relationship between markets and data to a pedagogical strategy: "The approach in these chapters is to introduce statistical concepts first and then to use them to describe the behavior of returns on securities. Thus, Chapter 1 studies probability distributions and the properties of samples and then uses the concepts to examine distributions of common stock returns. Chapters 2 and 3 take up the statistical tools that are needed to study the relationships between returns on securities and portfolios" (1976, x). A financial market, according to Fama, is best understood through the prism of statistical methods developed to analyze data—in this specific case, methods that are adapted to the analysis of data on the returns of securities and portfolios. Methods and theories about markets developed hand in hand because financial markets were to be approached through data analysis of relevant financial transactions.

On closer reading, the argument articulated by Fama that financial research could only develop in close relationship with progress made in the field of data analysis also implied that financial research should not require additional expertise beyond that involved in properly analyzing data. "The new finance men . . . have lost virtually all contact with terra firma. On the whole, they seem to be more interested in demonstrating their mathematical prowess than in solving genuine problems; often they seem to be playing mathematical games," complained David Durand (1968, 848), a professor of management at MIT, in his 1968 review of the state the field. What did such mathematical games look like? Once properly collected, formatted, assembled, and processed, data can be subjected to analysis, such that anyone with access to the same data should be able to independently replicate them (Gitelman 2013). In other words, data become like mathematics in the sense that the degree to which they can be trusted can be adjudicated in their own terms: the opportunity to check the accuracy and power of data analysis is open to all those who possess some degree of technical skill (mathematical or statistical). There is no need for substantive knowledge of the processes that the data describe, once the data are taken to have some validity. So in this respect, data do not fear scrutiny, nor do they require data analysts to be particularly trustworthy.

By defining the main object of financial analysis—financial markets—in terms of data, financial economics thus seemed set on producing the kind of knowledge that would invite external verification. Reliance on data would open financial research to outside audiences: those who knew how to interpret the data properly could reach the same conclusions as the financial economists themselves. Data would make the discipline transparent, and data-driven financial knowledge would become universalizing and expansive rather than tied to the specialized scholarly interests of a few experts.

In this story, reasonableness, affect, collaboration, and trust should not matter once data had become central to financial knowledge: data, by virtue of their accessibility, even threatened to make the personal qualities of the analyst irrelevant. Once financial economists started to collaborate so that they could properly interpret financial data, over time, their interpretation would become closely aligned to the data themselves because of the transparency of data as a source of empirical evidence. But an important problem still afflicts this plausible argument. The quotes that open this chapter paint a picture of human excitement in the face of new data and of the new technologies that make data manipulation possible. Data seemed to spur skilled analysts to make new discoveries, rather than making the skilled analyst obsolete. And it is not just that financial data need human interpreters, just as any other kind of data do. Rather, the interpreters seemed to have a visceral relationship with the data. They experienced individual fulfillment and joy—the opposite of the rationalization we would have expected. A certain affective economy seemed to be at work, defined by wonder, expectation, and even naïveté. How did this come to be? How did particular emotions become woven into the social structure of the discipline of financial economics when financial economists themselves seemed, at least on the surface, to discount the importance of scholarship and expertise?

The Network of Financial Economics and Its Affects

Emotions are central to how knowledge is produced: through emotion, scholars find motivation and energy and use those resources to focus on the research frontier of their field (R. Collins 1998; Parker and Hackett 2012). Emotions are also central to how intellectual fields develop. They are systematically connected to social structure in scholarly arenas. But do emotions develop in fields that wear technical prowess as a badge of honor? And if so, what kinds of emotions are they?

To foreground the role of affect in a field as centered on data analysis as financial economics is, I combine insights from Bruno Latour and Lorraine Daston. Latour, as we have seen, looks at scholarly collaboration as the building of a network, while Daston understands affect as a set of virtues that the network uses to adjudicate the competence and trustworthiness of its members. According to both authors, these dynamics characterize technical and scientific fields as well as more humanistic ones. This theoretical integration, then, paves the way for my more specific argument that in the case of finance, the experience of wonder at data was connected to a particular kind of social structure, or a broader economy of affect.

Scholars may be excited by data for several reasons. Some of these may be as idiosyncratic as individual personality, and some may be as contextual as the historical novelty of using computers to generate new knowledge, as was surely the case for Fama, among the first scholars to have the skills to program the new machines. I suggest, however, that the social organization of research was also crucial. How, and how often, scholars collaborated; how they received credit for their contributions; and how their work spoke to the broader research programs that would come to define a discipline—these social processes affected the experience of doing research, by infusing it with particular emotions.

A perspective in the sociology of science, for instance, emphasizes the importance of small groups to scientific research: such groups tend to form around productive scholars, especially as they get ready to overthrow a major position or propose a theoretical breakthrough; in the process, their members develop distinctive ways of interacting with one another (Mullins 1972; Parker and Hackett 2012). In financial economics, I suggest that the social organization of research hinged on the dyadic collaboration, which emerged as the dominant collaborative strategy in the wake of Fama's research program on market efficiency. The emergence of very small-group dynamics is surprising because financial economics was built on data analysis, which was explicitly framed as *independent* of the skills of the individual analysts themselves. Providing empirical evidence in support of this perspective is the main task of the remainder of this chapter.

An empirical operationalization of the argument reveals the importance of affect to the organization of the network, and it is helpful to draw on a set of arguments concerned with the broader issue of creativity before we proceed. Studies of creativity have faced problems similar to those we confront as soon as we focus attention on how new research is produced: what counts as creative work— work that others will consider innovative, relevant, and useful, as able, in short, to move a field forward? And in a similar vein, who has the authority to make such pronouncements? Creative work, whether in the arts or in financial economics, cannot be defined a priori, for it requires some understanding of the context within which such work takes place, the audiences to which it is directed, and how the work is perceived. So understanding creativity means developing an understanding of domain expertise, and of the community that finds a contribution useful, and therefore creative. Teresa Amabile calls this the "consensual approach" to creativity, whereby a "product or response is creative to the extent that appropriate observers independently agree it is creative" (Amabile and Pillemer 2012, 6; see also Cattani and Ferriani 2008; Cattani, Ferriani, and Allison 2014).

While from a definitional point of view the study of creativity appears challenging, from an empirical point of view there is a relatively straightforward solution to this problem, which makes this approach particularly useful for our analysis of financial economics. If a field consecrates some of its producers with recognition and honors, the consecration process itself can be invoked in one's empirical operationalization of creativity. Put in simpler terms, the product that gets awarded by a set of peers invested with the authority to make such judgments can be considered creative for the purposes of sociological analysis (see esp. Cattani, Ferriani, and Allison 2014; Bourdieu 1993).

Recognition is not simply a way of highlighting the research (i.e., cognitive) achievements of a scholar or group of scholars. Awards are given in the context of emotionally charged rituals: a committee is assembled to judge the quality of the submissions under consideration; the committee then deliberates (often at length) over the merits and pitfalls of the work; and in deciding which product will be granted the award, the committee also reflects on the achievements of the field as a whole and on the directions it should take in the future. An additional advantage to focusing on expert judgments of creative work taking place during such ceremonial celebrations is that we can expect affective considerations to be particularly relevant. The selected work will embody both cognitive and affective criteria that resonate with the evaluation standards of peer judges. As the field collectively celebrates the work it considers most creative and cutting-edge, it renews its commitment to particular virtues, and particular ways of understanding the kind of research it pursues. Awards are therefore important not only because they signal the success of a particular research agenda or a particular way of constructing arguments; they also are important because they renew the commitment of the broader field to the values and virtues that are woven into its research practices.

In the case of financial economics, the flagship journals of the discipline highlight innovative research by giving awards for the best papers. Taking advantage of this aspect of the field, I focused on the top five journals of the field (the *Journal of Finance*, the *Journal of Financial Economics*, the *Financial Analysts Journal*, the *Journal of Financial and Quantitative Analysis*, and the *Review of Financial Studies*) and collected data on all the awards they granted in a variety of subfields (e.g., Investment, Corporate Finance, Financial Markets, and so on) over about two decades ending with 2013 (see appendix B for details).

I conducted a statistical analysis that, using five dependent variables, modeled separately for each award the impact of social structure on the likelihood of individual financial economists winning an award. My main goal was to tease out broader patterns in collaboration: whether scholars were likely to work with others they were already familiar with, or whether they selected collaborators based on other considerations, such as, for instance, the kind of expertise they held; whether scholars engaged in opportunistic collaborations or tended to be respectful of boundaries, careful not to invade the turf of their colleagues. In particular, I measured the degree to which each scholar worked with the same partners over time (*horizontal* collaborations, measured by the variable labeled "familiarity" in table 3.1), and also tracked collaborations where one of the coauthors had a much stronger and visible reputation than the other (*vertical* collaborations, measured by the variable labeled "prestige"). Both types of collaborations involve intimacy in the sense that as collaborators continue working together over time, they get to know and trust each other.

Second, I added two measures that tracked the extent to which collaborations were more occasional and opportunistic in nature. One variable, labeled "constraint," is a well-known measure that captures the extent to which an author writes with coauthors who do not themselves, independently, collaborate with one another (Burt 1992). A second variable, which I labeled "homogeneity," measured how similar each author's broad collaborative network remained over time. These two measures tapped the extent to which, rather than by familiarity and personal trust, collaborations were motivated by opportunism or the need to involve collaborators with specialized skill sets. This is because scholars whose collaborations change over time are likely to think about collaboration in a different way than coauthors who work together repeatedly with the same people. Changes in collaborative partners suggest the pursuit of knowledge by putting together ideas in ways that others (even the originators of some of those ideas) had not quite thought about before, in a role that Burt defines as "broker." This individual, by

TABLE 3.1. Summary statistics

VARIABLE	OBS	MEAN	STD. DEV.	MIN	MAX
JOF awards	139146	0.002	0.040	0	1
FAJ awards	6653	0.050	0.217	0	1
J FinEc awards	30218	0.006	0.079	0	1
JFQA awards	56398	0.001	0.025	0	1
REVFS awards	17175	0.004	0.064	0	1
Familiarity (Yr)	732456	0.025	0.170	0	13.875
Familiarity & prestige (Yr)	741420	0.065	0.889	0	131
Homogeneity	893970	0.082	0.458	−13.784	23
Constraint	864702	0.068	0.244	0	1.125
Past awards	386784	0.032	0.177	0	1
Cites Fama	356853	0.722	3.001	0	246
Cites Black	356870	0.390	1.463	0	47
Chicago aff.	404859	0.006	0.080	0	1
MIT aff.	404859	0.003	0.057	0	1
Chicago PhD	404859	0.008	0.090	0	1
Economet.	356890	0.988	2.991	0	98
AER	132592	2.908	3.972	0	97
# of Couthored Papers.	361823	1.477	2.722	0	69
# of singles	361823	0.987	1.795	0	113
Time	404807	96.379	12.989	60	113
Time to/since first paper in . . .					
. . . JOF	407995	0.136	1.808	−47	49
. . . FAJ	10859	−2.699	9.745	−47	12
. . . JFIN	407995	0.521	3.710	−46	37
. . . JFQA	407995	1.968	6.889	−40	47
. . . REVFS	407995	0.123	2.434	−52	25

Note: JOF = *Journal of Finance*; FAJ = *Financial Analysts Journal*; JFIN = *Journal of Financial Economics*; JFQA = *Journal of Financial and Quantitative Analysis*; REVFS = *Review of Financial Studies*; AER = *American Economic Review*.

virtue of his or her position in a network, acts as a bridge over "structural holes," making connections among networks that would not exist without the broker herself.

Underlying these sets of measures, it is worth emphasizing, are two contrasting views of the nature of collaborative work in intellectual fields: one focused on solidarity in interaction, the other on brokerage and the pursuit of informational advantages. In the first instance, the emphasis is on repeated collaborations over time: interaction with creative others affords the innovator new energy; perception of the emotional valence of new ideas and perspectives rapidly draws the would-be innovator toward the frontier of a discipline (R. Collins 1998; Farrell 2003; Parker and Hackett 2012). This is consistent with the classical sociology of science perspective as well, whereby intellectual success has a cumulative nature. In this older perspective, creative work is motivated by a thirst for peer recognition, an aspect of intellectual life that scientific awards crystallize in a public and ceremonial way. The micro-sociological model draws attention to social interaction that turns this long-term motivation into a day-to-day driver of creative work. Social interaction turns the long-term desire for recognition into a set of habits and practices that equip the creative producers with the skills to navigate the mundane challenges of innovative work. In his monumental sociology of philosophical creativity, Randall Collins (1998) argues that successful pupils tend to pick up the emotional and presentational habits of their teachers, even as they reconstruct the philosophical tradition they are trained in in new ways.

Social interaction can affect creativity depending on the status of the participants: when social interaction involves collaborating with scholars who already enjoy recognition and success, it endows the creative producer with the cognitive and emotional skills with which he or she can pave the way to success. In the process, the status-hierarchy of the field is reproduced: creative superstars continue their successful legacy by fostering the creativity of their collaborators. But interaction can lead to creativity via an additional pathway. Interaction motivates everyday work: it sharpens focus and deepens commitment. This effect should not depend on the status of the producer's collaborators: it is analytically separable, though in real-life empirical cases, motivation and prestige can certainly go together. That is to say, collaboration, in principle, can lead to more creativity by building the conditions for mutual trust, regardless of the visibility and reputation already enjoyed by the collaborators (see also Ruef, Aldrich, and Carter 2003).

Coauthorships, especially those that are long term, can therefore provide the kind of motivation that sparks creative work, even when coauthorships connect individuals who are not particularly eminent early in the collaboration. A long-term coauthorship constitutes a vested, meaningful relationship, motivating each author to both live up to the expectations of the others and nurture that relationship so that it grows over time (see also Rossman, Esparza, and Bonacich 2010). Randall Collins (1998) identified coauthorships as a kind of collaborative alliance or "horizontal tie": in social environments where coauthorship is diffuse, intellectuals gain the confidence to fully develop their complex ideas, and in doing so, the meaning of their work comes to depend on the shared value orientations and virtues (i.e., affects) that make the collaborations durable and enjoyable.

To be sure, as discussed most effectively in Uzzi's work (Uzzi and Spiro 2005), dense ties by themselves have the potential to *stifle* rather than encourage creativity. The main reason is cognitive rather than affective: dense ties afford access to information that is likely to be similar to what one already knows. Burt's "structural hole" model radicalizes this perspective and constitutes an alternative to the previous model and its focus on solidarity, motivation, and commitment. Burt focuses on individuals who act as bridges across disconnected communities: "People connected across groups are more familiar with alternative ways of thinking and behaving, which gives them more options to select from and synthesize. New ideas emerge from selection and synthesis across the structural holes between groups" (2004, 349–50). Structural holes are network locations between communities with no overlapping membership. According to Burt, individuals positioned in such locations are more likely to develop good ideas. Solidarity, or mutual trust, is not an essential ingredient for creativity and recognition; connections that span across distant communities are.

The results of the statistical models are presented in table 3.2. In four out of the five publication outlets, the measure capturing the extent to which each author engages in repeated, long-term collaborations with others is a consistent predictor of awards and therefore creativity. This effect is *net* of collaboration with prestigious others: in other words, it has statistical significance even as one controls for collaborations involving scholars who have already received recognition. The evidence about the effect of collaborative structures on the likelihood of winning awards points toward the importance of sustained, small-group coauthorships for creativity, even in the absence of connections with high-status scholars.

Consistent with my argument about the importance of small groups, the networks of financial economists do not easily fit with Burt's model of "bridges over structural holes," as the constraint measure has the opposite effect of what we would expect from Burt. Burt makes a strong case that individuals spanning structural holes are the most creative, but the models show that, in at least three of the journals, individuals with more constrained networks are in fact also more creative. In three out of five models, situating oneself on a structural hole has a statistically significant but *negative* effect on one's creative output. This is not to say that there is a penalty to engaging in research projects with a wide range of coauthors: authors whose collaborative network does not change over time tend to be less creative, whereas authors who diversify their networks are more likely to produce creative research. But that this effect coexists with an effect from dyadic familiarity suggests that authors who develop a core of trusted collaborators, to whom they return over time to engage in long-term research projects, while also engaging in different strands of work with more temporary collaborators, are most likely to receive praise and recognition in the field. This is consistent with

TABLE 3.2. Random effects logit regressions of selected independent variables on best paper awards

VARIABLE	(1) J FINANCE	(2) FINANCIAL AN	(3) J FINANCIAL ECON	(4) JFQA	(5) REV. FIN.
Familiarity (Yr, Ar)	1.243***	1.265***	1.526***	1.971**	−0.175
	(0.229)	(0.319)	(0.195)	(0.922)	(0.414)
Prestig. collabs (Ar)	0.306**	0.453***	0.499***	1.453**	0.265
	(0.143)	(0.148)	(0.127)	(0.704)	(0.221)
Homogeneity	−0.094***	−0.048*	−0.077***	−0.340**	−0.018
	(0.030)	(0.028)	(0.027)	(0.147)	(0.043)
Constraint	1.051***	−0.411	0.559*	1.028	0.717*
	(0.244)	(0.409)	(0.292)	(0.984)	(0.435)
Past awards	−0.241	0.383***	−0.164	−4.854***	0.061
	(0.182)	(0.080)	(0.137)	(0.965)	(0.206)
# of Fama cites	−0.014	0.009	0.007	0.168**	−0.021
	(0.015)	(0.018)	(0.009)	(0.071)	(0.021)
# of Black cites	0.042	−0.030	0.035	−0.488	−0.048
	(0.049)	(0.041)	(0.035)	(0.298)	(0.068)
Chicago aff.	2.074***		0.877**		2.116***
	(0.389)		(0.447)		(0.812)
MIT aff.	1.897***	2.062*	0.286		0.455
	(0.554)	(1.140)	(0.799)		(1.254)
Chicago PhD	0.950**	1.137*	−0.400	2.768	0.521
	(0.442)	(0.617)	(0.524)	(2.994)	(0.684)
Econometrica	0.039***	−0.036*	−0.019	−0.008	0.011
	(0.015)	(0.021)	(0.014)	(0.074)	(0.024)
Am Ec Rev	0.059***	0.005	0.013	0.045	0.010
	(0.017)	(0.034)	(0.015)	(0.105)	(0.030)
Coauthored Pps.	−0.118***	−0.023	0.021	0.240*	0.034
	(0.035)	(0.028)	(0.022)	(0.143)	(0.038)
Single-aut. Pps.	−0.211***	0.012	0.014	−0.424	0.034
	(0.070)	(0.015)	(0.045)	(0.382)	(0.087)
Time	0.052***	−0.084*	0.072***	0.198**	−0.024
	(0.012)	(0.048)	(0.017)	(0.084)	(0.030)
Time first JOF	−0.032				
	(0.042)				
Time first FAJ		−0.489***			
		(0.075)			
Time first JFIN			−0.087***		
			(0.019)		
Time first JFQA				−0.188**	
				(0.079)	
Time first REV					−0.110***
					(0.043)
Log(sigma_u²)	0.720**	−0.339	0.560*	4.066***	1.082***
	(0.350)	(0.583)	(0.334)	(0.167)	(0.418)
Constant	−12.725***	5.551	−14.196***	−40.890***	−4.799
	(1.316)	(5.106)	(1.851)	(9.464)	(3.145)
Observations	47,890	2,498	19,885	26,407	11,725
Number of id	2,212	314	1,525	1,301	1,163
Auth. random effects	YES	YES	YES	YES	YES

Note: Standard errors in parentheses.

*** $p<0.01$; ** $p<0.05$; * $p<0.1$

efforts from network theorists of economic entrepreneurship to go beyond dichotomous characterizations of ties, and theorize the interpenetration of close and
dense ties with familiar but distant ones (see esp. Vedres and Stark 2010).

We can conclude from these models that prestige in financial economics is a
function of one's embeddedness in both *vertical and already prestigious* collaborations with high-status individuals, and *horizontal* collaborative network structures. In both cases, collaborative networks lead to success, especially when they
afford opportunities for repeated interactions. And while increasing one's collaboration with prestigious others improves the likelihood of one's work being
recognized as creative, so does increasing one's collaborations with others in
general, regardless of the prestige of one's collaborators. There is both what
Merton (1973) called a "Matthew effect" (such that those who succeed tend to
become even more successful over time, enjoying cumulative advantage) and a
more egalitarian effect of social relationships on creative output. The two occur
simultaneously.

Second, the quantitative measures of horizontal and vertical collaboration increase in value the more scholars continue working together over time, as repeated
collaborations are given more weight than sporadic ones. This means that collaborations (both horizontal and vertical ones) become more creative in the long
run. Intuitively, the data-driven nature of financial knowledge may have something to do with these dynamics. When working with data, a new finding is always at risk of being idiosyncratic to a particular dataset: change the assumptions
underlying the model, or use a different sample of data, if not an altogether different dataset, and the finding might disappear. Yet, critics of current ways of how
economic knowledge is produced point out that replication is not systematically
pursued (Mirowski 1995), which brings me to a second point: for scholars to build
a career out of findings through data analysis, they need to make a claim to originality. Replicating another scholar's findings is not a way to success in a quantitative field. When replication does happen, it is therefore likely to be incremental, and to be pursued by the same scholar, over time. In figure 3.1, I show an
example of this division of labor: the research communities working on two research topics—cross-sectional analysis and volatility—that employ similar techniques but draw from different datasets have very little overlap.

One way of interpreting our results is that the creative pair or small group
works on a dataset with a particular angle that the collaborators develop over time
into a more coherent perspective. Each finding can be substantiated with findings from previous work: data analysis turns into the springboard for a sustain-
able chain of discoveries stretching into the future. By contrast, expand the collaboration, and the perspective can no longer be attached to the pair that originated
it—data collectivize the finding, so to speak, thereby making attribution of the

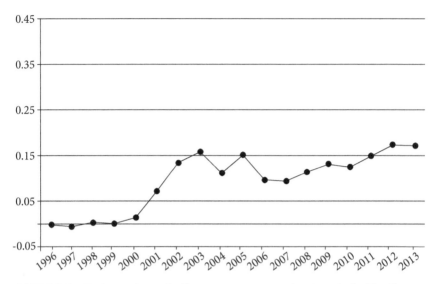

FIGURE 3.1 Topic overlap, volatility versus cross-sectional analysis. The figure plots the topic overlap between volatility and cross-sectional analysis in the *Journal of Finance*, with data on articles published between 1996 and 2013. Specifically, the plot compares the year-to-year vector of authors who publish a paper on the topic of volatility with the year-to-year vector of authors who publish a paper on the topic of cross-sectional analysis, calculating and mapping a yearly Pearson correlation coefficient. Correlations range from –0.002 to 0.17, suggesting a minimal overlap between the topics. Substantively, both topics concern the measurement of stock market returns; small overlap suggests the presence of a division of labor.

discovery to particular scholars difficult. Perhaps more important, increase the size of the collaboration and its emotional intensity will decrease: small groups, by contrast, generate more emotional energy around data analysis as personal relationships motivate scholars to participate in research activities while feeling personally invested in the data. As shown in figure 3.2, the average number of co-authors on award-winning papers increases in the 1990s and 2000s, but only by a small margin of about one author.

Might we not expect the presence of these small groups of empirical researchers to fragment the field rather than turn it into the kind of cumulative, data-oriented field I am describing? Andrew Abbott (2001a) makes the important point that social knowledge tends to have a "fractal" nature, in the sense that when scholars take contrasting positions and develop perspectives that divide the world into dichotomies, each side of the dichotomy then reproduces the pattern that generated it. Intellectual conflict repeats itself, with contending groups taking up

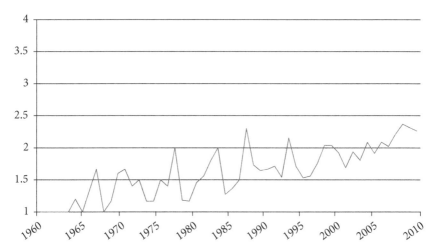

FIGURE 3.2 Number of authors per award-winning paper, 1960–2013 (*n* = 922 papers).

positions within the group that are similar to the one they take as a whole, against their opponents, while others are closer to the contenders. This cultural tendency generates important patterns, and a particularly relevant one for our present purposes is "fractionation," when in one side of a dichotomy, a group experiences a "rapid proliferation of distinctions" (see especially pp. 84–88). This happens when scholars on one side take a consistently dichotomous position at each level of debate: if they believe theory is more important than empiricism when speaking to methodologists, they similarly reject calls for engagement with the empirical world in conversations with fellow theorists, and so on. Fractionation also happens when one side of the dichotomy couples intellectual argument with a political stance. In both cases, intellectual rigor becomes a source of virtue, both intellectual and moral.

If we apply Abbott's argument to financial economics, why financial economics does not become fractionated constitutes a puzzle. One possible mechanism is the creation of cross-group collaborations. Dyadic and small-group ties, while they build confidence and trust among immediate collaborators, are also vulnerable to opportunistic exploitation. They should generate "structural holes," empty spaces among tightly knit communities of scholars that entrepreneurial individuals can exploit to their own advantage. But while we should expect collaborators to take advantage of such opportunities, we saw little evidence of such broader, opportunistic collaborations. Simplicity and communicability seem to push against fractionation because they help scholars find a niche, and remain in it, rather than going outside their area of specialization: the simple models preferred by financial economists—models that conform to the main tenets of the discipline—allow for long-term cumulative development. The emphasis on communicability and the persistence of long-term collaborations, in turn, are symptoms of interpersonal trust. We might therefore expect scholars to forgo opportunities to exploit new venues, when building financial knowledge piecemeal in small groups already offers a pathway to success, and when working with scholars outside one's network may make others suspicious of one's motives. In other words, through affect, scholars are able to sustain a collaborative network structure that, under a different moral economy, would likely lose its coherence.

The quantitative evidence we just considered suggests that in a field like financial economics, where knowledge is developed on the basis of data analysis, collaboration and coauthorship tend to take place in small groups. Further, small groups are the structural foundation for an affective economy that privileges a certain view of expertise and a certain orientation to how knowledge is made, where discoveries are couched in a language of reasonableness, simplicity, and communicability. Those values orient the research activities of scholars in that they generate a structure of opportunities for data analysts. The affective network of financial economics is a duality of small groups and intergroup communicative practices centered on particular virtues.

Qualitative Analysis: Creative Pairs

The analysis above shows that one of the predictors of creative success is intimacy in collaborations. But how important of a predictor is it? Statistical significance tells us that the association between two variables is not the result of chance and chance alone. However, the association between collaboration and creativity is not a spurious result of statistical models: collaborative pairs are more likely to be recognized than lone scholars or scholars with transient collaborators. For perspective, we can return to table 3.1 and note that, with no information about how much they collaborate, how long they have been working in the field, and so on, the likelihood of any given scholar winning an award ranges from 0.001 to 0.04, depending on the journal. If, however, we concentrate on the top one hundred authors with the highest score of horizontal collaboration, the number is astoundingly higher: forty of those highly collaborative authors have won two or more awards since 1990. To be sure, to apply the theory I am building in this book reflexively, the simple detection of a pattern turns into a significant finding only when it is translated into a language that is appropriate to standards of the network to which the researcher belongs. I can do a bit better by looking into relevant examples, using the statistical apparatus as a guide.

According to the argument I am making here, financial knowledge is developed on the basis of data analysis, where collaboration and coauthorship tend to take place in small groups, linked by an affective economy that privileges a certain view of expertise and a certain epistemology. When discoveries are couched in a language of reasonableness and simplicity, the field recognizes them as valuable, because adherence to those values marks the authors as trustworthy. Put differently, reasonableness and simplicity generate a structure of opportunities: scholars who infuse their research with such values have more credibility than scholars who do not. In the following section, I present more descriptive and qualitative data in support of the general point, using the quantitative data as a guide. I concentrate on the far tail of this distribution, where a more in-depth discussion of an example will be particularly meaningful. I then contrast this pair with a second case of a deeply collaborative duo who is not as successful.

Over the period under consideration, as shown in figure 3.3, the most collaborative pair in financial economics is Martin Gruber and Edwin J. Elton. Gruber holds a PhD from Columbia University, which he earned in 1966 for a dissertation titled "The Determinants of Common Stock Prices." Elton holds a PhD from Carnegie Mellon University, where he defended a dissertation titled "Studies in Financial Theory" in 1971. Their entire careers unfolded at New York University,

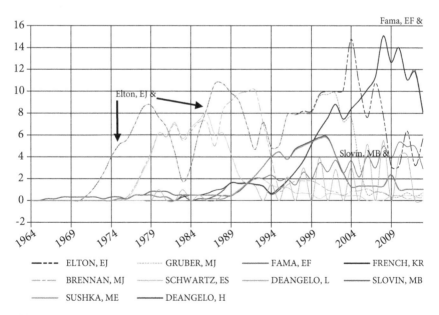

FIGURE 3.3 Top ten collaborative financial economists.

where they rose to the rank of full professors by the early 1970s. In 2004, Gruber won a James R. Vertin Award for lifetime achievement for producing a body of work with enduring value for investment professionals. Elton lists seven scholarly awards on his curriculum vitae (CV), including a lifetime achievement award from the European Finance Association. Together, the two share five best paper awards in the journals in my sample.[4]

Elton and Gruber did not coauthor with Eugene Fama or his close collaborators, but their area of specialization centers on the "characteristics and analysis of individual securities, as well as . . . the theory and practice of optimally combining securities into portfolios": modern portfolio theory, in a nutshell—the area in which Fama's research agenda was most transformative (Elton et al. 2006, v). One of the early outcomes of the two scholars' collaboration was a 1972 methodological paper titled "Earnings Estimates and the Accuracy of Expectational Data." In the paper, they investigate the accuracy of forecasts of the correlations among securities produced by different models, starting with the pragmatic point that historical data are the most likely source of such estimates. The language of the paper is particularly instructive, so let me provide two short examples:

> Although some work has been done on specifying sets of conditions under which particular mechanical techniques are optimum forecasters, the range and complexity of models investigated have been very narrow. Furthermore, very little research has been conducted on the underlying statistical properties of the process generating earnings. Rather than attempting to investigate the properties of alternative forecasting models and earnings streams, this study empirically determines which of several techniques produces the most accurate forecasts of earnings per share. (Elton and Gruber 1972, B410)

In other words, Elton and Gruber claimed that an empirically oriented strategy can be more instructive than further theorizing or further refinement of a methodological approach. They called for a deeper, empirical understanding of the models currently used. These are key characteristics of a mode of argument centered on data. Later, more substantively, the authors reveal why this exercise had important practical implications:

> The average data show that the best mechanical technique outperforms the security analysts at one financial institution, but is outperformed by the analysts at two others. However, none of the three differences is significant at even the 20% level, and two of the three differences are not even significant at the 35% level. In short, there is no statistically significant evidence to indicate that the forecasts made by analysts are

different from those made by an exponentially weighted moving average employing an additive trend. Insofar as better forecasts lead to better valuation models, the lack of such evidence would seem to indicate that mechanical techniques exist which can provide valid inputs to financial models and that these techniques (given their low cost) should be employed at least as a bench mark against which to judge analysts' performance. (B419)

Here the paper introduces the idea that data analysis, when properly conducted, contextualizes, if not altogether challenges, the analysts' performance. Elton and Gruber advocated for better use of statistics; through statistics, different truth claims can be compared and systematically evaluated. Financial economics could prove traders wrong by showing their strategies to be no better than mechanical techniques, devised without recourse to specialized knowledge of market variables.

Both Gruber and Elton went on to have very prolific careers: as shown by their respective CVs, Gruber authored or coauthored 8 books and over 110 articles, while Elton was involved in 11 book projects and over 120 articles. Of those articles, Elton's CV reports that 21 were coauthored, 8 of those solely by Elton and Gruber, while an additional 8 included a third coauthor, Christopher Blake. In 1979, Gruber and Elton's collaboration resulted in a jointly authored book titled *Portfolio Theory—25 Years Later*, a volume celebrating the legacy of Harry Markowitz (the founder of modern portfolio theory).

One of the common threads in their research output is attention to data and to the methodological innovations that new findings may warrant. Representative titles of Elton's papers, to this effect, include "Are Betas Best?" (1978, coauthored with Gruber), "Simple Rules for Optimal Portfolio Selection in Stable Paretian Markets" (1979), "A Simple Examination of the Empirical Relationship between Dividend Yields and Deviations from the CAPM" (1983), and "Professional Expectations: Accuracy and Diagnosis of Errors" (1984). "Simple rules" and "simple examination" are recurring themes in his work, deepening the perspective for which he laid out the foundations in collaborative work with Gruber. Thirty years into his career, in his 2001 "A First Look at the Accuracy of the CRSP Mutual Fund Database and a Comparison of the CRSP and Morningstar Mutual Fund Databases," he joined forces again with Gruber and a third coauthor to investigate the accuracy of newly available datasets. He returned to data analysis as an important exercise of its own accord.

Gruber's work includes papers with such titles as "Portfolio Theory When Investment Relatives Are Lognormally Distributed" (1974), "A Closer Look at the Implications of the Stable Paretian Hypothesis" (1975, coauthored with Elton and

Paul R. Kleindorfer), and "Cost of Capital Using Arbitrage Theory: A Case Study of Nine New York Utilities" (1994, a lengthier case study). As in Elton's case, as these titles suggest, Gruber's style of analysis centered on the discovery of empirical problems whose solutions required new analytical skills. But these skills were developed, and presented, incrementally: Gruber wrote about the consequences that the introduction of a new statistical distribution has for portfolio theory, without rewriting portfolio theory from scratch; he invited his readers to take a closer look; and he wrote case studies that included new but manageably small datasets. In his 1974 paper, he helped reformulate portfolio theory by introducing statistical assumptions that were becoming increasingly accepted in the economic literature.

A more telling example comes from the first paper in a sequence on portfolio selection strategies that Elton and Gruber coauthored with Manfred Padberg in 1976. This early paper opens by highlighting an irony: modern portfolio theory was motivated by efforts to devise "practical and implementable" suggestions. But "the primary outgrowth has been normative and theoretical," and "modern portfolio theory has rarely been implemented." After listing several reasons why this was the case, the three authors proposed a solution that had the practical and implementable qualities they praised, such that an "intuitive interpretation" of the technique is possible, so "its basis is easily understood." They continued: "This method not only allows one to determine which securities are included in an optimal portfolio but also how much to invest in each. Furthermore, the technique allows the definition of a cut-off rate defined solely in terms of the character of the individual security, such that the impact on the optimal portfolio of the introduction of any new security into the manager's decision set can easily be seen. Finally, the technique makes clear to the manager what characteristic of a security are desirable" (Elton, Gruber, and Padberg 1976, 1341). Elton and his collaborators highlighted the importance of proposing methods of data analysis that could be easily implemented. Such methods should not pose difficult technical challenges or create confusion about what the methods were actually measuring and what aspects of the data they made more central to the analysis. It is tempting to contextualize their strategy of making data and empirical relationships visible and accessible in Fama's larger point that financial economics should be reasonable. In Fama's mind, as we saw, being reasonable meant seeing the relationship between theory and data in terms of how well a model accounted for some aspects of empirical reality that were useful for the purposes at hand. From the perspective of Elton and his collaborators, financial economics should also strive to reach out to informed practitioners: reasonability meant proposing simple solutions to complex problems, so that reasonable people could understand and adopt those solutions and get on with their business!

In other words, Elton and Gruber are powerful examples of the positions made possible by the rise of data analysis in financial economics: theorizing takes to the background while data become the apex of the data-method-theory triad, all in the name of helping hands-on financial practitioners gain better insight into the unpredictable nature of markets. Their suspicion of analysts who claimed to have better knowledge than the markets themselves, coupled with their preference for methods that could be implemented in real financial practice, highlight this characteristic of financial economics, a discipline that attempts to study markets scientifically so as to make them more accessible to the people who operate in them.

Elton and Gruber's work reveals another important aspect of data analysis: letting the data speak means relying on simple algorithms, which go on to replace complex and counterintuitive models. Techniques of data analysis do not need to be more accurate than these complex models: simplicity suffices because it makes the techniques potentially implementable. The practical effects of simple techniques for analyzing financial data give value to such techniques. Understanding the practical quality of data analysis is important for two additional reasons. Practicality makes the techniques more likely to be accepted by other scholars, as it speaks to affective dispositions that circulate within the discipline. Second, and relatedly, scholars who put forward practical techniques say something about themselves: they take a moral position in that they implicitly frame the role of the scholar as being about producing simple solutions. To the extent that scholars orient their research around these values, they can better impress on others that they can be trusted.

Orienting one's research toward values that others consider appropriate and use as signals of trustworthiness, in sum, constitutes a successful strategy, and Elton and Gruber represent a particularly striking example of these dynamics. But not all scholars can follow this pathway. A second, negative case helps make this point, and it also helps us better understand why the affective network matches virtues and research. Reasonableness and simplicity made it easier to produce incremental work, focus on the accumulation of knowledge, and pursue piecemeal innovation. They made it harder to make discontinuous contributions or introduce theoretical points that sat uneasily with the core of the discipline.

The second case is a collaborative pair also characterized by a deep and durable relationship that nevertheless failed to achieve the kind of recognition afforded to scholars like Elton and Gruber. The pair is Myron B. Slovin and Marie Sushka. Slovin received his PhD from Princeton in 1972 with a dissertation titled "Deposit Rate Setting at Financial Intermediaries: Theoretical Models and Econometric Analyses with Additional Focus on Savings and Loan Associations." His academic website at Louisiana State University lists his teaching interests as commercial banking and financial institutions and markets, and his research interests as corporate finance, financial institutions and markets, and commercial banking. One overarching empirical interest that characterizes several of his publications is in mergers and acquisitions.

Sushka received her PhD from Georgetown in 1974 with a dissertation titled "An Econometric Model of the Money Market in the United States, 1823–1859." She lists her areas of specialization as corporate finance, banking, and financial markets and institutions, and she currently teaches at the W.P. Carey College of Business at Arizona State University. In addition to the interests she shares with Slovin, Sushka was trained as an economic historian. Phillys Keys and Pamela Turner (2006), using data on finance articles written between 1988 and 2003, rank her among the top four women scholars in the field.

Between 1974 and 2012, Slovin and Sushka coauthored thirty-six papers (some of which include a third author). They also coauthored two monographs (in 1975 and 1977, titled *Interest Rates on Savings Deposits: Theory, Estimation, and Policy* and *Money and Economic Activity: An Analytical Approach*, respectively) and a textbook titled *Macroeconomics for Managers* (1987). According to the collaborative index I calculated for the financial economists in my sample, this pair ranks among the top ten most collaborative scholars in the field. Neither, however, won a best paper award in any of the top five journals I am tracking. Why not?

I submit that the mismatch between their research and the moral economy of the network is one reason behind their lack of recognition. Their work, I suggest, was empirical but not cumulative. And rather than concerning itself with refinement of the core model, it would look for exceptions. There was a gap between the affective economy of the network and the affective orientation of their work, and this gap was consequential to the kind of recognition these authors received.

Sushka and Slovin's collaboration began with a focus on the intersection between regulation (especially monetary regulation on deposits enforced by the Fed) and monetary outcomes. Their first joint paper is titled "The Structural Shift in the Demand for Money," which they wrote in 1975 while they were both economists at the Federal Reserve. A later paper, titled "The Macroeconomic Impact of Changes in the Ceilings on Savings Deposit Rates," appeared in the *Journal of Finance* in 1977. In both cases, they carried out applied work in an area of financial economics that was removed from the field's primary concern with financial markets.

Their turn toward topics that are more central to the discipline took place in 1986 with a paper titled "Tender Offer Premia and Managerial Signaling," which appeared in the journal *Managerial and Decision Economics* (J. Polonchek is the third, leading coauthor on this paper). The three scholars conceived their contribution as an extension of "asymmetric information-signalling models, such as Spence and Riley (1975)" (Polonchek, Slovin, and Sushka 1986, 69). They therefore mounted a critique of the idea that market equilibrium can be accomplished "in the presence of asymmetric information and signaling," proposing a skeptical assessment of the standard model in financial economics.

In 1993, Slovin and Sushka's paper "Ownership Concentration, Corporate Control Activity, and Firm Value: Evidence from the Death of Inside Blockholders," published in the *Journal of Finance*, was nominated for a best paper award but did not win (Sushka reports this on her CV). The award went to a paper focused on a similar problem, authored by Lisa K. Meulbroek and titled "An Empirical Analysis of Illegal Insider Trading." I report the abstracts of the two papers below for comparison, with the winning paper first.

> Whether insider trading affects stock prices is central to both the current debate over whether insider trading is harmful or pervasive, and to the broader public policy issue of how best to regulate securities markets. Using previously unexplored data on illegal insider trading from the Securities and Exchange Commission, this paper finds that the stock market detects the possibility of informed trading and impounds this information into the stock price. Specifically, the abnormal return on an insider trading day averages 3%, and almost half of the pre-announcement stock price run-up observed before takeovers occurs on insider trading days. Both the amount traded by the insider and additional trade-specific characteristics lead to the market's recognition of the informed trading. (Meulbroek 1992, 1661)
>
> We analyze how ownership concentration affects firm value and control of public companies by examining effects of deaths of inside blockholders. We find shareholder wealth increases, ownership concentration falls, and extensive corporate control activity ensues. Share price responses are related to the deceased's equity stake. Control group holdings fall for two-thirds of the firms due to either the estate's dispersal or inheritors selling stock. A majority of firms become targets of control bids: three-quarters of bids are successful; one-third are hostile. Our evidence is broadly consistent with Stulz's (1988) model of the relationship between ownership concentration and firm value. (Slovin and Sushka 1993, 1293)

The abstracts of the two papers appear quite similar in terms of research focus; both papers use new datasets, originally assembled for the purpose at hand. It is, of course, difficult to say why the first is a winner: we cannot attribute the differential success of these two papers to any one set of conditions with some accuracy, since we do not know what other papers were considered for this award, how close the Slovin-Sushka paper was to winning, who served on the committee, and so forth. But one major difference between the papers that becomes clear on a closer reading is that the Meulbroek paper is supportive of the standard model. Her results lead her to conclude that "insider trading is beneficial. The extent to which insider trading aids in price discovery in the sample can be substantial. The cumulative abnormal return on insider trading days is half as large as the price reaction to the public revelation of the information on which the insider trades. This ratio suggests that the stock market detects informed trading and impounds a large proportion of the information into the stock price before it becomes public" (Meulbroek 1992, 1663). Later, she adds by way of policy implications: "Since trading leads to the incorporation of private information in stock prices, regulation that impedes trading may also result in less informative prices. Thus, regulation designed to decrease stock price volatility, such as the proposed tax on securities transactions, may actually result in noisier, less-informative stock prices" (1697). In other words, it is faith in the efficiency of the market that underlies her research and that the empirical analysis helps solidify.

In the case of the Slovin and Sushka paper, by contrast, the emphasis is on critique. The paper's main point is that managers, at least in US firms, concentrate power in their hands through equity ownership that, were it to be released to the public, would increase the value of the firm. The argument is therefore at odds with claims that market processes by themselves correct imperfections in managerial practice. Rather, the paper provides substantive support for a theory of management entrenchment that identifies in the protected position of managers a cause of persistent mispricings.

I do not believe Slovin and Sushka's lack of recognition by the mainstream of the field can be simply attributed to ideology or compliance with orthodoxy, as if a scholar's position on the question of efficiency and market equilibrium were sufficient to determine whether one would have a successful career. Rather, the quantitative analysis presented above suggests that long-term collaborations increased the odds of success in this field, and that, at the same time, the field was less open to strategic collaborations (less open to the exploitation of Burt's "structural holes") than we might expect from studies of creativity in other fields. Putting the two observations together amounts to saying that scholars who collaborated on similar projects over long periods of time were more likely to be successful than scholars who moved from topic to topic in search of new discoveries. And focusing on the costs of deviating from one's area of long-term expertise gives us new insight into a potential stumbling block facing Slovin and Sushka as they strove to achieve recognition from the field.

A critical review of one of their early works gives more substance to this claim. The piece appeared in the *Journal of Finance* in 1976 and was authored by Franklin Edwards, at the time a professor at the Graduate School of Business at Columbia University. The work under review is Slovin and Sushka's 1975 coauthored book,

Interest Rates on Savings Deposits. Edwards focused on a number of points he found problematic, but for our purposes, the following two are particularly important. First, Edwards objected to what he perceived to be the authors' skepticism toward the competitive nature of the market for savings deposits: "In particular, their model of firm behavior implies (or requires) that savings institutions be monopsonists in the savings market, or that they be price-setters rather than price-takers. This assumption is difficult to accept. Indeed, competition for savings deposits would seem to be quite keen among banks, savings and loan associations, and mutual savings banks" (1976, 1524). Alternative perspectives, added Edwards, would introduce further problems, leaving him somewhat dumbfounded. So he complained about a proof that "cannot possibly be correct in its present form," about "a number of annoying features" in the empirical work presented in the book, about "dubious measures of the degree of competition," and about a lack of statistical tests for important assumptions (1524).

A second critical point emerged around Edwards's perception of Slovin and Sushka's work as technically inadequate and imprecise. To this effect, he argued: "Although the authors frequently employ quite sophisticated econometric techniques, they inexplicably fail to apply the standard statistical tests of structural stability, preferring to 'eyeball' the estimated parameters for evidence of instability." He continued:

> A particularly disturbing aspect of this analysis is the absence of a discussion of what is meant by "effectiveness of monetary policy." The authors appear to argue that "effectiveness" is to be judged by the size of the respective money multipliers (e.g., the magnitude of the impact of a change in money supply on income and open market rates). They say: ". . . the size of each of the money multipliers in case B is likely to be smaller than in Case A. This suggests that the impact of monetary policy on economic activity is less effective if . . ." (p. 133). This is not a meaningful criterion of effectiveness. . . . Surely monetary policy effectiveness is a concept having to do with the predictability (or variability) of the money multipliers, rather than with their magnitudes. About this the authors have nothing to say. (1525)

Edwards's critique may seem unnecessarily harsh, but the tone is suggestive of an underlying problem: the values toward which Slovin and Sushka oriented their work were clearly different from Edwards's. Terms that Slovin and Sushka took for granted (like "effectiveness") appeared mysterious to Edwards. Statistical tests they did not deem necessary appeared to Edwards to be absolutely essential, and their absence led him to question the integrity of their entire work. There was a mismatch between the affect of the authors and the affect of the critic.

We can generalize from this point. The book was Slovin and Sushka's area of expertise, where, conceivably, they would be able to mount a defense and build toward changing the affective economy within which Edwards's critiques were articulated, were they joining forces with others in the subversion of orthodoxy. But Slovin and Sushka's strategy, by contrast, was to branch out over time into other areas of specialization. Rather than focusing on banking regulation and its intersection with market forces, they went on to write about corporate finance and corporate management, among other things. What seemed to remain constant throughout their work was their penchant for unfavorable assessments of the competitive model. But because their line of research was at odds with the core model that increasingly defined the discipline of financial economics, they could not pursue a strategy of simplicity and reasonable results. And their work, as a consequence, veered too close to the edge of reasonableness, failing to achieve the kind of recognition that the network model I am proposing here would predict for them.

Conclusions: Why Is Fama So Happy to Work with Data?

In this chapter, I demonstrate that the network of financial economics developed on the basis of small collaborations, collaborations that were often as small as dyads. These collaborative pairs worked with data by engaging in nonoverlapping projects: scholars did not exploit gaps in the broader research networks of finance in order to build their own individual reputation. They oriented their work toward reasonableness over other values, so that communicability across projects in the simple language of data analysis could be achieved.

Theoretically, we should expect this compromise, where collaborative pairs and small groups specialize in lines of research that tend not to overlap with work done by others, to generate motivation to engage in data-heavy projects. Working with data means that the potential for being scooped is high, so an affective economy that prevents scholars from exploiting such opportunities gives the field stability. And as Shapin (1989) remarks, technically skilled scholars have historically been subordinated to the scientist proper, whose creative vision they undergird and implement through their actions, without receiving proper recognition. The problem of having one's contribution properly recognized is therefore particularly salient in empirically driven fields. Affect, I suggested, can protect technicians from these dangers.

Investigating the social structure of collaboration in financial economics raises compelling questions about how research works when it starts from big and unexplored datasets—when the theory-data-method triad is reconfigured, with data at its apex. Financial economics teaches us that the alleged anonymity, portability, and depersonalized nature of data are in fact fully compatible with deep, intimate ties of collaboration among scholars. To be sure, further layers of depersonalization can be added through "little analytics"; yet, even when techniques of data filtering, clustering, and reduction, on which data increasingly rely, would seem to redefine the role of human observers (Amoore and Piotukh 2015), financial economics demonstrates the resilience of social structure. Seemingly untrained analysts, complex datasets, and increasingly standardized procedures to make the datasets legible can all be mobilized toward the organization of knowledge into a discipline. Perhaps this is true of big data as well: add expertise, and big data and small groups can go hand in hand too. We explore these themes in the conclusion.

In the previous chapter, I showed that reasonableness became a particular virtue for financial economists, with particular rules set by scholars who occupied the core of the data-processing networks that moved the field forward. Financial economists justified their contributions in terms of how they fit into a loosely defined, general framework. Reasonableness was an affect in Daston's sense: enmeshed in a "web of affect-saturated values that stand and function in well-defined relationship to one another," reasonableness helped turn financial economics into a "balanced system of emotional forces, with equilibrium points and constraints" (1995, 4).

In line with Daston, this chapter emphasizes the constitutive role affects play with respect to scientific networks, and proposes an empirical characterization of such networks for the case of financial economics. In financial economics, reasonableness and data analysis went together as the discipline crystallized because financial research came to be tethered to data. This gave scholars an incentive to couch their findings in a common framework so that they could build on each other's work but maintain some degree of control over their own turf. Where datasets are contested, as Daston would predict, doubts about data are also doubts about data analysts. Daston suggests that the rhetorical moves scholars make as they communicate to others serve as a solution to this problem of uncertainty. She sees measurement in terms of relationships of trust that can be reproduced only to the extent that participants in those relationships abide by a broader moral economy. And in doing so, she paints a world of self-discipline, of scientists exercising power over themselves as much as they do over the flow of traces and inscriptions that a center of calculation may or may not rise to manage.

Financial scholarship became team-based because data needed to be stabilized, made uniform, and formatted in ways that would appear universally valid before they could be put to work. The kinds of tacit choices that would drive data analysis in one direction as opposed to others generated opportunities for the same investigators, making the same assumptions and knowing what assumptions would be less credible to the broader community, to specialize in particular lines of research and analysis. My point is simply that data expertise must be developed over time, and that it often takes a career to do so, especially when data themselves must be processed in order to negotiate potential objections about their credibility.

Do all disciplines work on the basis of affectively cohesive networks? Or, do disciplines need to display some unity and centralization before they adopt shared orientations to affects? To the second question, Daston says no. When she discusses how quantification in science takes different forms, ranging from counting to the production of mathematical models more or less tethered to data, the underlying argument is that the structure of the community is intimately related to the forms of quantification the community takes up. This plurality in forms is matched by plurality in objectives. Accuracy, precision, communicability, and impartiality become more or less central to quantification under different periods and social circumstances. In other words, each objective may or may not be valued, but sometimes it is, even as a virtue, worth pursuing for its own good, depending on the social processes that animate quantification, and the structure of social relationships that connect scientists to one another.

I agree with Daston, for one main reason. Financial economics is not particularly unified as a social structure, since scholars collaborate in small groups, but it is nevertheless coherent; what gives the field coherence is belief in data, in the sense that scholars developed a common orientation to how data should work and how data could be mobilized in the pursuit of new knowledge. The direction of causality therefore appears to be reversed: it is the affect that allowed for centralization of knowledge in this diffuse network, rather than a centralized network producing pressure toward common affects. This leads me to suggest that affect may be particularly important for decentralized disciplines that could easily, in the absence of shared affect, fragment.

Sociology serves as an interesting contrast. We are fragmented, and so are our affects, with endless fights between public sociologists and social physicists, quantitative scholars versus ethnographers, and so on. Unlike financial economists, however, we sociologists never anchored our discipline to one type of data. And our collaborative networks are much more diverse than the collaborative networks of economists (Moody 2004). The network structure of our discipline, in the absence of successful efforts to make one kind central to sociological knowledge, tends to multiply the number of values sociologists pursue.

Let us return to financial economics to remind ourselves that people like Fama were (and remain) so happy to work with data. Why? If my argument is correct,

Fama's happiness was not just excitement about working with new technology, though certainly that played a role. The excitement was also about a new vision in the field of finance, one where computers would allow scholars to collaborate, unfettered by theory or method, and turn datasets into the bedrock for future financial knowledge, in a language that was both simple and reasonable. Fama himself, responding to the structural pressure the field puts on scholars to join a partner in a collaborative pair, made new friends on the way. His collaboration with Kenneth French built stronger foundations for the efficient-market hypothesis, and Fama is not only one of the founding fathers of finance but also one of its most collaborative figures. To how his work defeats the one challenge that could have ended the dominance of market efficiency way before the behavioral revolution to come, we now turn.

WINNERS AND LOSERS IN FINANCIAL ECONOMICS, OR FAMA VERSUS BLACK

How Markets Became Efficient and Equilibrium Was Defeated

In a 1985 critique of the seemingly unbridgeable chasm between research on finance in *economics* and research on finance in *financial* economics, Larry Summers likened the study of finance to the systematic study of ketchup. In a thought experiment, he invited his readers to imagine a new field, "ketchup economics." This field would have two groups of researchers: general economists, working in economics departments, and "ketchup economists," "located in Department of Ketchup where they receive much higher salaries than do general economists." (As a sociologist, I do not feel much empathy toward the plight of the latter.) He continued: "Each group has a research program." General economists would study the fundamental determinants of prices and quantities in the ketchup market, paying attention to things like the cost of tomatoes. Ketchup economists, by contrast, would counter that "ketchup transactions prices are the only hard data worth studying" (Summers 1985, 634). And they would base their entire research program on such data.

Summers concluded: "Financial economists like ketchupal economists work only with hard data and are concerned with the interrelationships between the prices of different financial assets. They ignore what seems to many to be the more important question of what determines the overall level of asset prices. It would surely come as a surprise to a layman to learn that virtually no mainstream research in the field of finance in the last decade has attempted to account for the stock market boom of the 1960s or the spectacular decline in real stock prices during the mid-1970s" (634).

Summers was not alone, or the first, in articulating such a critique: the complaint that financial economists' success in building a new discipline had come at a great cost—ignorance of the underlying determinants of financial value—was already widespread in the late 1960s, when an older, institutionally oriented generation of scholars was looking at the rising new finance with suspicion, if not disdain. And the complaint would resurface later in the development of the discipline, when behavioral economists rekindled academic interest in the role that limited rationality plays in financial processes. We explore this theme in greater depth in the next chapter.

But Summers's more specific point that it was a fascination with hard data that underlay the success of the discipline deserves further scrutiny, as it points to a set of dynamics that reflect different concerns than anxiety about whether finance should be considered a science and practiced in accordance with the scientific method. Building a discipline around a consensus about the importance of hard data to knowledge entails settling a number of important issues, including, for instance, how the data should be analyzed, how generalizable such analyses may be, and what scholars might be in a position to say in the absence of data. Faced with the same hard data, and equipped with the same belief about the importance of hard data to knowledge, scholars may still apply different inferential criteria and propose results that, to those less steeped in the same assumptions, may seem unwarranted (Abbott 2001b). Data analysis conducted on the basis of assumptions not shared by others may therefore raise suspicion and mistrust rather than create consensus. Setting hard data at the foundations of a discipline, in other words, is a social process of building trust across a network.

When do scholars who work with hard data succeed in articulating a perspective on its analysis that wins enough consensus for the discipline to move forward, such that data analysts come to be trusted? In this chapter, I answer this question by comparing two research trajectories: Eugene Fama's and Fischer Black's. Eugene Fama, as we have seen in previous chapters, is considered the father of modern finance for his work on market efficiency. I claimed that this recognition is also warranted on account of both his leadership in the computer revolution and his articulation of a set of affective values that would foster increased, creative use of financial data. Fischer Black is a more controversial, even enigmatic figure: his influence in the field is best exemplified by the Black-Scholes-Merton option-pricing formula. In 1997, Scholes and Merton won a Nobel Prize for this work, and Black would have enjoyed the same recognition had it been possible for the prize to be awarded posthumously. Unfortunately, Black passed away in 1995. But Black was also a staunch proponent of the Capital Asset Pricing Model (CAPM), a theoretical framework on the prices of financial securities, based on the importance of properly taking risk into account, that failed to generate the kind of long-standing scholarly attention market efficiency was able to draw.

I show how Eugene Fama's research program, centered on the idea that markets are unpredictable and efficient, generated a stream of research, whereas Fischer Black's, centered on the idea that markets reflect a society's tolerance (or preference) for risk, did not. The two notions—efficiency and risk—are not incompatible: in fact, they are a powerful instance of the type of problem posed by the joint hypothesis, namely, uncertainty about what empirical tests actually falsify in such cases. And yet, efficiency became canonical, whereas risk did not. To explain this difference in outcomes, I look at the specific tools and affective orientations these two scholars built into their work. Fama used *data analysis* to carefully demarcate the object of analysis over which financial economics claimed jurisdiction, in a way that allowed him to emphasize what was distinctive about his approach while minimizing opportunities for conflict with adjoining disciplines.

Fischer Black, by contrast, believed that data should be used instrumentally, in efforts to *build new theoretical frameworks*. Data were but a stepping-stone to broader questions. In other words, Fama actively worked toward building "ketchup economics," as Summers put it, by making the data as hard as possible. By using methodological techniques that had legitimacy, he made data legitimate as well, and put data at the apex of the data-method-theory triad. Black, on the other hand, understood data analysis to be one component of the research process. But proposing innovative methodological tools, for data whose suitability to the analysis of finance had yet to be established, constituted a reconfiguration of the data-method-theory triad. And this limited the size of the network Black could build around his research program.

Efficiency: From Hypothesis to Theory

Though roots of the concept of efficiency extend beyond economics, economics has fully embraced this notion for a long time, traditionally in reference to issues of performance measurement (J. Alexander 2008; Dimson and Mussavian 1998). When it was imported into financial economics, efficiency took the different and narrower (though remarkably ambiguous and flexible) meaning we discussed in previous chapters. It served to highlight a property of financial markets— namely, that they are devoid of opportunities for excess profit because they always, already incorporate all relevant information into prices. Efficiency describes markets as perfect (or tending toward perfection) in processing information (Fama 1970, 1991).

The hypothesis that financial markets are informationally efficient, as we saw, built on the discovery of the *statistical* property of asset prices that prices are independent over time: the price of a stock is serially independent, meaning that it fluctuates "randomly" and therefore impedes systematic prediction of its future values (Bernstein 1992). With Eugene Fama, efficiency and random walks became inextricably tied. His main claim that stock price movements could not be predicted was based on the idea that prices already reflect all available information. But if only new information affects stock prices, to the extent that such information emerges randomly, changes in stock prices are random too. Statistical independence could therefore be "endowed with implicit economic content" (Mehrling 2005, 63).

Fama's success in turning the efficient-market hypothesis (EMH) into an intellectual innovation coupling random walks and efficiency was not the result of his methodological prowess. His ability to draw from new datasets, his timing, and his connections were the most important factors. Fama's thesis on stock price behavior was published in its entirety, something Fama himself did not expect—but the intellectual environment was ripe, which made Fama's work the subject of great interest on the part of the financial community (Bernstein 1992). Fama followed up by publishing an extensive (but partial) review of the literature, proposing a classification between different degrees of efficiency that forever moved the debate away from dichotomy (efficient/nonefficient) and toward a matter of degree (how efficient) (Mehrling 2005, 91).

The ideological fit between the Chicago school and Fama's approach is important too. By the 1960s, Chicago had grown into a powerhouse for research on markets that emphasized their self-correcting properties; to the Chicago school, efficiency had become a foundational assumption not to be disputed (Fourcade 2009). Fama worked at the newly professionalized business school, which benefited from proximity to the Chicago economics department, and thus was the context of important intellectual exchange as well as resource sharing (Overtveldt 2009; Samuels, Biddle, and Emmett 2008). But as we shall see, ideology alone is not sufficient in securing the success of a theory, as the case of CAPM illustrates.

CAPM: From Model to Empirical Approach

To this day, many consider CAPM one of the most revolutionary ideas in finance, but not in the same sense as efficiency. CAPM is at the roots of foundational concepts in investment theory, like the distinction between "unsystematic" and "systematic" risk, where the former is specific to the asset and thus possible to control through diversification, and the latter describes how the asset price varies as the market fluctuates, as captured by measures such as "beta" and the volatility of stocks (Dempsey 2013; Smith and Walsh 2013). Moreover, from the viewpoint of CAPM, the price of risk always reflects market equilibrium: prices indicate the propensity of certain investors to take on more risk than others, thereby commanding a higher premium than would be the case with safer portfolios. Risk, in this view, is a core aspect of financial behavior, not an aberration to be corrected (Mehrling 2005).

Unlike efficiency, however, CAPM does not occupy a core place in the financial canon, or, put more precisely, it does not constitute the basis for a research program in the same way EMH does. Partly, this is because Fama invented a research tradition in which to couch EMH, making it appear the uncontroversial result of a long stream of analysis (Jovanovic 2008). By contrast, CAPM originated with several independent efforts addressing different kinds of problems, and it took quite some time before analysts even understood that they were working on a similar problem. Jack Treynor is credited with developing the essential insight behind CAPM in 1962, as part of a broader attempt to value a risky stream of future earnings. His central insight was an understanding of risk as deriving from some underlying economic variables (Mehrling 2005, 57). But that the result of this investigation was a version of CAPM only became clear to economists after Harry Markowitz, William Sharpe, and Merton Miller (all central figures in financial economics) shared a Nobel Prize in the 1990s, prompting the field to reflect on the origins of the model (French 2003). Sharpe and John Lintner were initially credited with the discovery of CAPM, and neither of their models had fully worked out the relationship between risk and equilibrium (Fama and MacBeth 1973). Why such an accomplished group of scholars did not develop a systematic perspective on their shared intellectual agenda is puzzling.

With so many scholars working on the same model to begin with, what is not surprising is that few followed Fischer Black's lead. Yet Black would become the most tireless advocate of CAPM and remain so even when other theorists had moved on (Lehmann 2004, 9). Understanding Fischer Black's academic agenda can thus give us insight into the remarkable trajectory of CAPM. The main contribution of Fischer Black, initially articulated when he worked alongside Jack Treynor at the consulting firm Arthur D. Little in Cambridge, was to develop the original intuition behind this model into a full-fledged worldview, in which financial markets play the central role of pricing risk and thereby faithfully mirror how much risk a society is willing to tolerate.

Fischer Black

Black (1938–1995) looms as a seminal figure in financial economics, renowned as much for his accomplishments as he is for his iconoclasm. His career was characterized by an unwillingness to commit to one professional trajectory, and in his early life, to even one intellectual discipline. Having taken classes in physics, logic, mathematics, and psychology at Harvard, as both an undergraduate and a graduate student—switching majors, attempting to switch his graduate program in the process, and eventually moving to MIT (something that earned him an accusation of "dilettantism" by his PhD adviser in mathematics)—Black familiarized himself with several theoretical and analytical traditions without being committed exclusively to any one of them. This unusual trajectory afforded him the opportunity to develop a style of reasoning that involved tackling any given problem from different directions and angles. Also, importantly, in the course of his eclectic education Black developed a taste for freedom from intellectual and social constraints.[1]

In 1965, a year after earning a PhD in mathematics from MIT, Black took a job at Arthur D. Little (ADL), a consulting firm in Boston, in what turned out to be both an opportunity for intellectual development and a source of disappointment. At ADL, Black involved himself in some of the most important early cases that financial firms were then building against the regulatory efforts by the New York Fed. Black cut his analytical teeth on a study of mutual funds, with the goal of investigating their performance, and specifically their ability to generate returns above the market average. Mutual funds had commissioned the study, and expected it to provide evidence for their superiority. But Black, by then increasingly convinced of the efficiency of markets, wrote a scathing report.

Also at ADL, Black worked on a Ford Foundation project tailored to devise new investment strategies for college and university endowments in the United States, so that the foundation itself could divert resources to new projects. The burgeoning derivative industry would develop out of studies such as this. His work as a consultant, in short, exposed Black to some of the most cutting-edge work in financial economics at a time of great intellectual creativity. This, given his unorthodox theoretical background, gave him a sense of the intellectual stakes of the debate. It was also the context in which Black began to pull together the many intellectual threads he had been following during his disorganized academic career.

Jack Treynor, his colleague and mentor at ADL, was then building a sophisticated understanding of finance on the basic intuition that, to calculate the future value of an investment, risk must be accounted for and priced accordingly. This project involved a radical reconstruction of some of the basic (and up to that point, quite rudimentary) tools on which the financial industry had been built. Treynor's CAPM was a first attempt at such a repositioning of financial theory. CAPM essentially posited the price of a security to depend on its *covariance* with a market portfolio, or the extent to which its return moved in the same direction as the return on the market as a whole. Intellectually, CAPM meant grappling with questions of uncertainty and risk that contemporary economic models had simply bracketed off; and it also meant developing a theory of the characteristics of that "market portfolio." More practically, CAPM could be used to identify deviations from predicted prices on the basis of the riskiness of the asset, and to profit from them through arbitrage.

Black was drawn to CAPM by his belief in market efficiency. By efficiency, though, Black did not mean *informational* efficiency in the manner advocated by Fama. Markets would always be in equilibrium, he argued, if it were not for real-world constraints (such as costly selling, information, and management). For the purposes of analysis, such constraints could be bracketed off because, more fundamentally, price volatility, economic fluctuations, and business cycles are the result not of market failures but of risk. In other words, the kind of efficiency Black was interested in was the ability inherent in markets to price risk. And this was nothing short of radical: from the assumption of market equilibrium, Black "was busy spinning a counter cultural vision of his own. . . . The ideal CAPM world that Fischer imagined was not perhaps the 'brotherhood of man' famously imagined by John Lennon. Indeed, it was the opposite of a world with 'no possessions.' But it was arguably just as utopian" (Mehrling 2005, 92). Fischer Black dedicated his career to devising methods to decide what risk was worth embracing (11). It was a vision in which individuals were radically free to pursue their economic strategies without being subjected to the power of existing arrangements and power structures. This vision had practical implications for Black: he even developed safer driving habits and a healthy diet as soon as he realized that the risks associated with more careless approaches afforded low rewards.

From the perspective of CAPM and market efficiency, Black developed an intuitive sense of what the most important debates in those networks were (see R. Collins 1998 for why star intellectuals develop this feel for the attention space). Would-be intellectual stars, such as Michael Jensen and Myron Scholes, sought him out at ADL. In 1971, when he eventually accepted a position at the Chicago Business School and moved to the Midwest, Black's favorite pursuit was sparring with Milton Friedman—not over the desirability or efficiency of markets, which they both took for granted, but over the nature of money.

His intellectual engagement in academia, however, was short-lived. When, for personal reasons, he left Chicago for a position at MIT, where Keynesianism was the dominant framework, he became an isolate rather than modifying his theory of money so as to take better advantage of the intellectual environment of the East Coast. His theory, developed in the midst of the stagflation of the 1970s, was both antimonetarist and anti-Keynesian—which made him suspicious to and rejected by both Chicago acolytes and MIT neo-Keynesians. At Chicago, however, he had at least benefited from an intense, shared belief about the efficiency of markets. At MIT, this theoretical common denominator was no longer present. During this period, he developed "contemplative" tendencies that Max Weber would have recognized as mystical. "Fischer adapted to the resulting sense of intellectual isolation [at MIT] by embracing a certain degree of physical isolation as well" (Mehrling 2005, 198). He would work in an office with the curtains always drawn, the door always shut, communicating only by phone with the outside world. Ultimately, he decided to pursue a new career altogether.

In 1984, Black left academia for a position at Goldman Sachs. Employment at Goldman, while of course being a more remunerative alternative, was also an opportunity for Black to put his broader vision into practice. "The decision to leave academia thus involved as much pull as push. Thenceforth, instead of producing theories about an ideal world not yet achieved, Fischer would be producing business products to move the actual world closer to the ideal" (Mehrling 2005, 240). From the quasi-monastic detachment of his days at MIT, Black threw himself back into the practical world of financial innovation. He did this without compromising his dedication to CAPM as a quasi-philosophical perspective on the world. Black, for instance, declined to become involved in the Chicago Board, even though the market for derivatives the board wanted to build was to be based on his option-pricing formula: this, to him, was simply "an exciting way to gamble" (138; see also Blackburn 2008, 89).

Black, in short, saw CAPM as a model of how financial markets in equilibrium shape the economic world. In his eyes, CAPM naturally implied that only unfettered financial markets can generate a proper balance between risk and safety, for financial markets are the source of interest rates that match demand for, and supply of, risky assets. Black considered equilibrium between risk and returns a foundational matter of philosophical importance, not a matter of mere technicality (Derman 2007; Lehmann 2004).

Efficiency versus Equilibrium

How different are EMH and CAPM? It is important to note that equilibrium in the relationship between risk and return is consistent with the idea of informationally efficient markets, and the two are often discussed together (Dempsey

2013). But CAPM, because it is a theory of risk, can also accommodate financial processes in inefficient markets. EMH, because it is a theory of information, is by like token not committed to any specific model of stock price evaluation: it can be consistent with CAPM, positing price to result from a balance between risk and return; but it is consistent with other models too, introducing factors beyond the risk-return equilibrium to explain stock prices—something Fama recognized as early as 1973 (see esp. Fama and MacBeth 1973).

Perhaps even more worrisome, whether financial markets are defined by an equilibrium between risk and return, in fact, cannot be empirically tested (Roll 1977). This joint-hypothesis problem is a general one and constitutes the core of the Duhem-Quine thesis. As is often the case with complex theories, flawed or incomplete data, or gaps in the auxiliary assumptions necessary to operationalize key constructs, can be blamed for failing to bear out their central predictions (MacKenzie 2006, 23). Rarely are theories dismissed on empirical grounds alone. In accordance with this thesis, empirical tests of EMH were often jointly testing CAPM, and vice versa: there was no a priori reason why the tests should disconfirm the former rather than the latter (23). Nevertheless, it was CAPM and its assumption of equilibrium between risk and return that were ultimately abandoned. The model itself came to be seen less as a worldview on which to reground financial economics, and more of a useful and rich approach that new models with superior accuracy were bound to supersede. In fact, the formula with which Fischer Black's name is most iconically associated, the Black-Scholes option-pricing formula, relied not on an asset-pricing theory but on a no-arbitrage assumption coming from a different theoretical lineage, provided by Robert C. Merton, who would later share a Nobel Prize with Myron Scholes on this account (Lehmann 2004). Awareness of CAPM's empirical inadequacies hindered the acceptance of work that depended on it; it was therefore preferable to build option theory on a different foundation.

The fate of CAPM was sealed by empirical attacks carried out by Fama himself. In joint papers, he and Kenneth French (1992, 1993) published a famous alternative that, instead of restricting its focus to risk and return as the two essential parameters of stock market valuation, introduced additional factors. Once these factors were taken into account, Fama argued, the augmented model provided a better fit to the data and thus proved market efficiency. In spite of Black's and Treynor's protestations, "beta" was declared dead (Black 1998). Fischer Black stuck to his intuition, but from then on he was virtually alone in applying a CAPM logic to such disparate phenomena as money and banking, currency exchange rates, and of course options and warrants (Mehrling 2005), while others went on to develop more sophisticated models of efficient portfolios (and specifically, arbitrage portfolio theory).

In sum, the puzzling aspect of CAPM's rise and decline is that, in spite of CAPM never being falsified in any definitive manner *independently* of efficiency, the empirical burden was put on the former, not the latter, even prompting the futile protests of the model's most steadfast proponents (Treynor 1987). CAPM's failure was ultimately epistemological: CAPM was not perceived as a theoretical alternative to efficiency; rather, it became an auxiliary model to be discarded once its predictions clashed with EMH, and thus CAPM was sacrificed on the altar of EMH. EMH, explicitly described as a *hypothesis*, became the main theoretical lynchpin of financial economics. CAPM, explicitly described as a *model*, became a practical tool in aid of concrete financial decisions.

As we saw in chapter 2, part of what made EMH successful was that it was embraced by a new guard of financial economists, eager to subvert the status quo of the discipline (Jovanovic 2008; Poitras and Jovanovic 2010); among them, Eugene Fama is the most renowned scholar. Led by Fama, financial economists used EMH to build a relationship with the larger field of economics on more equal foundations, freeing their discipline from an earlier association with practical concerns and vocational training that undermined its seriousness as an academic discipline (Fourcade and Khurana 2013; Whitley 1986a). In this vein, through EMH, financial economists put their discipline on what they believed to be more scientific grounds: efficient markets served to launch a new style of doing research, where systematic analysis of quantitative data, couched in a language of axioms, mathematical proofs, and hypothesis testing, became the dominant format for presenting new financial knowledge.

These explanations do not go far enough, because they treat the hypothesis in isolation, as if other theories were not also available, serving as potential candidates for this process of theoretical and disciplinary consolidation. They focus on the epistemological question of what theory would be more appropriate to a larger project of making finance scientific, systematic, and abstract. But EMH did not emerge in isolation, and in fact, its rise is inextricably related to the defeat of CAPM (MacKenzie 2003; MacKenzie and Millo 2003). Just like EMH, which was concerned with how markets price correctly and instantaneously new information and therefore constitute an important stepping-stone for the development of the discipline of financial economics, CAPM provided a theoretical rationale for, and gave a mathematical formulation to, the long-held intuition that the riskiness of an asset influences its expected return. Because CAPM was a model of how to price assets in the face of uncertainty, it too provided a potentially generative opportunity for new research, especially given how far-reaching its practical implications were, so much so that, according to critics, "its theoretical significance is equaled if not surpassed by its widespread use in business and finance" (Bernstein 1992, 201). Perhaps more so than efficiency, CAPM constituted a central part of the framework "for managing the transition from traditional craft practice to the modern scientific methods that would transform investment management over the ensuing 30 years" (Mehrling 2005, 5).

It is therefore puzzling that, spurred by dissatisfaction with its empirical shortcomings (Roll 1977), finance theorists grew more aware over time of the theoretical limitations of CAPM, and that, ultimately, they relegated CAPM to the status of one among many competing and, allegedly, more empirically accurate methods of portfolio selection. Market practitioners continue to use it to make quick, back-of-the-envelope calculations; academic scholars, however, have largely abandoned it as a theoretical framework (but see Dempsey 2013). While recognized as a centerpiece of modern financial economics, CAPM is now mainly discussed in terms of historical significance, practical implications, and empirical shortcomings.

If lack of empirical fit alone cannot explain CAPM's short life cycle and why its implications were not worked out in subsequent models in the radical way advocated by Black and Treynor, whereas EMH thrived, what does? EMH's longevity may derive from its successful application in financial markets: by finding in what ways markets were efficient and in what ways they were not, EMH research often opened up profit opportunities for practitioners to exploit (MacKenzie 2006, 94–97). Further, Fama's work became the basis for, among other things, fair value and rational pricing. But Fischer Black, in his early work with Myron Scholes, similarly suggested how CAPM pointed to specific profit opportunities (what he called the "alpha effect"). Nevertheless, financial market agents refused to implement his investment strategy. Academics similarly questioned whether the effect he described was plausible (Mehrling 2005, 108). I submit that understanding what made Fama's research strategy seem worth pursuing, while making Black's appear less valuable, requires an analysis of both the social networks in which their research was embedded, and the affect through which their respective models were built.

EMH and CAPM: A Network Analysis

The importance of an idea, much like the reputation of a scholar, not only grows over time but is often outright established "downstream": its fate is in the hands of future scholarly networks, who retroactively construct the idea as important as they weave it into a broader research program and credit it for making new moves possible (R. Collins 1998; Frickel and Gross 2005; Lang and Lang 1988). Of course, differences exist across disciplines in terms of how long it takes for an important idea to emerge (Cole 1992; Hargens 2000). In general, scholars receive recognition and enjoy success when they write papers that are not only highly cited but also cited alongside other successful papers, generating broad research programs. As papers are linked together by citations, they give rise to more or less coherent subspecialties, reflecting an underlying social structure characterized by increased communication within emerging scholarly communities (Crane 1969). When those connections grow in number and tightness, consensus crystallizes around the "facts" that underlie these ideas, in a process similar to that of creating "black boxes" (Shwed and Bearman 2010). Links among arguments across papers serve as the framework on which a disciplinary common sense is built over time.

One way of operationalizing empirically the argument that the importance of an idea depends on how that idea is used by a scholarly community is the construction of cocitation networks (Gmür 2003; Mullins et al. 1977). Papers are cocited when they appear together in the same citing paper; cocitation, when repeated across several papers, establishes commonality in terms of shared specialization. Moreover, papers that receive the most number of cocitations in these specialized clusters become central to the kinds of arguments that circulate in them. Cocitations allow papers to move to the core of a community of research, establishing them as necessary references for those who want to contribute to its conversation.

Examination of cocitation networks in the financial economics literature illuminates an important aspect of the puzzle of why EMH and CAPM achieved different status. In figures 4.1–4.4a and b, I show cocitation networks of the literature referenced by all articles published in the top four journals in financial economics, namely, *Financial Management*, the *Journal of Finance*, the *Journal of Financial and Quantitative Analysis*, and the *Journal of Financial Economics*, from 1981 to 2004 (Heck and Cooley 1988).[2] Each network takes a snapshot of cumulative cocitations of papers during a particular time frame (papers cited fewer than thirty times are not shown). Specifically, the figures display the papers financial economists cite from different time periods, and their cocitation patterns. To make the graphical layout of the networks meaningful, I implement a community detection algorithm (the Louvain algorithm) that spatially groups together authors depending on what papers are more frequently cocited. Further, in figure 4.1, where the network is sufficiently small to allow it, I scale the size of each node to its eigenvector centrality in the network.

The graphs reveal important aspects of the financial economics literature. I first highlight the two papers that have among the highest centrality scores in figure 4.1, Fama and MacBeth (1973) and Black and Scholes (1973). They both sit at the intersection of two research communities, and their high centrality indicates that they are "obligatory points of passage" for subsequent work (Latour 1987; Yonay 1998). The paper coauthored by Fama is an early, influential investigation

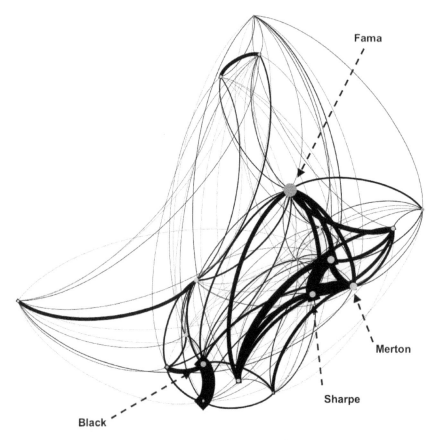

FIGURE 4.1   Fama and Black cocitation networks, 1973.

of the relationship between risk and return where Fama tests the EMH empirically with data on the New York Stock Exchange common stocks. The paper coauthored by Black is the classic statement on the pricing of options and corporate liabilities.

Second, note how the cocitation networks evolve around these papers over time, as reflected in the sequence of networks developed to depict how cocitations accumulate (refer to table 4.1 for a list of prominent papers in each cocitation network). Both papers can rely on strong, contemporary allies—most notably, two different papers written in 1973 by the same author, Robert Merton; one paper deals with the theory of rational option pricing (cocited with Black and Scholes, not labeled in the figure), and the other proposes an "intertemporal capital asset pricing model" (cocited with Fama and MacBeth). One difference immediately jumps out: Fama's work is part of a cluster of papers, of which Merton's rep-

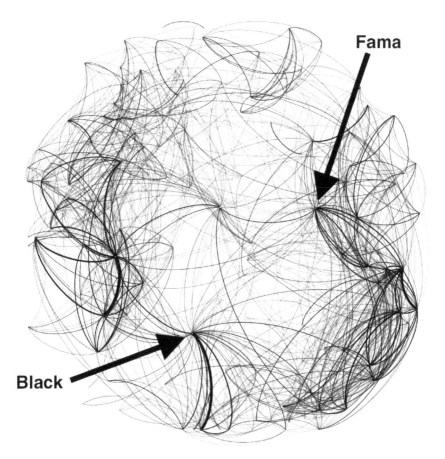

FIGURE 4.2   Fama and Black cocitation networks, 1983.

resents one, that propose different approaches to the valuation of capital assets; it should be noted that Fischer Black's 1972 "Capital Market Equilibrium with Restricted Borrowing" is also part of that cluster, but its centrality is lower and it is therefore not visible in the figure. Markowitz and Sharpe are more influential scholars who are also cited within this cluster. Black's work, by contrast, is embedded in a research cluster that is more narrowly concerned with the specific problem of options pricing (Merton's paper is the most important example).

Both Black and Fama continue to publish a great deal over time; but, in Black's case, his subsequent work fails to meet the citation threshold that would make it visible in the citation networks, whereas Fama succeeds again with his 1993 paper with French that debunks CAPM. Black's work, by contrast, is not followed by work pursuing his research agenda and developing it into a broader perspective.

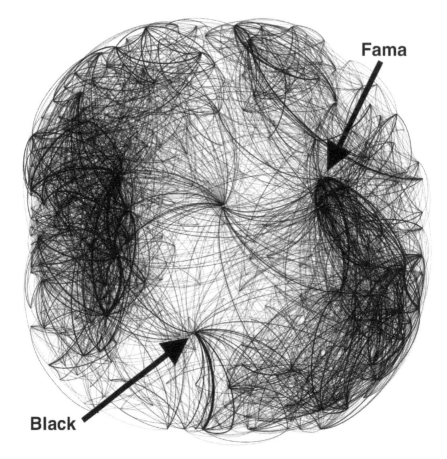

FIGURE 4.3   Fama and Black cocitation networks, 1993.

Thus, it does not generate a coherent research program, as none of his subsequent papers acquires as much prominence in the network as Black-Scholes. As a consequence, Black-Scholes becomes canonical, whereas Fama successfully seizes the attention space of the discipline with his empirical debunking of CAPM. Black-Scholes is recognized as *a* model of option pricing, not as one piece within a larger theoretical framework provided by Black's vision of finance as the analysis of equilibrium between risk and return. Eugene Fama shapes the direction of research and the character of the debate in financial economics over a longer period of time than does Fischer Black; this, moreover, in the wake of Fama's falsification of CAPM, thus at Black's expense. By 2003, a dense cocitation network has developed around Fama's work, whereas the research community around Fischer Black appears sparse and loosely knit.

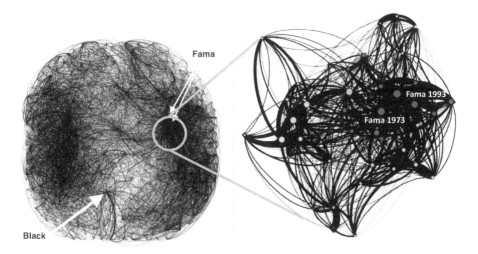

FIGURE 4.4A Fama's cocitation networks, 2003.

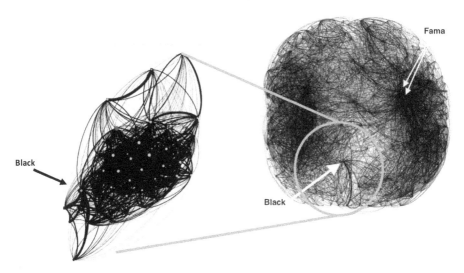

FIGURE 4.4B Black's cocitation networks, 2003.

One problem with cocitation analysis is that, even though density in cocitations suggests some degree of consensus, it is still hard to distinguish between networks where citations are in agreement with the source paper and networks where citations are used as foils for critique. The picture gains more focus if we shift attention to networks of prestige, as suggested by Collins and Guillén (2012) as a part of their model of "mutual halos." Mutual halos capture the degree to which prestigious innovators are linked to other prestigious innovators, thereby

TABLE 4.1. Most eigen-vector central papers in Fama's and Black's networks

highlighting how innovative ideas emerge in the context of dense networks endowed with creative energy, as opposed to being the product of lone innovators (contra Burt 2004). As we saw in the previous chapter, financial economists are not likely to take opportunistic advantage of brokerage opportunities in the scholarly network; deep, repeated collaborations are a better pathway to success. Over time, these collaborative patterns should give rise to densely connected networks of prestige.

The prestige of an innovative intellectual, according to the mutual halo model, can be measured in three steps: First, prestige is the amount of attention the intellectual is given in the relevant literature, which indicates how successful the innovation is. Second, through the same method one can measure the amount of attention the intellectual's immediate masters, disciples, and collaborators enjoy, thus highlighting the importance of his or her research programs among contemporaries. Third, one can measure the cumulative prestige enjoyed by the network two links away from the focal intellectual, which gives an indication of how diffuse the prestige of the intellectual is in the time span of roughly a generation. (Beyond two links, it becomes more difficult to distinguish between rival research programs/schools of thought.) These extended measures of prestige reveal the degree to which the successful intellectual is embedded in successful networks.

Focusing on the top twenty theorists, I show in table 4.2 that both Fama and Black are part of the financial canon, in that discussion of their work receives a significant amount of exposure in a variety of venues (see the note to the table for details on sources). They both belong to the top five of financial theorists by all measures of prestige. Black's prestige is canonical and self-reinforcing: his work is recognized in the field, and Black is connected to other prestigious innovators, both in his immediate network and in the larger, two-link network. Similarly, Fama's prestige is tied to, and enhanced by, a lineage of subsequent innovators, coupling Fama's focus on the efficiency of markets with a market model of portfolio evaluation (Arbitrage Portfolio Theory [APT]).

While Black and Fama enjoy high recognition in the field, differences between the two lurk just beneath the surface and can be appreciated by comparing the mutual halo rankings with the network citation data discussed above, and paying attention to chronology. Fama's work constitutes the foundation for the work of other prestigious theorists, and there is an important generational component to this: younger analysts who could have pursued CAPM chose to deepen Fama's hypothesis by providing alternative methods of asset pricing (thus effectively striving to replace Black's model). By like token, Fama's direct competitors (theorists such as Sanford Grossman and Andrei Shleifer, who are critical of EMH and make that critique central to their work), while they are certainly prestigious, do not rank as high as his disciples and followers. Fama's lineage is strong even in the

TABLE 4.2. Prestige ranking, top twenty financial economists

RANKING		ECONOMIST	AFFILIATION	PHD	YEAR	PRESTIGE	MUTUAL HALO		RESEARCH
ONE LINK	TWO LINKS					(PERCENTILE RANK)	ONE LINK	TWO LINKS	
1	1	Fama	Chicago	Chicago	1964	1.00	1050	4291	EMH
2	2	Scholes	Stanford	Chicago	1969	0.89	906	3667	CAPM
3	3	Jensen	HBS	Chicago	1968	0.94	874	3625	EMH/ AGENCY
4	4	Miller	Chicago	Hopkins	1952	0.98	867	3355	APT
5	5	Black	MIT, Chicago	Harvard	1964	0.97	720	3348	CAPM
6	13	Roll	UCLA	Chicago	1968	0.86	641	2363	APT
7	6	Ingersoll	Yale	MIT	1976	0.64	604	2743	APT
8	21	MacKinlay	Wharton	Chicago	1985	0.64	595	1928	EMH (Critical)
9	16	Schwert	Rochester	Chicago	1975	0.38	583	2219	EMH
10	17	French	Dartmouth	Rochester	1983	0.96	559	2141	EMH/APT
11	18	Cox	MIT	Wharton	1975	0.83	545	2109	APT
12	9	Harvey	Duke	Chicago	1986	0.70	540	2585	APT
13	8	Brav	Duke	Chicago	1998	0.31	518	2587	EMH and Beyond
14	27	Asquith	MIT	Chicago	1982	0.00	485	1793	EMH
15	26	Shleifer	Harvard	MIT	1986	0.95	474	1799	Behavioral Econ.
16	19	Grossman	Wharton	Chicago	1975	0.52	468	2043	EMH (Critical)
17	14	Sharpe	RAND	UCLA	1961	0.79	449	2310	CAPM
17	11	Treynor	Goldman	Harvard	1955	0.10	449	2411	CAPM
19	34	Ross	MIT	Harvard	1970	0.99	436	1598	APT

Note: Prestige scores are derived by counting the pages the following books dedicate to each author's work: Bailey 2005; Berk, DeMarzo, and Harford 2011; Bernstein 1992; Bodie, Kane, and Marcus 2008; Brealey and Myers 2003; Campbell et al. 1996; Constantinides, Harris, and Stulz 2003; Eckbo 2008; Houthakker and Williamson 1996; Huang and Litzenberger 1988; Hull 2005; Kettell 2001; Ross, Westerfield, and Jaffe 2008; Thorsten IV and Schenk-Hoppe 2009; Vernimmen and Quiry, 2009.

face of important critiques; Black's network is not. The one, potentially major source of prestige in Fischer Black's network, Jack Treynor, is barely mentioned in the financial economics literature. His prestige score ranks in the bottom tenth percentile, and it is his relationship with Fischer Black that gives him some visibility in the field, rather than the other way around. Tellingly, Perry Mehrling's masterful biography of Fischer Black starts with a vignette illustrating how much the field undervalued Jack Treynor's contribution, and how that was in part due to Treynor's failure to secure the support of established scholars (like Franco

Modigliani, who knew about Treynor's research but failed to understand its implications).

It is possible, then, to attribute Black's relative failure at impacting his discipline to biographical trajectories, both his and those of the members of his network. Jack Treynor formulated his version of CAPM while employed at ADL; he then went on to work for Goldman Sachs. As a result, he never had the chance of producing students; though in and of itself, this criterion does not serve as a particularly convincing explanation of his weak legacy. Treynor, presumably, could have advised students affiliated with different departments or universities. To be sure, John Lintner, a more distant member of Black's circle, taught at Harvard Business School, which put him at some distance from Chicago, the main center of financial innovation in the 1960s and 1970s, where one might expect interest in CAPM to be potentially stronger.

If Lintner and Treynor did not occupy sufficiently powerful institutional positions for the launching of CAPM as an agenda-setting theoretical model, Myron Scholes did. Scholes taught at MIT from 1968, right after earning his PhD at Chicago, until 1972, when he moved back to Chicago. One of Fischer Black's main collaborators, especially with respect to the development of options-pricing theory, Scholes is perhaps the most prestigious member of his academic network. Why didn't he work toward making CAPM an intellectual rival to market efficiency? It is not because of lack of interest: "Fischer Black and I were interested in all aspects of finance but loved the capital-asset pricing model as a way to describe the trade-off between risk and return. It gave us the insights to figure out how to value options," Scholes would later recall (in Breit and Hirsch 2004, 243). Upon returning to Chicago, however, Scholes became heavily involved in the Center for Research in Security Prices (CRSP): "As director of the center, I led the development of large research data files containing daily security prices and related information on all New York and American Stock Exchange securities from 1962–1985 (now updated by others through the present), and merged these data with monthly data files back to 1926. This effort added immeasurably to the research output of colleagues around the world conducting research in financial economics. I believe that great empirical work leads to additional theory and new theory leads, in turn, to new empirical testing" (244). CRSP, of course, was one of the research pillars of Chicago financial economics, and Scholes's leadership solidified his connection with Fama (conversely, his overlap at Chicago with Black was minimal). More importantly, Scholes had widely spanning research interests, and his contributions were numerous and eclectic; he did not devote his efforts to the single-minded development of CAPM. The model was left without a leader, a vacuum others did not step in to fill. Even William Sharpe, one of the forefathers of CAPM, conceded that the model could not be shown to be valid

(MacKenzie 2006, 93). And as we saw, Fischer Black himself had an erratic career, moving from Chicago to MIT and then to the private sector, owing both to personal reasons and to his inability to find sufficiently supportive colleagues. By contrast, Fama's entire career took place at Chicago, which gave him unequaled access to resources, both material and intellectual, as well as to students.

Network data, in short, help us make two points. First, the finance theorists who developed Fama's approach to financial markets were a coherent group: a "small, tightly woven [group] of researchers oriented toward common intellectual goals who work together in opposition to current intellectual trends" (Parker and Hackett 2012, 22)—in this case, popular and professional perceptions of markets as inefficient, and at least initially, mainstream economics' refusal to recognize financial economics as a legitimate intellectual discipline. The group pushed forward Fama's agenda while putting it on a collision course with CAPM.

Second, Fama's work created controversy but was not displaced by it: Fama's network occupies a durable position in the field, which reproduces its relevance to intellectual debate. Fischer Black's work, by contrast, sits at the intersection of several debates, and while it produced a theoretical controversy of its own, as evidenced by Fama and French's work in the 1990s, scholars who were inspired by Black's approach were more likely to attempt to transcend it empirically than to use it as a theoretical building block. In fact, Black's network is notable for its failure to produce such a common orientation toward finance, in spite of Black's efforts. It is not that other financial economists did not pursue his insights. But they did it in a different and more theoretically modest way than Black intended.

Statistics and Affect

A network-based explanation would focus on Black's failure to establish a network due to his mobile career. In light of our quantitative analysis in the previous chapter, we would make an analogy between Black's career and the career of a broker: as we just learned, the field does not seem to be particularly open to such roles, leading us toward the conclusion that Black could not thrive in a discipline structured around a few key centers of innovation. A network-based account would nevertheless run into a problem: Fischer Black, like his more prestigious colleagues, also taught at Chicago, but failed to build a coherent network around him while working there. This is not because of doubts about his intellectual abilities or because of ideological differences: even though he often gave the impression that he did not hold consistent views on any topic (Mehrling 2005), his Chicago colleagues respected him.

Black's relationship with Chicago scholars, in fact, deepens the puzzle that CAPM's focus on equilibrium was defeated through empirical work, whereas efficiency continues being defended, not just on empirical but on normative grounds (Brav, Heaton, and Rosenberg 2004). In fact, while in terms of theory Fama was as entrenched in the Chicago school approach as Black was, this was not the case from a methodological point of view, where Fischer Black and Chicago spoke the same language. Black understood empirical work as an "engine of discovery," meant to make theory more "plausible," where plausibility was defined as the property of a theory that does not "imply consistent, easy to exploit profit opportunities" (Black 1982, 32; Lehmann 2004). While there is much debate as to whether the Chicago school (and economics at large) holds a coherent view on methodology (Reay 2012), the idea that theory does not require fit with empirical data is a central tenet of Friedman's approach. Black was very much in agreement with this point.

Fama, by contrast, adopted an approach to data (data dredging) of which the Chicago school was very critical (see esp. Black 1982). This problem afflicted Fama and French's refutation of CAPM in particular (and the broader network in which Fama's research was located as well, e.g., Merton's 1973 Intertemporal Capital Asset Pricing Model [ICAPM] and Ross's arbitrage pricing theory). As Lo and MacKinlay put it:

> The conclusion that additional risk factors are required may be premature. One of several explanations consistent with the presence of deviations is data-snooping. . . . The argument is that on an ex post basis one will always be able to find deviations from the CAPM. Such deviations considered in a group will appear statistically significant. However, they are merely a result of grouping assets with common disturbance terms. Since in financial economics our empirical analysis is ex post in nature, this problem is difficult to control. Direct adjustments for potential snooping are difficult to implement and, when implemented, make it very difficult to find real deviations. (2002, 190)

In sum, it is not just that the validity of EMH, much like that of CAPM, could not be proved: Fama's early and seminal statement on EMH conceded as much, and a theory's lack of realism would not have raised eyebrows at Chicago (MacKenzie 2006, 95–96). Fama's work, however, relied on econometric techniques in ways that put him at odds with the Chicago approach; Black's, by contrast, did not.

To explain both puzzles—Black's lack of students and collaborators at Chicago, and CAPM's capitulation to empirical falsification—attention should be drawn to the intersection among methods, data, and theory in the particular landscape of financial economics, and to the affects that circulated in the network. The entry point for such an analysis is the different ways that the two networks—Black's and Fama's—framed quantification. In general, analysts of quantification have shown that fields in search of legitimacy resort to quantification to establish their credentials. Faced with skeptical audiences, and a low level of trust among colleagues, contested fields rely on quantification as a source of "mechanical objectivity" and impersonal knowledge, hiding ambiguities behind the seemingly objective quality of numbers (R. Collins 1984; Daston 1992; Espeland and Stevens 1998; Porter 1995). The discipline of economics has perhaps profited the most from this framing strategy (Breslau 1997; Breslau and Yonay 1999; Fourcade 2009).

Quantification, however, is a capacious term that contains several potentially contrasting approaches or "modes": a particularly important distinction can be made between frequentist and subjectivist methods. The former attempt to establish the context within which knowledge and expertise can be exercised, and demarcate that zone as outside the influence of other chains of events, thus buffering it from the intrusion of other kinds of expertise (Camic and Xie 1994; R. Collins 1984; Hacking 1984).

On the other end of the continuum, subjectivist methods are captured by Friedman's writings (Hammond 1990). For instance, in an important discussion Friedman paraphrases Savage and states: "The role of statistics is not to discover truth. The role of statistics is to resolve disagreements among people. . . . The role of statistical analysis is to lead us to reconsider our personal probabilities in the hope that our personal probabilities will come closer and closer together" (Hammond 1990, 167; see also McCloskey 1998).

Subjectivist methods, in spite of their quantitative credentials, present the same problems and contradictions commonly found in nonquantitative techniques: they require trust and tacit knowledge to become authoritative. Thus, it is not surprising to find appeals to subjectivist methods in the most cohesive approach to economics, the Chicago school, whereas in less elite parts of the discipline, methods tend to appeal to objectivity to bolster their power to persuade (Reay 2012).

Focusing on the relationship between trust and methods helps us shed light on the EMH-CAPM controversy. Fama's use of frequentist statistics to produce a test of efficiency that falsified CAPM implied that financial phenomena were real and objective, independently of the analyst's interpretation. The implications were not only ontological but practical as well. Within this framework, seemingly intractable problems could be swept to the side. For instance, as noted by Mehrling (2005) and MacKenzie (2006), it was initially unclear whether random-walk models could be easily incorporated into the emerging financial canon. As we have seen, Benoit Mandelbrot, who worked on the research frontier in this area, was calling for the complete abandonment of Gaussian models, leading Paul Cootner to compare him to Churchill: "Mandelbrot . . . promises us not utopia but blood, sweat, toil, and tears" (Cootner 1964a, 337).

But Fama was undeterred by such fatalistic scenarios. He ignored some of the unsettling implications brought by the hypothesis that the distribution of stock prices was nonnormal. Thus Mehrling (2005, 90) writes: Fama's "only intellectual investment was in efficient markets and, so far as he could see, the Mandelbrot hypothesis did not require giving up efficient markets. Quite the contrary, efficient markets (in the sense of serial independence) plus the Mandelbrot hypothesis (in the sense of fat tails) together seemed like a pretty good empirical characterization of the data." How far, indeed, could Fama see? Standard statistical models, because they were "mechanically objective," substituted for the low trust among financial scholars, and between financial economists and economists in the larger discipline, allowing Fama to connect his research program to the concerns of a larger community. Coupled with the appeal to wide audiences of his writings, Fama used statistics to build bridges with others.

Black, by contrast, used statistical analysis as an "engine of discovery," in the way advocated by Friedman and by the Savage/De Finetti tradition of statistical analysis. In his view, "a plausible theory is one that fits both everyday experience and correlations that come out of statistical analysis. There just isn't any easy way to test a theory . . . all we can do is to keep our theories more plausible, and to keep testing the theories against measured correlations" (Black 1982, 32). Note how, on the surface, this is very similar to the very approach advocated by Fama himself, when he argued, as we saw in chapter 2: "Remember that no null hypothesis, such as the hypothesis that the market is efficient, is a literally accurate view of the world. It is not meaningful to interpret the tests of such a hypothesis on a strict true-false basis. Rather, one is concerned with testing whether the model at hand is a reasonable approximation to the world, which can be taken as true, or at least until a better approximation comes along. What is a reasonable approximation depends on the use to which the model is to be put" (Fama 1976, 142).

The difference between the two approaches, I believe, is revealed by the last sentence: the idea that a model is reasonable depending on what it tries to achieve. In the absence of shared epistemological and practical orientations, scholars disagree about what constitutes a plausible theory. In line, Black's methodological affinity with Chicago was insufficient to build enthusiasm and consensus around his intellectual approach: there was no shared orientation in his network allowing for research to move forward. As one financial scholar noted, "It is distressing to discover that . . . viewed in isolation, the hypothesis that asset markets are in equilibrium is just so much empty rhetoric. But we do not view markets in isolation; we implicitly and explicitly bring a mixture of intuition, conjecture, and knowledge to our research" (Lehmann 2004, 30). The problem for Fischer Black was that he did not have a network closely focused on similar objectives and goals to rely on (as Friedman did), so using this mode of quantification as a tool of persuasion skirted the larger issue of how to construct expertise in a low-trust environment. Black is therefore remembered as a genial but idiosyncratic and individualistic innovator.[3]

In short, the difference between Fama's and Black's use of methods lay in Fama's pragmatic approach, which led him to privilege frequentism and data dredging. By contrast, rather than focusing on organizing new networks, Black looked to individual innovation but adopted a set of research techniques that exacerbated the individualism of the group around him. As both symptom and result of this strategy, Emanuel Derman, a colleague of Black's at Goldman Sachs, notes, "Fischer . . . always preferred applied research to academic," because in that context his "independent thinking" and "unorthodox but well thought-out ideas" could flourish (2007, 171). The paradoxical result of this approach was that it further undermined the already weak cohesion of the group rallied around CAPM, opening the door for alternative approaches to circumscribe its influence.

Affect, Networks, and the Production of Knowledge

Could it simply be the case that Fama and his collaborators were savvier and more strategic than Black and his collaborators? Is the different reception of CAPM and EMH to be understood in terms of entrepreneurial success in an academic setting? The evidence I presented in this chapter points in a different direction. Fama and his collaborators had access to new data sources they could claim as an original contribution. The complex architecture of piecemeal discoveries in a cumulative language that was described in chapter 3 was made possible precisely by the control EMHers exercised over data. Starting in an environment characterized by low trust and ongoing controversy, Fama and colleagues made controversy less intense as they mobilized data, theory, and method to strive for consensus. Black and CAPMers, by contrast, did not control the machinery that produced and aggregated the data. And the broader disciplinary environment within which they worked prevented them from making new theoretical or methodological moves *as a network*. In a discipline like financial economics, where collaboration is small-group oriented, often dyadic, emphasizing the distinctiveness of one's position was problematic, and Black had few venues open to him in terms of building a broader community of scholars. Black, in many a respect, adopted the strategy articulated by Mandelbrot a few decades earlier, and wanted to find new ways of putting data and theory in conversation with each other. But he could not make durable allies for this project.

Financial economists, under the influence of the network that formed around Fama, allowed innovations in data analysis to take the lead, whereas theory and methods were used more conservatively in attempts to link the emerging discipline to economics. They recombined the theory-data-method triad so that data would ascend to its apex. To consolidate the centrality of data to their work, financial economists fostered certain kinds of debates and areas of inquiries while blocking others. In particular, as the availability of financial data increased, in a format that was easy to analyze, financial economists built their understanding of markets on those data. To do so, they bracketed off approaches to the study of markets that required data not yet available. Data, in other words, came to be understood as *sufficient* for the analysis of markets to proceed.

Data, of course, are supposed to facilitate tests for multiple theories, and not simply provide support for one theory at the expense of others. But in this chapter, we see once again that data are not so easily disembedded from the configuration of theory, methods, and previous understandings of data that lay behind the assemblage of data. The volume of research using Fama's work as a jump-off point, as a result, vastly overshadowed the volume of research permitted by Black's work. By like token, Fama enabled new generations of scholars to become successful too. Proposing new theories, in the context of financial economics, meant attacking data networks. But disciplines that define innovation in terms of evidence-based moves create scant opportunities for those pushing for such alternatives.

Conclusions: Affect, Networks, and Differential Success

I have conceptualized scholarly networks in terms of social relationships and emotional attachments to particular values—or affective dispositions—through which scholars build trust in one another. Focusing on trust serves to emphasize collective processes, but, as this chapter reveals, this does not come at the expense of recognizing the importance of individual success and individual careers. Networks help scholars map out the venues that are worth making innovative moves in, and the venues that, on the other hand, appear less amenable to new, creative approaches. Because creativity is a matter of recognition—of relevant and appropriate audiences finding one's products useful—affect promotes innovative research when it allows scholarly networks to expand and spur new research. As we saw in chapter 2 and as further documented here, this can be a matter of sheer research *volume*: financial economists in the late 1950s started writing cumulative papers that made use of innovative datasets, and the stream of research they produced helped them set aside problematic questions about the limits of their data. The more general point is that emotion-laden values—the kinds of standards, criteria, and objectives a network cares about—promote creativity as long as they allow a network's recognition to increase: the more appropriate others pay attention, the more the network can draw new resources and allies.

But this is not the same as allowing individual careers to flourish: there is a collective action problem at the heart of this dynamic, having to deal with inequality and stratification in the attention any given scholar can draw to his or her work. For a network to grow creatively, it is not necessary that all its members contribute to the creative process equally or be rewarded for their input and efforts proportionally. Affect establishes a set of values with which the network positions itself in relation to other networks. But from the point of view of the internal dynamics of a network, depending on its specific social structure, affect may benefit a small elite of scholars while failing to reward the efforts of the majority;[4] or it may help reward confirmation of a finding rather than a new discovery, therefore privileging a kind of work that would not exist without other, less duly recognized activities, just to give two examples. The pursuit of precision, accuracy, and the many other objectives an affective network may determine to be important creates opportunities for the network that are not necessarily equally available to all its members. Affect, in short, gives scholars values to strive for and communicate with, but it does not guarantee individual success.

Individual-level approaches to the question of creativity point to an innovation/tradition trade-off (Foster, Rzhetsky, and Evans 2015) dating back to Thomas Kuhn's (2011) famous formulation of the problem in terms of an "essential tension." A scholar's output, in this perspective, is a matter of a decision to pursue more or less innovative strategies. But it is also true that a discipline as a whole can be more or less open to innovation, and, to put a finer grain on it, to certain kinds of innovations as opposed to others. It is the intersection between individual strategies and what a discipline considers an appropriate mode of analysis that we must focus on. Those who put their field on well-established pathways and traditions will find it easier to have their work accepted, but at the cost of appearing as lacking in originality. Those who, by contrast, pursue new discoveries while upending tradition may seem more original but will also find it difficult to have their work accepted. Nevertheless, scholars who figure out working compromises between innovation and tradition put themselves in a position of strength.

This way of thinking about the relationship between knowledge and affect invites us to look, first, at concrete structures of collaborations characterizing a discipline—focusing on what scholars work on, and how they conduct their work—because this constitutes the practical level within which research takes place. One practical strategy to seek out innovative research agendas is to rearrange the theory-method-data triad. Putting data analysis at the apex, for instance, can help scholars turn a field in new direction. So, too, can methodological or theoretical innovations. The choice of a particular strategy can be traced back to the specific arrangements of a given field.

Second, an approach to knowledge that is sensitive to affect invites us to expand our attention to the affective dispositions scholars develop to situate their work in a broader context, where the affect of other networks must be taken into account too in order to create the conditions for one's work to generate a developing research agenda. And third, it invites us to assess the extent to which the affect of the network, once established, generates opportunities for certain research trajectories while making others more difficult. Each aspect is never predetermined or fixed; more importantly, multiple pathways may be open at any given time, making it difficult for individual scholars to predict what trajectory will lead to success. Such a framework, however, allows the analyst to reconstruct the pathways that do indeed work.

By alerting us to the processes involved in making a field creative, and generating career opportunities for those involved, this framework opened a new perspective on the success and failure of ideas, in this case, the success of EMH and the failure of CAPM. EMH became the banner of a network where the values orienting the work of scholars within this tradition allowed for collective expansion of the network. EMH scholars understood that the cutting edge for the kind of work they were proposing rested on data management. Coupling data management with new analytical techniques would pit financial scholars against the "econometric" network; thus, investing in cutting-edge methodological work could potentially slow down the pace of research. Coupling data management with new theory, by the same token, would put finance in a debate with "model" builders. EMH scholars chose neither of these two paths, sticking close to stock market analysis and investing their creative energies in this area while fostering conciliatory relationships with others. Accordingly, Fama and his collaborators used standard statistical methods conveying "mechanical objectivity" (Porter 1995) to frame efficiency as real and discoverable by anyone using conventional methodological tools.

By contrast, Fischer Black and (some of) his colleagues understood CAPM as an ideal state of the world that had not yet fully come into existence, but one that scholars could nevertheless theorize about using quantitative analysis as an "engine of discovery." First, they understood statistics not as a method to prove or falsify theory but rather as a method to change one's beliefs about the world.

CAPM was constructed in a "mode of statistical analysis" that emphasized subjective discovery. Second, scholars also hoped to find ways to make the world more congruent with CAPM (Lehmann 2004; MacKenzie 2006; Porter 1995). But this methodology and research approach made the CAPM network self-limiting. Because it encouraged an individualistic intellectual style, it detached itself from the data-processing networks that were building up at the center of financial economics, privileging instead theorizing and model building even in the absence of data. This hindered the creation of a research group invested enough in CAPM to defend it from criticism (Parker and Hackett 2012). As a consequence, the network was unable to generate trust in its findings.

As studies of quantification have shown, scholars adopt analytical methods not only when they are suitable for the data at hand but also when legitimacy is of concern: powerful external forces are at play when influential outsiders and gatekeepers frame a particular methodological practice as desirable (Leahey 2005). Moreover, in spite of their alleged uniformity and universality, quantitative methods make it possible for scholars to "display a general conformity with defensible scientific practices" while differentiating their discipline from other research programs by using different subsets of the statistical toolkit (Camic and Xie 1994, 776).

A comparison of the trajectories of the scholarly networks around Fama and Black reveals that methods have to be suitable for the networks in which data circulate as well: internal forces come into play when data analysis is framed as a resource that can give the network distinctive advantages. These scholars' differential success tells us something about how academic networks develop around data. Once an infrastructure is built to facilitate the collection of data, a discipline is under pressure to use such data; networks can grow by specializing in data analysis. Claims that the data are appropriate for the kinds of questions the discipline anchors its research agenda on are buttressed not only by conforming to accepted scientific methods but also by using methods that allow for the network to expand. Put differently, techniques of quantitative analysis are not a substitute for relationships of trust among knowledge producers: getting a network of data analysis to produce new research programs means adopting *collectivist* approaches to data. This is the topic of the next chapter.

HOW FINANCIAL ECONOMICS GOT ITS SCIENCE

In the beginning, praising the methodological advances achieved by the field seemed like a good idea. Surely, if there was a way forward, it would involve reliance on new techniques, new data, and new analytical approaches—or so argued Fred Weston, then editor of the *Journal of Finance*, the top journal of the field.

> The emerging problems and issues of finance make it unsatisfactory for us to expect that we can contribute to the improvement of economic and business decisions solely by generalization and judgment. We now have at our command improved techniques for formulating models; we have developed improved tools for observation, for gathering data, and for careful statistical testing of alternative propositions. The older methodologies are useful for suggesting hypotheses and propositions, but inadequate for the systematic formulation of models and their testing. (Weston 1967, 540)

But would the old guard quietly stand by as the "new finance men" took over? There were some who did not feel threatened by the new methods, and even pointed to ways that, in spite of claims to the contrary, the old guard was indispensable to new finance, just as new finance was making itself indispensable to the old guard.

> Mathematical analysts are not only contributing to the advancement of our discipline by using their own methods and concepts, but they are

also imposing upon institutionalists some requirements that are for the good of the profession. They are requiring us to be more careful in our generalizations and more precise in our definitions. They are asking us to describe more clearly the elements of a problem, to estimate more exactly how several influences operate to produce a given result, and even to think about the relative importance of these several influences under different sets of conditions. . . .

One of the problems of mathematical analysts is to select and evaluate empirical data, and generally the data are about institutions, instruments and markets. What data are most significant for a particular purpose? What are the limitations of the data? Or, more broadly, how important is the question, how useful is a test of an hypothesis [*sic*], or how realistic is a model for the real world of finance? Sometimes institutionalists can draw inferences from quantitative analysis that are not readily apparent to those who make such analyses. What we need most in finance is a good mathematician-theoretician on one end of a log, a good institutionalist on the other, and an adequate vocabulary for communication between them. (Sauvain 1967, 541–42)

Others, however, were far less conciliatory. When they looked at "new finance," they saw only a set of recycled techniques, used more often than not to cover up one's ignorance of substantive financial processes.

The quantitative approach is anything but new in finance; in the hands of the actuaries, it dates back to the eighteenth century. What, then, is the difference?
. . . The difference, as I see it, is the effectiveness with which quantitative methods are used. The actuaries have managed to keep at least one foot on the ground by addressing themselves to workaday problems requiring mathematical solutions; and although these problems may seem dull and uninteresting to the new finance men, they are at least tractable, and usable solutions are forthcoming. The new finance men, on the other hand, have lost virtually all contact with terra firma. On the whole, they seem to be more interested in demonstrating their mathematical prowess than in solving genuine problems; often they seem to be playing mathematical games. . . .
When they build models, they often become so infatuated with the product that they will plug in any data, no matter how inappropriate, just to obtain numerical results. When they engage in what Weston calls "the careful statistical testing of hypotheses," they are anything but careful in their selection of data. The idea of adapting their analytical ap-

proach to the limitations of available data hardly ever occurs to them. (Durand 1968, 848)

The new finance men were quick to point out that they followed the same, sound principles of research as their predecessors. But their techniques, they promised, were far superior in reducing uncertainty.

> The actuaries which Professor Durand champions must surely offer a similar justification for their labors. Namely, that they reduce ignorance so as to improve decision making. No more than the rest of us are they blessed with the clean, stable processes of theoretical construct. This process appears to be the rule in empirical economic research. Typically, seemingly less significant variables are dropped when it is impossible to reject the hypothesis that their coefficients are zero. This is true even though a tight confidence interval cannot be formed about zero for the coefficients on the basis of the data. The question at issue is whether one would feel more confident about the results if some other procedure were followed. (Pye 1968, 853)

Calls for a conciliatory perspective, all in all, seemed more prevalent than critique.

> The history of method in economics shows that power of economic analysis and equipment of analytical tools grow only by painfully slow accretions of knowledge and technique; that never has there been a time in which a generation has made such vast strides that it could afford to discard or even to neglect the achievements of the preceding generations. (Bicksler 1972, 917, quoting Jacob Viner)

But the methods marched forward. Old approaches would still be used, but only for the description of special cases. If you did not want to miss the proverbial forest for the trees, new finance was the right tool.

> Some are concerned that the new finance theory discards much of the traditional, particularly the institutional and descriptive materials. This is not true. Rather, what we are seeing is a more complete statement of the theory showing previous models to be either special cases of a more general theory or formulations under alternative assumptions. Thus the new theory provides an effective framework for determining the relevant institutional and descriptive materials, leading to their more effective utilization. (Weston 1974, 240)

Did finance theory succeed in providing the expansive, effective framework advocated by sympathizers of the new approach? Did the new finance men accomplish what they set out to do, and through their mastery of new data and new analytical techniques, did they turn finance into a science? To answer these questions, we have to dig deeper into how a discipline becomes a science, paying particular attention to how scholars build trust in quantitative analysis and hard data.

Defining and Contesting "Scientific"

If there is a hierarchy to the social and human sciences, it hinges on the extent to which a discipline can fashion itself as a follower of the scientific method. Financial economists, by virtue of their reliance on analytical methods common in the hard sciences, would likely put themselves close to the top of this hierarchy (Fourcade, Ollion, and Algan 2015). The "study of business finance . . . has developed a highly mathematical and formal approach. . . . Adopting statistical and economic techniques, contemporary finance has become an abstract and esoteric field of research concerned with highly 'restricted' . . . and limited objects which seems far removed from the everyday functioning of particular institutions," argues Richard Whitley (1986b, 172), echoing, with more than a hint of criticism, the fears expressed by the old institutionalist guard. In a preface of an influential textbook, Copeland and Weston confirm this view:

> Finance [used to be] largely a descriptive field of endeavor. . . . [M]ajor theoretical thrusts have transformed the field into a positive science. . . . Fifty years ago the faculty were drawn from the ranks of business and government. They were respected and experienced statesmen within their fields. Today, finance faculty are predominantly academicians in the traditional sense of the word. The majority of them have no business experience except for consulting. Their interest and training is in developing theories to explain economic behavior, then testing them with the tools provided by statistics and econometrics. Anecdotal evidence and individual business experience have been superseded by the analytic approach of modern finance theory. (1988, iii–iv)

The claim that the discipline is scientific—"a positive science"—is strengthened by the fact that finance has generated not only new techniques but also new *objects* of analysis, allowing analysts to uncover new phenomena: terms like "implied volatility" and "beta" have become fundamental features of financial trades. Market agents have therefore been able to directly incorporate financial theory into their professional practices. As the sociologist of finance Preda argues, there is a long history to this practice. Over the past two hundred years, traders and investors have mastered specific observational skills and technologies with which they revealed particular aspects of financial markets to broader publics while likening themselves to disinterested experts and scientists (Preda 2009, 23). To Preda, "the effort to transform investment knowledge into a science was crowned by the formulation of basic tenets of the random walk hypothesis, which was to dominate the second half of the twentieth century" (25).

And yet, many would find the idea that finance is scientific problematic. Some adopt critical arguments that originate with the institutionalists, and point to finance's dependence on broader social forces: "Unlike other technologies, the ability of finance to work depends critically on both laws and perceptions. . . . [F]inancial markets are like orchids, requiring a very specialized institutional climate to flourish. . . . Moreover, perceptions and norms are essential to finance in ways that they are not for other technologies. Perceptions can hold Boeing shares aloft, but perception alone cannot hold Boeing jets aloft" (Davis 2009, 55). Others reflect on what financial economists gain by portraying themselves as scientists—and worry that their real interest is in shutting down public debate and staving off political challenges to their power and expertise: "Finance and economics are among modern society's most depoliticized areas of activity. . . . [M]odern finance, perhaps more than any other area of politics, has acquired a logic of calculability and an appearance of scientific objectivity that places its fundamental assumptions—such as its indicators of performance—beyond discussion and debate" (Goede 2005, 2, 3). Similarly, highlighting the danger of using scientific objectivity to bolster its appearance, some economists, especially those critical of the mainstream (including finance), warn us that there are "many worldly and logical gaps in neoclassical economics," and denounce "its hidden ideological agendas, its disregard for the environment and inability to consider economic issues in an ecological context, its habitual misuse of mathematics and statistics, its inability to address the major issues of economic globalization, its ethical cynicism concerning poverty, racism and sexism, and its misrepresentation of economic history" (Fullbrook 2004, 6).

These are important and difficult conversations, as the term "science" serves to connote not only scientific knowledge but also the social prestige and power that accrue to those who succeed in gaining scientific recognition for their activities. Thus, there is much at stake in attempts to define financial economics as a science or criticize financial economists for appropriating a term that does not capture the nature of their knowledge. As sociologists of science have long warned, however, beyond its use as a marker of boundaries (Gieryn 1983), what makes the term "science" especially problematic is that there is no one, set-upon definition of science that holds for all disciplines to begin with. Crucial aspects initially thought to be distinct to the hard sciences—like the strength of scientific consensus over a set of well-established facts, or the ability of scientists to make rapid discoveries—turn out not only to characterize the soft sciences too but also to be unevenly present in the hard sciences (Cole 1983, 1992). And as a consequence, attempts to codify general differences between human and natural sciences have produced mixed results at best (Cozzens 1985, 128; though see Simonton 2004).

Revisiting public debates among scholars often helps us retrieve points and reveal aspects that get lost as the debate moves forward (or, as is more often the case, the debate stops as scholars move on to do other things, and whatever was debated is simply forgotten). And on deeper reading, the brief series of exchanges I reported at the beginning of the chapter helps us reconstruct key issues that, as the discipline consolidates, cease to draw the attention of financial economists but nevertheless yield useful insights into what it might mean to define financial economics as scientific.

Scholars involved in this debate worried about the effects of introducing the scientific method to financial research: they were especially concerned that science would displace history and institutional analysis. But they also had more specific anxieties about the effects of introducing into the discipline particular methods, analytical techniques, and ways of gathering data. Not unlike the debate around Richard Roll's work we discussed in chapter 2, questions that emerged from this particular set of debates include the following: Would the new methods and data improve the ability of finance scholars to guide "economic and business decisions"? How would "accretions of technique" relate to "accretions of knowledge"? What would be forgotten as the discipline moved away from traditional approaches, like those that emphasized institutional history and description, and embraced the "quantitative approach" as practiced by the "new finance men"? How would methods, theory, and data intersect in the new configuration of *practices* proposed by the leaders of mathematical financial economics?

We saw in chapter 2 that Eugene Fama succeeded in sidestepping many of these thorny issues by proposing that the fit between theory and evidence should be *reasonable*. Through this move, Fama helped change the affective dispositions that held the scholarly network of finance together; this opened the door to a new stream of research on market efficiency. The focus was on rhetoric and justification, aimed at winning legitimacy for a new theoretical perspective. Yet, the problem of data, and precisely the role that financial scholars would expect data to play in the construction of their discipline, was not confined to one theoretical perspective; it was more pervasive. With the rise of modern finance theory, would "any data, no matter how inappropriate," be plugged into models "just to obtain numerical results," as David Durand worried? Would, by contrast, data analysis become just a better way of reducing uncertainty, thus serving the same objectives earlier analysts had found worth pursuing, even though they had access to inferior methods, as suggested by Gordon Pye? Questions about the extent to which finance could make a claim to scientific status, in short, were inextricably linked with questions about the effects of new data and techniques on knowledge making in finance.

This chapter focuses on the practices financial economists built around data and technique, and on their approach to and presentation of the analysis of financial data. Since it is on the basis of their technical proficiency and access to new data that financial economists built the case that their discipline was scientific, investigating the forms financial economists used to communicate with one another can yield important insights into their relationship with their new analytical practices. Building on the work of scholars who deepen Latour's thesis that science produces facts by employing particular techniques of presentation— particular ways of *visualizing* data (Cleveland 1984; Latour 1986; Simonton 2004; Smith et al. 2000)—I am specifically interested in the *devices* financial economists turned to in order to produce numerical knowledge, as their work became increasingly focused on the analysis of quantitative data.

I propose a typology of research communicative practices—from graphs to tables and equations—and theorize about the kinds of social structures that are more likely to adopt these practices. The level of trust within a scholarly network, and the degree to which the network relies on technology, produce a preference for different ways of handling numbers. When experts trust one another, and trust the technology through which they produce new knowledge, their research outcomes are presented as graphs bringing together theory and measurement. Remove trust in expertise, and graphs are used to represent only empirical relationships; remove trust in technology as well, and graphs disappear, and knowledge is communicated in the shape of numerical tables. Finally, mutual trust among experts with little reliance on technology tends to generate a preference for equations—mathematical representations of theoretical arguments.

I suggest that focusing on these different modes of communicating the results of technical analyses gives us insight into the kinds of knowledge claims that financial economists came to make, and how they built trust in those knowledge claims. To substantiate this point, I offer an analysis of a random sample of close to three hundred articles published in the top journal of financial economics— the *Journal of Finance*. I show that some financial articles, especially in an early period, made use of devices characteristic of the hard sciences, specifically, graphical representations of theoretical and empirical relationships. But this is by no means indicative of a broader trend. In fact, finance papers quickly came to rely on statistical tables and equations, preferring long lists of symbols and numbers over graphs and charts. That this specific format became dominant is revealing of a broader structural pattern in this discipline, one characterized by low trust.

More broadly, then, attention to the devices for communicating quantitative outcomes gives us a framework to grasp variation in the ways quantification is used in knowledge-making projects. The main thrust in theories of knowledge is to confine numbers to the process of verification, or falsification, of knowledge claims. Analyses more attuned to the politics of numbers, and its relationship to expertise, have uncovered two additional roles: First, numbers serve as a tool of political control, for when mobilized in support of specific projects, numbers can help define new sites of political intervention by, for instance, allowing policy-makers to implement new policies based on census data. Second, and more internal to disciplines, numbers help knowledge producers convey an objective stance. Numbers substantiate scholarly claims to objectivity intended as lack of personal motives, in ways that shore up weak expertise. Experts rely on numbers to communicate with a public that demands their authority be justified and rationalized. Quantification is a response to public insistence that experts be made accountable.

A focus on how numbers are constructed from within, however, reveals that the problem of trusting numbers extends to the producers of knowledge themselves. Simple use of techniques of quantitative analysis cannot substitute for relationships of trust among knowledge producers: numbers play a limited in the construction of social knowledge when they are not backed by social relationships.

Data and Visualization in the Pursuit of Science

Since the turn toward practice in the sociology of knowledge, empirical approaches focused on what scientists do (rather than, say, philosophical approaches to the scientific method) have become dominant. One of Latour's lasting contributions to this turn is his recognition of the importance of technologies of calculation to scientific activity. In fact, Latour's concept of the center of calculation serves as a way to systematize analysis of local practices into a more general theory of science. As we have seen in previous chapters, a center of calculation is a hierarchical network where the systematic collection of information at lower levels generates data that are fed to levels higher up. As data are linked together, transported, and manipulated to generate new, more synthetic data, the network builds up more and more layers of abstraction. Data, in this model, are traces that move up and down a vertically integrated network of communication, affording more control with less cumbersome and more condensed information the more one moves toward the core.

Central to the flow of information are strategies and tools of persuasion. Latour focuses in particular on *inscription devices*. These are "any item of apparatus or particular configuration of such items which can transform a material substance into a figure or diagram which is directly usable by one of the members of the office space" (Latour and Woolgar 1986, 51). The product of an inscription device is a graphical representation, which makes "the 'things' you gathered and displaced . . . presentable all at once to those you want to convince. . . . You have to invent objects which have the properties of being *mobile* but also *immutable, presentable, readable* and *combinable* with one another" (Latour 1986, 7). In other words, graphs fix the results of an analysis into formats that allow for further manipulations: graphs can be compared with other graphs, they can be built on to produce new discoveries, and most importantly, they can be used to focus the audience's attention on specific features while ignoring less relevant aspects.

Graphs are accomplishments that signal the power of a discipline to raise the stakes of a debate. And graphs turn things into facts, because when socially sanctioned visualizations come into play, they become more difficult to disprove. Disagreement is no longer just a matter of marshaling contrasting evidence or building solid arguments. Rather, critics must produce their own charts and graphs if they want their own analysis to gain attention and support.

There are at least two related reasons that make this process arduous and rigorous. First, graphs help scientists understand the fit between theory and data efficiently, as visual representations convey relevant information in a compelling way. Unlike textual representations of data, graphs make the detection of patterns easy to perform (Bastide 1990; Bazerman 1988). Therefore, not all graphs will do: it is graphs that promote theory-evidence integration that succeed. Second, precisely because graphs afford quicker understanding, they also serve as heuristics for the detection of new patterns—they serve as instruments of discovery (Lynch 1988).

Latour points to the "extraordinary obsession of scientists with papers, prints, diagrams, archives, abstracts and curves on graph paper. No matter what they talk about, they start talking with some degree of confidence and being believed by colleagues, only once they point at simple geometrized two-dimensional shapes" (1986, 15–16). And while Latour is reluctant to make the case that the social/ human sciences part ways with the natural sciences in this respect, others (Chua 1995; Cleveland 1984; Smith et al. 2000) argue that this obsession with graphical inscriptions is more pronounced with the hard sciences. "Methods of graphical display have come to encompass a wide range of techniques for enlisting allies. . . . That the use of such methods has not been evenly distributed across the spectrum of the sciences may well speak directly to the perennial question of why the harder sciences seem to experience higher degrees of facticity and theoretical integration than their softer counterparts" (Smith et al. 2000, 87).

If graphs have such important effects, why do they tend to characterize research in the hard sciences but are less prevalent in the soft sciences? As Cleveland (1984) shows, the differences are significant: whereas a physics paper is likely to dedicate from one-fifth to one-third of the total space to figures, a psychology paper will dedicate one in every ten pages, and a sociology paper will dedicate one in every fifty pages. A discipline's structure as a center of calculation provides one answer. For graphs to help "draw things together," an established structure that gives scholars confidence in the data underlying graphical representations surely helps. We may venture to say that techno-science and "graphism" work together in sustaining trust relationships among scientists. As Peterson shows for the case of biology, scientists spend as much time manipulating the apparatus that generates data (the laboratory) as they do discussing the accuracy of their findings. This is not because they take each other at their word. Rather, it is because, "when the possibilities of research are constantly receding, labs funnel their resources into developing the techniques and technology to maintain their position along the cutting edge. Consensus and stability are sacrificed under the faith that ambiguous, local research will eventually solidify" (Peterson 2015, 1219).

As new critical scholarship makes clear (Gitelman 2013; Poovey 1993, 1998), however, graphs are not the exclusive province of science, and thinking about the intersection between trust and technology gives us purchase on potential differences across fields. A good example is the rise of big data, which complicates the point that only centers of calculation have a natural affinity with graphs. Big-data networks exhibit a similar affinity, but this happens in spite of a fundamental uncertainty about what data actually measure. In the case of big data, pattern recognition through data dredging is strongly allied with visualization precisely because, with big-data enthusiasts, it is correlations that matter, even when the underlying mechanisms are unknown (boyd and Crawford 2012). Finance as it is practiced in the profit-making centers of capitalism is perhaps the most illustrious example. Here data analysis generates a new visual economy where a deluge of numbers is filtered through graphs and charts, the point of which is not to afford new theoretical insight but rather to help traders and investors make money. Emphasis is on making discoveries with short-term payoffs, while the algorithms that make such discoveries possible are black boxed (Amoore and Piotukh 2015).

Rather than "drawing things together," such approaches potentially impair theoretical and empirical integration. Particularly problematic is that the sheer size of a dataset is no substitute for knowledge of how the data are produced, and thus of the biases implicit in the dataset. But while this insight has fundamental implications for a wide variety of practices that big data is quickly revolutionizing (for policing, see Brayne 2017; for lending practices, see Fourcade and Healy 2016), proponents of big data seem to take little stock in the biases they are embedding into their analyses. In sum, whereas Latour's image of the center of calculation emphasizes the movement of information up and down a centralized network, big data does not quite fit this centralized model where different levels of the center hold each other accountable. But it produces a culture of visualization that is similar to that of science (Coopmans et al. 2014; Knorr Cetina and Bruegger 2002).

Science uses and depends on inscription devices, but in ways that are not quite captured by Latour's insights. Yes, scientists obsess about graphs, but so do data analysts. Big data, like science, depends on technologies for pattern recognition, a relationship that promotes a culture of visualization. But unlike science, big data is also characterized by mistrust. It embodies an extreme form of "mechanical objectivity," predicated on a deep suspicion of the expert. In big data, unlike in science, data are increasingly understood to be *autonomous from, and even substitutive of, theory*—and, more radically, superior to it. Their increased volume, variety, and velocity of circulation allegedly make big data unaffected by human intervention, especially expert interpretation. Evidence-based claims become simply more credible than professional perspectives because they seem unmediated.

Trust in expertise, in short, remains hidden in Latour's concept of the center of calculation. But visualization practices, like any other research practice, take place in communities of inquiry and expertise. Variation in inscription devices is therefore the result not only of different calculative practices but of underlying patterns of trust that make the adoption of such practices more or less likely. This becomes further apparent once we expand our focus to quantitative practices that, unlike science but in similar ways to big data, do not benefit from a network of trust. As we have learned from Porter (1995) and critics of quantification, trust in experts by outside audiences is not a necessary condition for the production of social knowledge, but lack of trust does produce a pronounced demand for statistics. It is precisely when scholars do not trust one another that appeals to objectivity as impersonal judgment become more common. As Randall Collins (1984, 349) puts it, "We set stringent statistical criteria not because logically they are crucial for establishing the truth of a theory but because our intellectual community is socially distrustful of the honesty of investigators."

Latour's logic invites us to extend the intuition that science visualizes to other media of communication likely to emerge in such instances. Again, a brief comparison with big data is helpful, as there is some similarity between the use of statistics in social research and in big data: in both cases, expertise is perceived to be weaker than the formalized, objective methods through which numerical knowledge is produced. Why, then, does big data produce graphs, whereas statistics tends not to? One important difference, I would suggest, is the degree to which these practices are embedded in technology. The "data" of big data are complex assemblages of fine-grained data collected for purposes that have little to do with the question at hand; what holds them together are "algorithms." Visuals are an extension of this logic: graphs represent the empirical relationships discovered by the algorithms so that human interpreters can make sense of these patterns. But the detection of the patterns themselves is black boxed.

By contrast, statistics relies on methods that are controlled and monitored by experts. And when experts do not trust the numbers, tables come in handy as communicative techniques.[1] Without a technology that enables a culture of visualization, we see low trust and use of statistics resulting in inscription devices that present numerical displays in tabular format. This type of display would reflect the logic of the statistician: uncertainty about the quality of the data and the trustworthiness of the expert means more attention to the limits of and problems inherent to the data, and more value on, for instance, the accurate reporting of errors. Graphs, from this point of view, may actually be misleading precisely because they make data appear as facts. Tables with numbers, on the other hand, may seem more truthful as they foreground the limitations of the data and the analysis itself (Gelman, Pasarica, and Dodhia 2002; Meyer, Shamo, and Gopher 1999).

Trust in expertise, in short, is decoupled from trust in the technology. Experts who do not trust one other may rely on technology to overcome the limits they see in expert knowledge, and in the process, come to treat their research outcomes as if they were objective facts. By contrast, experts who do not trust other experts but who are also critical of the analytical apparatus built into technology may cultivate a preference for numerical representations of their findings, discouraging others from taking the analysis at face value. Experts who put value in expertise can also have different perspectives on technology. When they value and depend on technology, bringing about the tight relationship that Latour christens as "techno-science," numbers will give rise to theoretically meaningful graphs. When, however, expert practices are not mediated by techno-science, quantification will likely take a different form than graphs or tables. We can generalize from the cases of high-energy physics, described by Sharon Traweek (2009), and economics, described by Breslau and Yonay (1999). It is not that these fields are disembedded from or critical of technology. It is rather that they privilege the symbolic manipulation of logically coherent systems of equations, or mathematics, as a way to produce new knowledge. In fact, the latter authors show how mathematical models in economics serve a function similar to that of the laboratories in the life sciences: they help economists distinguish their own actions from the agency of what they study, thereby increasing trust in their results by claiming

TABLE 5.1. Inscription devices as a function of trust in expertise and reliance on technology

	LOW TECHNOLOGY	HIGH TECHNOLOGY
High trust	Mathematics (models with equations)	Big science (graphs advancing theory)
Low trust	Statistics (tables)	Big data (graphs of correlations)

objectivity for their findings. Data do not drive their research; rather, the logical consistency of their models drives their research. In table 5.1, I summarize this argument.

Armed with these distinctions, we can return to the case of financial economics both to investigate Weston's claim—that financial economics becomes more scientific over time—in an empirically sound manner and to assess the extent to which *changes* in the communicative practices and types of inscriptions reflect changes in the roles played by data and technology in the production of financial knowledge. What kinds of techniques do financial economists deploy to communicate their results? What do changes in practices tell us about the status of the field? What does it take for financial economists to believe their data?

Saying Things with Numbers

Let us first look at how financial economics compares with other disciplines, and then look at the historical development of the field. I rely on Cleveland's (1984) extensive survey of several disciplines across the human and natural sciences, and apply his methodology to the top journal of the field of financial economics (the *Journal of Finance*) in order to quantify finance's reliance on graphs and compare it with other disciplines. Specifically, Cleveland draws a random sample of papers published between 1980 and 1981 from top journals from each field and calculates the proportion of each paper occupied by graphical representations. Figure 5.1 presents selected results of his investigation: it reports results for the journal in each discipline that has the highest fraction of papers occupied by graphs. To Cleveland's data, I add my own coding of the *Journal of Finance* (with a sample of eighteen papers).

The figure groups the results by category of scientific discipline (social, mathematical, or natural). Focusing our comparison on the social sciences reveals that financial economics makes slightly more use of graphs than the average: a forty-page article will have about one full page of graphs, whereas an average social

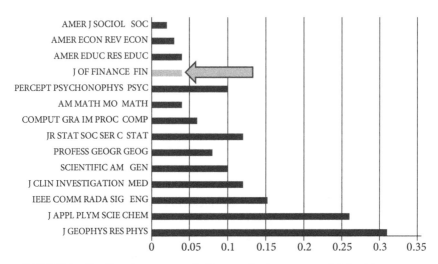

FIGURE 5.1   Fractional area occupied by graphs in papers published by top journals across disciplines, 1980–1981. Data from Cleveland (1984) and author's calculations.

science article of similar length will have less than a full page of graphs. Sociology is the lowest among the social sciences, with an average fraction of 0.02 of total space of articles appearing in the *American Journal of Sociology* occupied by graphs (2%, or about one page in a fifty-page article). Psychology, with 0.10, is the highest. Finance, with a fractional graph area of 0.04, is slightly higher than the 0.03 mean for the social sciences as a whole (Smith et al. 2002, 753). Economics, at 0.03, is lower than finance, and right at the average.

How does financial economics compare with the mathematical and physical sciences, the "positive" disciplines it strives to imitate? The differences are striking but not surprising, in that they are consistent with broader patterns. The mathematical sciences range from a low of 0.04 (mathematics) to a high of 0.12 (statistics). Thus, financial economics resembles mathematics more than it does statistics, as papers in this discipline have three times as much space assigned to graphs as papers in financial economics. The physical sciences, in turn, range from a low of 0.10 (for the general-audience journal *Scientific American*) to a high of 0.31 for physics. The comparison with physics is particularly dramatic: the fractional graph area in physics is about eight times larger than that in financial economics. The difference is large, though, of course, it is not unique to financial economics. If we just compare the average for financial economics with the average for the physical sciences (as reported by Cleveland), the latter number is 0.12, thus three times as large—still, quite a significant gap.

It seems reasonable to conclude from this analysis that financial economics makes far less use of graphical representations than the hard sciences do. If we accept Latour's thesis, classifying financial economics as a "positive science" would seem an exaggeration. Financial economists rely on graphical inscription devices marginally more than economists do, about as much as education researchers, and less than psychologists—disciplines we would be hard-pressed to classify as hard sciences. Research in finance, much like its social scientific counterparts, simply does not focus on producing the "immutable mobiles" that Latour believes to be so important to scientific knowledge.

Does this mean that Fred Weston's dreams for financial economics were never realized, and that knowledge and technique never came together in the way desired by many of the new finance men? Were the institutionalists right all along that the techniques of their opponents would turn out to be ineffective and ephemeral? Jumping to such conclusions, while tempting, is premature. Our cross-disciplinary comparison is based on a small sample. And it is based on only two years, with little justification offered for selecting 1980–1981, and no effort to understand whether the broader sociopolitical context affects knowledge production in particular ways in that period, which is especially problematic for the social sciences (Zald 1995). Though the *Journal of Finance* is the top journal in the field, generalizing from such a limited sample to an entire discipline seems misguided.

Between 1945 and 2000, the *Journal of Finance* published 3,247 articles. To address the small-sample problem, and to stretch the temporal framework of the analysis so as to weaken the effects of specific external events on the sample, I took a random sample of 293 articles (about 9% of the total) to gain a better grasp of the prevalence of graphs in financial economics.[2] I did not restrict myself to tracking visualization alone but recorded the use of two additional techniques of quantitative display over time: tables and equations. Overall, I assembled data for the following three variables:

FGA = proportion of a paper taken up by graphs
FTA = proportion of a paper taken up by tables
FEA = proportion of a paper taken up by equations

Tables and equations are two additional methods of quantitative analysis (besides graphs), but they have different effects and signal a different relationship between numbers and disciplines than do graphs. Tables, as we have seen, are less effective at communicating results or inviting pattern recognition. On the other hand, tables allow better understanding of details (and errors); they go hand in hand with statistical analysis. Equations, by contrast, can be formalized representations of theoretical arguments, or they can aid statistical analysis, backing the construction of complex variables.

Figure 5.2 confirms the original finding that financial economics is not a discipline saturated with graphs. The highest proportion of total space occupied by graphs occurs around the early 1960s, when the sample drawn from this period averages a peak value of 0.09. This is about as much as psychology or general science journals. But it is an exception to a long-term trend where graphs receive far less use. By the 1970s, graphs become less frequent, with an FGA barely exceeding 0.05 until the early 1990s, and even then, never reaching the peak of the 1960s. What becomes more prevalent is tables, which by the 1990s take up about 18 percent of paper space, on average; and equations, averaging 8 percent of paper space in the late 1970s and early 1980s, to decrease to about 4 percent in the 1990s.

Another way of understanding the relative frequency of these different inscription devices over time is to count their average occurrence in papers by year. I do this in figure 5.3, which shows the average frequency of graphs, tables, and equations over the 1952–2000 period. On average, through the late 1950s, a paper has about a 70 percent chance of having a graph; in the 1960s, the average number of graphs per paper increases to more than one (but less than two). It hovers around 1.5 until the early 1990s, when the average number increases to over two. Given the small size of these frequencies, the conclusion that graphs do not play a central role to financial knowledge seems warranted.

The story for tables and equations is different. Whereas a paper from the 1950s has a 50 percent chance of having a table, the average number of tables per paper increases to about 2 through the mid-1970s, 2.5 through the 1980s, and about 4.6 through the 1990s. Similarly, the average number of equations in a paper increases dramatically over this period. From less than 2 equations per paper on average in the 1950s, their frequency increases to about 10 in the 1960s, 14 in the 1970s and 1980s, and about 11.5 in the 1990s. Thus, a typical twenty-page paper published in the *Journal of Finance* in the 1970s would have four pages of tables (totaling about two tables), more than half a page of equations (about nine equations), and more than half a page of graphs, with a 20 percent chance of having no graphs at all. A paper from the 1990s, for the sake of comparison, would have three and a half pages of tables (totaling about five tables) and more than half a page of equations (about twelve equations). The paper would be about as likely to have a graph as not to have one; if it did, that graph would take up less than a half page. While there are year-to-year variations in these frequencies, the trend toward a handful of tables extending over several pages and an increasing number of equations strikes me as the most important feature of these figures.

Of course, a sample drawn from the entire population of articles is not representative of cutting-edge research in the field (though the average citation count of the sample is a respectable 118.4). In figures 5.4 and 5.5, I perform the same

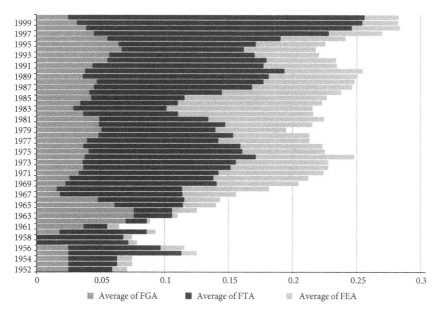

FIGURE 5.2 Fractional graph area, fractional table area, and fractional equation area in sample of papers published in the *Journal of Finance*, 1952–2000 (*n* = 293 articles, five-year moving averages).

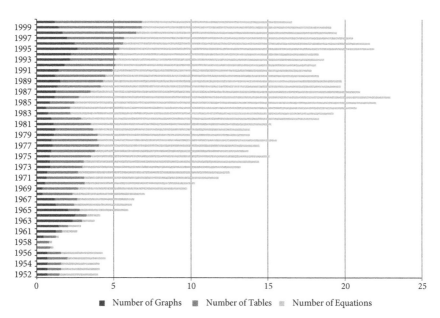

FIGURE 5.3 Yearly average number of graphs, tables, and equations in sample of papers published in the *Journal of Finance*, 1952–2000 (*n* = 293 articles, five-year moving averages).

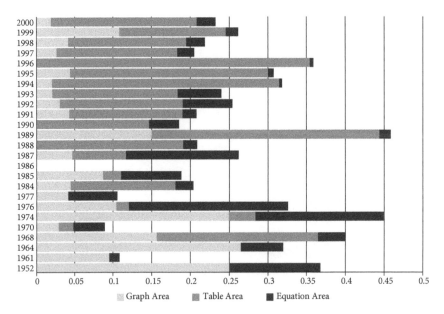

FIGURE 5.4 Fractional graph area, fractional table area, and fractional equation area in the top fifty most-cited papers published in the *Journal of Finance*, 1952–2000.

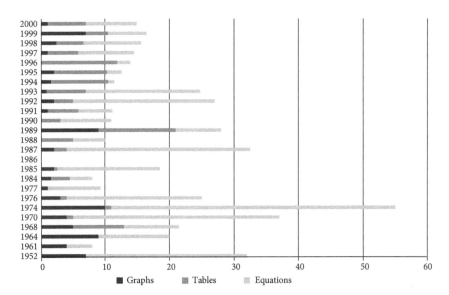

FIGURE 5.5 Yearly average number of graphs, tables, and equations in the top fifty most-cited papers published in the *Journal of Finance*, 1952–2000.

analysis on a different sample of papers: I focus on the fifty most-cited articles from the same time period. The average citation count of this sample increases to 1,498, thus capturing papers that have had wide influence on the field and beyond.

An analysis of these influential papers reveals a pattern similar to that characterizing the broader literature: an early period dominated by relatively heavy use of graphs and minimal use of statistics, which gives way to a later period where the papers make heavy use of tables and equations and, with some exceptions, very limited use of graphs, if at all. Looking at the sample as a whole, on average, a highly cited paper in financial economics will have one full page of graphs for every 20 pages, 2.6 pages of tables, and slightly less than one page of equations. That one page of graphs will have two or three graphs, tables will likely number four or five, and the paper will have about eleven equations overall.

In support of Latour's thesis, influential papers do indeed make more use of graphs than do all other papers; but the difference is small, on average, and does not change our discussion of cross-disciplinary comparisons. If anything, what the diachronic analysis of the frequency of inscription devices reveals is that financial economics becomes *less scientific* over time, at least in the specific sense of relying less and less on graphs as a way of communicating research results. What accounts for this variation over time? Why do tables and equations become the preferred way of conducting quantitative analysis in papers written by financial economists?

The Social Sources of Graphs

If my theoretical model is correct, we should expect financial economics' shifting reliance on different inscription devices to be a function of how trust and technology intersect. We should expect periods of optimism and enthusiasm around new technological developments to encourage financial economists to produce graphs. By contrast, we should expect moments of conflict—when trusting one's colleagues means trusting only one's immediate collaborators—or periods of technological stagnation to invite a focus on statistics or mathematics. In table 5.2, I select from the top fifty papers a few examples that serve to illustrate this point. I discuss each quadrant below.

Technological Optimism
(High Technology, High Trust)

Papers in the high technology–high trust quadrant are characterized by high levels of trust, both in the measurements and results produced by other papers, and

TABLE 5.2. Inscription devices, exemplary papers, *Journal of Finance*

	LOW TECHNOLOGY	HIGH TECHNOLOGY
High trust	Leland, H. E., and D. H. Pyle. 1977. "Informational Asymmetries, Financial Structure, and Financial Intermediation." 32 (2): 371–87.	Markowitz, H. 1952. "Portfolio Selection." 7 (1): 77–91.
	Merton, R. C. 1987. "A Simple-Model of Capital-Market Equilibrium with Incomplete Information." 42 (3): 483–510.	Sharpe, W. F. 1964. "Capital Asset Prices: A Theory of Market Equilibrium under Conditions of Risk." 19 (3): 425–42.
	Froot, K. A., D. S. Scharfstein, and J. C. Stein. 1993. "Risk Management: Coordinating Corporate Investment and Financing Policies." 48 (5): 1629–58.	Merton, R. C. 1974. "On the Pricing of Corporate Debt: The Risk Structure of Interest Rates." 29 (2): 449–70.
	Average FGA: .02, Average FTA: .01, Average FEA: .13	Average FGA: .25, Average FTA: .01, Average FEA: .10
Low trust	Ritter, J. R. 1991. "The Long-Run Performance of Initial Public Offerings." 46 (1): 3–27.	Jensen, M. C. 1968. "Problems in Selection of Security Portfolios - Performance of Mutual Funds in Period 1945–1964 - .1. Introduction." 23 (2): 389–416.
	Fama, E. F., and K. R. French. 1992. "The Cross-Section of Expected Stock Returns." 47 (2): 427–465.	Schwert, G. W. 1989. "Why Does Stock Market Volatility Change over Time?" 44 (5): 1115–53.
	Lakonishok, J., A. Shleifer, and R. W. Vishny. 1994. "Contrarian Investment, Extrapolation, and Risk." 49 (5): 1541–78.	Lee, C. M. C., and M. J. Ready. 1991. "Inferring Trade Direction from Intraday Data." 46 (2): 733–46.
	Average FGA: .01, Average FTA: .29, Average FEA: .01	Average FGA: .19, Average FTA: .23, Average FEA: .01

in the power of technology to move the discipline forward. There is both optimism in technology's role in the advancement of knowledge and a belief that scholars will stand to benefit from incorporating new techniques into their work. Of the three illustrative papers I selected, those by Markowitz and Sharpe were written by their respective authors as they held positions at research institutes (the Cowles Commission and the RAND Corporation) that were at the forefront of infusing economic and social knowledge with a new technological ethos (Mirowski 2001). The Merton paper is an extension of their model. The three papers have a high fractional area used for graphs, very few tables, and a fair amount of space taken by equations.

Technology Challenges Experts (High Technology, Low Trust)

Moving clockwise, the main theme in the high technology–low trust quadrant is that technology is not a friendly ally but an agonistic tool that scholars can mobilize as they fight common wisdom or the flawed research of their colleagues. Illustrative papers include a study by Michael Jensen, an instantly classic attack on fund managers that uses quantitative techniques to show why their strategies are misguided; a paper by William Schwert that uses a newly assembled dataset to challenge previous understandings of important economic phenomena; and a paper by Charles Lee and Mark Ready that uses new quantitative techniques to infer stock market data with more accuracy than that achieved by previous attempts.

Technology Has Done Its Job; It Is Time to Fight! (Low Technology, Low Trust)

One of the main themes in the low technology–low trust quadrant is satisfaction with the current state of technology. This does not mean a rejection of technology or of new analytical techniques but rather a sense that the technical state of development of the field is secure enough to warrant theoretical consolidation. In some cases, the argument is that technological developments may have helped in the past, but they are no longer needed to make new theoretical points; or, that existing data have not been interpreted correctly and that new theories are needed to shed light on anomalies. The Fama-French paper is illustrative of the first point. It is the classic paper that questions Black's alternative model of capital asset evaluation; the story of this fight was told in the previous chapter. The Lakonishok, Shleifer, and Vishny paper and the Ritter paper are a case of the latter. They reanalyze stock market data to shake confidence in dominant theories informed by efficiency. This is, in short, a quadrant of intellectual conflict, where technology is not seen as a one-size-fits-all solution to the problem of innovation. Papers in this quadrant are characterized by large tables taking up much space, and very few equations or graphs. Tables, one may argue, increase openness and transparency: long and detailed lists of numbers and coefficients ostensibly allow the critical reader to gain better understanding of the strength and limits of the analysis. Yet, we are very far from the world of graphs and equations of the top-right quadrant. The proliferation of numbers and statistical tests that characterizes this quadrant suggests that few scholars expect that others will take their own results seriously.

What Assumptions Can We Tweak? (High Trust, Low Technology)

The high trust–low technology quadrant is characterized by limited use of technology and high trust in one's colleagues. This is reflected in greater use of formal models (and mathematics), low use of graphs, and limited use of tables.

Arguments in this quadrant are constructed following logical rules dictated by models. The common theme is one of trust and optimism; scholars use mathematics and formal modeling to add more nuance to existing models, tweak core assumptions, or expand the purchase of their explanatory frameworks. In the process, they may entertain the possibility that competing theories need to be incorporated into the standard model; but this is in the spirit of building all-encompassing explanations, rather than as critique. Illustrative papers are Leland and Pyle's paper on informational asymmetries, Merton's paper on imperfect information, and Froot, Scharfstein, and Stein's paper on risk management: they are all incremental contributions that aim at strengthening financial economics' understanding of market phenomena.

Conclusions: What Kind of Science Is Financial Economics?

The old institutionalist guard we encountered at the beginning of this chapter—scholars who, like Durand and Bicksler, were invested in understanding the broader political and economic conditions affecting the rise of markets—worried about financial economics turning into a discipline of formal methods and sophisticated techniques. Such a development, they predicted, would ultimately weaken the ability of the discipline to explain and understand the kinds of phenomena it cared about. It would turn the discipline into an empty exercise of analyzing data for the sake of analyzing data, regardless of the data's ability to shed light on relevant financial phenomena. These scholars also felt that they were on the losing side of the debate. The allure of new formal methods, they intimated, was too strong to resist.

The analysis I presented in this chapter cannot speak directly to the question of content—the issue of whether financial economics became less and less able to produce meaningful knowledge over time. But it does provide important hints about substance. By saying something about form, putting financial economics in comparative perspective with other disciplines, as well as paying attention to temporal variation within financial economics itself, this chapter provides evidence about substantive shifts as well.

First of all, my analysis of the prevalence of different techniques of quantitative communication revealed a shifting landscape, with graphs being replaced over time as a dominant template by equations and tables. And it was once scholars of finance began focusing on data analysis and the discovery of new statistical relationships that this strategic preference for tables and equations specifying statistical relationships emerged. As this type of quantification came to be accepted, it produced new affective relationships with datasets, which came to be seen as the main pathway to knowledge.

We saw in chapter 3 that the overall structure of the affective network, with pairs of scholars working together on data analysis, provided the foundation for research on market efficiency. In this chapter, the evidence points in a similar direction: over time, financial economics became a discipline focused on data analysis, using techniques of persuasion (Latour's inscription devices) aimed at fending off critiques from skeptical opponents rather than building new and more comprehensive theories. Thus, explaining finance's inability to shed its seeming obsession with standard models, to be sure, requires an understanding of the ideological/institutional background in which it emerges. But, I suggest, it also requires an understanding of the processes that consolidated its underlying structure and, more specifically, of the kinds of communicative techniques the networks developed to disseminate their research.

This chapter also deepened our understanding of trust in affective networks that rely on quantitative analysis. It proposed an expanded notion of trust, where trust in other scholars matters, but so does trust in whether technologies can help knowledge production. Scholars like Fama might trust the technology more than the people using it, and so end up being critical of technical innovations promoted by others. Other scholars may trust the work of their colleagues especially when it incorporates new technology; yet others might think that technology can only restrict the kinds of questions asked.

Using this expanded notion of trust, I think, is warranted both theoretically and empirically. The influential, now-classic approach to trust proposed by Giddens (1990) differentiates between interpersonal trust and trust in "abstract systems," types of expert systems that people must rely on in modern society but that, simultaneously, people have little knowledge about or control over. Whereas the first kind of trust is based on mutual knowledge, the second is predicated on ignorance. As we have learned from Latour, however, objects and technology are part and parcel of scientific networks. Trusting technology, then, can go hand in hand with trusting the experts who use it—which, from the point of view of scholars, means mixing interpersonal and abstract trust. Technology can also be mobilized against experts. Once a pattern of trust is established, it produces legacies that are difficult to dislodge. The pattern persists until new conditions come into play.

What kind of science, then, is financial economics? I would venture to say that it is not the same kind of physics-envy-filled discipline as mainstream economics (Mirowski 1991). Rather, financial economics turns out to be a science of data. Over time, its focus on data becomes so narrow that financial economists forget that what data analysis can do can be overshadowed by what data analysis cannot do; financial economists forget to ask themselves what the discipline could gain by going beyond the data at hand. This is the lasting legacy of research of market efficiency, one that survives later critiques of the efficient-market hypothesis and that continues to characterize knowledge in this field. Larry Summers is right in thinking of financial economics as the analysis of ketchup. And he is also right in pointing to the peculiar patterns of collaboration that emerged within this discipline as having something to do with its narrow focus. We will return to this theme, for one last time, in the conclusion.

CONCLUSION

A Network Sociology of Scholarly Affects

Financial economists described markets as efficient on the basis of the alleged un-predictability of price changes over time. They could not test efficiency directly without making further assumptions about how markets work—without a joint hypothesis, that is. How, then, did they come to accept efficiency as a valid repre-sentation of market processes when tests of market efficiency inevitably were tests of other processes as well? And more specifically, how did they go about rein-venting finance as a science in the process of testing this elusive notion of market efficiency?

As we investigated these questions, we met some of the most prominent mem-bers of the scholarly networks that turned financial economics into a discipline with scientific ambitions, looked into the controversies that helped consolidate its core assumptions, and scrutinized the methodological devices that gave finan-cial economics its distinctive epistemology. To be sure, modern-day financial eco-nomics is no longer the exclusive domain of market-efficiency scholars; with the rise of behavioral economics, markets do not seem so rational and efficient as they did to the cohort of scholars who coalesced around Fama. And yet, behavioral economics remains within a terrain broadly defined by rationality and efficiency: it is a theory of why people deviate from the rational model of action, not a new way of grasping human behavior that dispenses with rational-actor assumptions. Even an event as catastrophic as the 2007–2008 financial crisis failed to uproot market efficiency from the canon. Markets, in spite of it all, continue being un-predictable, and their unpredictability is still taken as evidence that markets are working efficiently.

Financial economists accomplished this feat by producing a durable model of financial market behavior according to which unpredictability was an inherent and desirable quality of efficient markets. Scholars who saw data analysis as a pathway to new knowledge were attracted to this model because it was based on new data. Armed with their data-analytic techniques, these scholars translated *lack* of evidence of patterns into evidence of the *absence* of patterns in stock price movements. Making this shift entailed winning methodological fights, turning computers into useful and reliable sources of new knowledge, and accepting data mining as a legitimate technique for gathering new evidence: it entailed putting data analysis at the apex of the data-method-theory triad.

Three episodes capture this trajectory: the methodological fight between Cootner and Mandelbrot we saw in chapter 2, a series of articles on the changes that computerization was bringing to financial knowledge, and the Fama-Black controversy over the appropriateness of data mining.

> *Episode #1.* In 1964, in his pioneering effort to consolidate new work on statistical models of security prices into one volume, the editor and economist Paul Cootner calls for more research before some of the more radical hypotheses stemming from this research are canonized. He specifically singles out Mandelbrot's work on securities, whose acceptance, he argues, would render "almost all our statistical models . . . obsolete. . . . Almost without exception, past economic work [would be] meaningless." Cootner is made uncomfortable by the "causal empiricism" displayed by Mandelbrot. "Much of the evidence is graphical and involves slopes of lines which are not given precise numerical values in the paper. . . . At one of the few places where numbers are mentioned, some data are dismissed as 'absurdly large,' are 'corrected,' and in the new data a number, 18, is accepted as reasonably close to another number which should be somewhere between 21 and 31." (Cootner 1964a, 333–34)
>
> *Episode #2.* In 1969, the *Financial Analyst Journal* publishes the first installment of a series of articles analyzing the rise of the data service industry—a new set of companies offering computer-based data management and insight. Striking a critical tone, the author Joseph H. Spigelman warns against underestimating the problem of complexity and "radical discontinuity" in computerized databases. "At the very least, systems involve people who operate them—people who enter data onto tape, and then into the computer, inaccurately (permitting the computer to compound the error at incredible speed); who resist change of accustomed routines, even where the change is presented as beneficial to

them; who fight—and if possible, sabotage—any threat, real or fancied, to their values, their security, their power. To computerize meaningfully, the system must be enlarged to embrace the 'man-machine interface.'" Spigelman goes on to make many additional critical remarks, with another example being what he identifies as "misplaced precision and overconfidence in the breadth of one's knowledge," which, he argues, results from the fact that "only what can be specifically defined—at least in terms of logical relations . . . and preferably in quantitative terms, either deterministic or stochastic—can be computerized. What is inexact must be made exact" (1969, 93).

Episode #3. Fischer Black is renowned for proposing in 1973 a new method for pricing options—a type of financial instrument that allows the holder to buy or sell an asset at a set price on a set date—that is based on a sophisticated formula that quantifies the risk of the underlying asset. In 1992, Eugene Fama and Kenneth French, however, using new data, show the model behind the method to be too limited: more factors than risk alone go into the pricing of options. Black accuses Fama and French of arriving at their conclusions through data mining. The *Economist* reports on the controversy by declaring the crowning achievement of Black's model—a coefficient of risk famously termed "beta"—"dead."

These three episodes—Paul Cootner, the economist warning against untried methods; Joseph Spigelman, the financial commentator delineating the potential pitfalls of computerized databases; and Fischer Black, the financial theorist complaining about undue confidence in datasets as arbiters of knowledge—all involve people on the losing side of a debate. These individuals tried to stem the tide of change that was sweeping through the field, but did not succeed. For new models did emerge in financial economics—even though Cootner's conservatism characterized the field for a long time, and it is only very recently that Mandelbrot's methods were fully incorporated into research, while, of course, Mandelbrot's own suggestions about the future course of financial economics were initially rejected. It is also the case that Fama's research agenda did overshadow Fischer Black's, and turned into the canonical framework on which the discipline of financial economics rose to prominence—though Fama was often invested in presenting innovation in terms of data analysis, not in terms of new statistical methods. Finally, computerized datasets not only became the basis of much social science knowledge but also went on to constitute a technological innovation of their own (as the boom of Internet companies and the rise of big data testify).

These examples thus have at least another important feature in common: they highlight a preoccupation with data and methods, especially with how data and methods may affect social knowledge. And in this respect, this preoccupation was prescient. For better or worse, the model of financial markets around which financial economics came to be structured—the *efficient-market hypothesis*—was the outcome of such statistical and data-driven methods. Financial economics was made possible by the new relationships with data and methods established by its scholarly networks. Theories of markets as efficient and *unpredictable*, on the basis of evidence that only backed those theories after many manipulations and assumptions (as is the case with all data analysis), were the outcome of social structure: the social structure of collaboration that underlay financial economists' efforts at producing new knowledge on financial dynamics. Digging deeper into the processes that made such relationships possible affords new insights into not only the constitution and growth of financial economics and unpredictable markets but the making of social knowledge as well.

The Collaborative Structure of the Efficient-Market Hypothesis

In this book, I showed that financial economists recombined the theory-method-data triad so that data would be the cutting edge of their research agenda. To do so, they organized themselves into a scholarly network characterized by the following, shared understandings: that financial knowledge would need to establish a reasonable link between data and theory, that research outcomes should be communicable to others, and that research that appeared to be cumulative and incremental was preferable to research that claimed to make big breaks with the past. I also argued that such shared understandings were not the results of some initial consensus about the state of knowledge in the field, as if it were an orthodoxy that financial economists worked hard to protect.[1]

My analysis showed that the core ideas of this field derived from the specific collaborative patterns, backed up by shared methodological arrangements, that allowed for data to be taken seriously. The theory of market efficiency was the result of a particular way of collaborating, characterized by small groups of finance scholars working on compatible but nonoverlapping projects and speaking a common language developed from data analysis and frequentist statistics.

Drawing attention to the issue of *trust*, I suggested that financial economists sought to gain trust from their colleagues in adjacent disciplines and professions (especially economics), while building trust among themselves, in order to create a disciplinary niche for financial economics. Given this strategy, pursuing theoretically innovative approaches seemed ill advised; and given the opposition faced by scholars like Mandelbrot who also advocated for methodological innovations, pursuing new methods also appeared challenging and even counterproductive. What financial scholars did instead was to capitalize on the technological means at their disposal: their ability to assemble and analyze security-price datasets. And they used statistical theory, and its accompanying, widely available statistical tools, as a way to link data analysis with economic theory. They took a conservative stance toward theory and methods, and considered data analysis their main strength and source of innovative potential. Conservatism, especially with regard to methods, created an important opening.

Financial economics is not the only instance where the theoretical framework behind statistics (and more precisely, frequentist statistics) functioned as a source of legitimacy when experts face distrustful audiences. Randall Collins (1984) goes as far as suggesting that the popularity of statistical approaches among social sciences derives from the systemic lack of trust that characterizes social science networks. Given financial economists' data-analytic advantages, however, statistics also served as a tool to stave off criticism and gain sufficient credibility in the process of building an identifiable body of work. Financial economists put their efforts into turning the market into an "open" object of analysis; if that meant that the market was unpredictable, that was what current technology allowed financial economists to establish. The efficient market was born from this specific configuration of trust-seeking and credibility-building practices.

Trust and Social Knowledge through Scholarly Virtues

It takes a massive amount of work to make knowledge seem like a transparent and necessary representation of the world, and experts accomplish this difficult feat by enlisting heterogeneous networks in their support, aligning their interests with those of powerful constituencies, and creating technologies (both physical and symbolic, like new systems of accounting) through which their knowledge can be made relevant to the myriad problems their users may face (Çalışkan and Callon 2009; Callon 1998; Jasanoff 2004). Seminal contributions by Latour and Callon have enhanced our understanding of expert networks, including scholarly networks, by drawing attention to their weaknesses: experts, on their own, do not have the power to influence the world over which they claim to have specialized knowledge—Callon refers to such weaknesses as "disabilities" (in Pinch and Swedberg 2008, 29–56). The problem of trust underlies this new approach of expertise, leading to renewed attention to questions about how outside audiences come to trust experts, and how experts come to trust one another.

It is this second problem, how trust works and the forms it might take, that this book addresses. We examine the mechanisms of trust in the context of knowledge making, when scholars themselves are not simply embroiled in controversy but also divided about the ways controversy can be overcome. We know from the social history of science that, particularly in instances of deep uncertainty, scholars shift their focus from the controversy itself to the character and reputation of the scholars involved in it. Because interpersonal relationships and interactions play a crucial role in the making of *scholars*, character and reputation are built up over time through mutual trust. Mentorship ties and collaborations act in the long term as determinants of trust; interpersonal trust thus has practical importance for knowledge making.

One way of answering the question of what helps scholars solve controversy, in short, is to pay attention to the reputation of those involved: to the network processes that help establish it, and the processes through which scholars preserve it. Rational-choice theorists would argue that scholars build their reputation through time as they "encapsulate" the interests of their colleagues (Hardin 2002): the more they confirm attributions of trust conferred by others (i.e., the more they prove themselves to be *trustworthy*), the stronger their reputation, giving rise to processes of self-sustaining, cumulative advantage of the kinds classically discussed by Robert Merton. Reputation, however, is not just a matter of prominence. It is also a matter of truthfulness, a social accomplishment that scholars work toward by mobilizing particular social values. Reputation, too, is the outcome of interpersonal trust.

As shown by studies by Shapin (1994) and Gooday (2004), among others, a focus on the importance of mutual trust to the division of intellectual labor reveals that truthfulness and virtuous performance, through which the individual scientist establishes his or her integrity and competence, are part and parcel of scholarly life. Daston's concept of the moral economy of science also highlights intellectual virtues as fundamental to the development of notions of the "scientific self" through which scholars get others to trust their work. These perspectives already cover quite a bit of ground, but a focus on affect as it attaches to networks adds new elements to the conversation.

Moral economy points to the transactional processes of scholarly life. As an early formulation clarifies, the focus is on "experimental workplaces" and how the "unstated moral rules define the mutual expectations and obligations of the various participants in the production process: principal scientists and their assistants, mentors and students, well-placed and peripheral producers—researchers who may be collaborators one day and competitors the next. Moral conventions regulate access to the tools of the trade and the distribution of credit and rewards for achievement" (Kohler 1994, 12).

With Shapin's (1994) intervention, the focus expands to the problem of the relationship between the broader culture and the social background of scientists, to show that the social construction of truth is about judging the competence of investigators by relying on social values through which science gains legitimacy. Daston's elaboration takes the concept in a similar direction, with more focus on the affect-laden values scholars pursue in order to not only assess the competence of their colleagues but position themselves in a broader scholarly community. These diverse perspectives converge toward two broad questions: How do scholars accomplish what Goffman (1983) would call a "working consensus" among themselves about the kinds of claims that can be taken "on faith" and those that are subject to controversy? When such controversy does take place, how do they adjudicate between claims that can be attributed to competent work and claims that are attributed to mistakes, problems, or misunderstandings? The joint hypothesis faced by financial economists is not a plight unique to their particular discipline. Scholarly competence and trustworthiness in research are the other side of academic virtues and norms. As scholars articulate their commitment to particular goals and values, they use morality in order to back up their knowledge claims. It may be a rather narrowly construed kind of morality, as Shapin reminds us, but it is morality nevertheless.

Zeroing in on the affect that circulates within particular networks means deepening the concept of the moral economy so as to understand how scholars pursue innovative venues.[2] The unit of analysis is smaller than society as a whole, even though the adoption of broader societal values—for example, gentlemanly culture in the lab—in order to regulate access to technical skills and means of scientific production remains important: in line with this, I showed that financial economists became indebted to Fama's standard of reasonableness, when that standard was obviously a societal value. But it is not just about specifying the relationship between scientific exchange and broader society: it is about figuring out the set of emotions that allow scholars to identify new, innovative research in the course of their day-to-day research activities.

A dual focus on *affects* and *networks* helps us systematize our understanding of these relationships. This focus reveals the role played by shared emotional dispositions in motivating scholars to work in similar directions, while closing off other collaborative venues. Unlike the kinds of moral virtues and scholarly reputations highlighted by scholars of trust, which refer to individual scholars, affect characterizes scholarly *networks*. It is a public performance, in the sense that scholars express their affective dispositions in order to position their work within a broader field of inquiry.

Drawing attention to the relationship between scholarly reputations and collaborative networks, for similar reasons, allows us to see how broader power structures might affect the development of a discipline. For instance, between 1989 and 2013 the *Journal of Finance* published work authored by 1,286 scholars, and only about 6 percent of them are women: the new finance men *have literally been men*. My argument implies that a fuller understanding of why men dominated the field of financial economics in its formative period and beyond can be achieved by paying more attention to the interplay between the identity of individual scholars and the collaborative opportunities the field offered to them. The data-analytic roots of financial economics certainly set the ground for the overrepresentation of men in the field; so did financial economics' relationship with another male-dominated field, economics at large. But it is also the mechanisms underlying the formation of collaborative groups that turn the identity of a scholar into a marker of insider (or outsider) status (see also Polillo in Weininger, Lareau, and Lizardo 2018, 136–46). And because of the durability of collaborative networks in financial economics (as shown especially in chapter 3), overrepresentation of men in the early stages of the formation of the discipline likely locked in gender patterns over time.

I use the term "affect" as opposed to "emotions" because I want to connect emotions to values articulated in the context of specific configurations of theory, method, and data networks. This is a second way we can theorize the impact that more general systems of stratification exert on disciplinary formation, but it is necessary to clarify our concepts before doing so. It is not that emotions are personal and subjective whereas affect is structural or emergent.[3] Emotions, in fact, are dynamic and change in intensity depending on collective processes: drawing on Durkheim (1995), we could say that personhood is constituted by such collective processes, and that therefore emotions are pre-personal. Rather than being private, emotions contribute to the quality of one's individual experience in the context of social rituals. As the sociology of emotions has long argued, emotions are the mechanism that connects individuals to broader social coalitions: they are the basic ingredient out of which social bonds are made, loyalty to larger groups is solidified, and boundaries between insiders and outsiders are drawn (Scheff 1994). When individuals participate in social rituals that reaffirm the strength of their social bonds, they experience collective effervescence and thereby increase their stock of emotional energy, Randall Collins's (2004) term for the emotional arousal and charge people gain from increased social solidarity.

As argued by theorists of affect, moreover, emotions are "stored" in the body: participation in rituals increases one's emotional energy especially when the shared mood of the collective assembly matches the emotions of the participants, though the ritual itself can transform those emotions (Summers-Effler 2010). In other words, emotions predispose the individual to react in particular ways to particular experiences, without fully determining that reaction (Bandelj 2009). Rituals create boundaries that individuals associate with a sense of sacredness: insiders to the ritual are invested with solidarity, and in turn, to make that sense of sacredness more permanent—to produce long-term collective effervescence—they invest distinctive *symbols* with the sacred sense of belonging to the group. Such symbols can be material objects (like a flag), but they can also be labels, slogans, and so on. Attacking those symbols means attacking the group that ritually identifies with the symbol. Scholars of affect are less likely to emphasize these dynamics.

Affect, nevertheless, is a particularly useful term to characterize crystallizations of emotions that develop around particular kinds of symbols, eliciting certain kinds of behaviors and practices in response (Barnwell 2017). When the rituals under analysis are scholarly rituals, as is the case in this book, affect can point us to the set of emotions that scholars attach to particular scholarly experiences and draw from in order to increase solidarity toward themselves and trust around their work. In other words, trust in other scholars derives from the solidarity that circulates within a scholarly network.[4] One increases one's trustworthiness by signaling with some credibility a commitment to a set of shared values or virtues, so as to persuade others to follow in one's footsteps; trust undergirds collective mobilization. Heuristically, trust alerts scholars to the kinds of venues they might want to pursue to have their contribution recognized. Affect is the collective, public face of a strategy for scholarly recognition.

Affect develops around the virtues a scholarly network expresses as a necessary token of membership: once emotions crystallize around the symbols a group invests with collective effervescence, they establish an affective relationship between the symbols and the participants to the ritual. An empirical strategy to investigate the distribution of affects in a scholarly network is therefore to track the scholarly virtues through which scholars manage to develop long-term collaborations. Crucially, this also means tracking who is excluded from collaborative structures because they express different virtues. The shared pursuit of accuracy, of technical sophistication, or, in our case, of reasonable models not only serves to rally a group of scholars around similar goals. It also socializes members of the network into a shared style of conducting arguments, where certain emotions are more likely to be expressed than others (such as, for instance, the passionate rejection of rival arguments as opposed to the painstaking but friendly critique). The pursuit of other values, as a consequence, marks the scholars who uphold them as outsiders. As we saw in the case of Sushka (a female financial scholar) and Slovin, even productive collaborations fail to be recognized by the field when they articulate affective values not recognized by the larger network.

The link between broader patterns of stratification and the hierarchies and exclusions that characterize a given discipline is not a direct one. Under certain conditions, for instance, affect dramatizes the isolation of a scholarly network, facilitating the development of trust among insiders and a sense of suspicion toward outsiders: it motivates scholars to engage in intellectual conflict with opposing factions. Under other conditions, however, affect may help scholars avoid conflict and open up new venues for collaboration—or so I argued for the case of financial economics, where the emphasis on reasonable, communicable results based on standard methods allowed finance scholars to come to a compromise over theory with their colleagues in economics (without, however, succeeding in the long run, as Summers's quip about *ketchupal* economics reminds us). In the process, financial scholars reproduced a distribution of power based on gendered boundaries that we might not necessarily expect in fields with different affective relationships to adjacent disciplines. In other words, a focus on affect reveals how trust is distributed within and across networks. Thus, affect draws attention to the emotional processes through which a scholarly network develops a focus on particular problems, and a sense of the kinds of projects that might be useful in providing adequate solutions.

We must, then, be aware of the historical specificity of the moral virtues that scholars articulate to bolster their scientific authority and their relationship with power. But once we consider affect in relational terms, we can say something about how creative work gets done, as well as whose work tends to be systematically discounted as not creative enough.

Affect Allows for the Creative Crystallization of Scholarly Networks

An affective network emerges as successful scholarly interactions generate shared (but not neutral) values, and in the process increase mutual trust among those who subscribe to those values. These shared values are not Mertonian values, like universalism, or value-free science (Merton 1973). It is not that those are unimportant but rather that they are detached from the practical experience of researchers. Mertonian values are usually mobilized in boundary work, when one's task is that of defending a science from outside attacks. The shared values produced through interaction, by contrast, are shared orientations toward recurring problems that emerge in the course of research. One way to grasp these orientations is to simplify them into one of three forms: as theoretical, methodological, or data-analytic problems. This is not because of some continuity to or essential quality of these terms, or to the activities they point to. This is rather because theory, methods, and data constitute, for historical and institutional reasons, potentially separate streams of intellectual production, in the human sciences in particular.

They usually form a triad, as scholars tend to take distinctive perspectives on the role played by each in a research agenda.

That theory, methods, and data have intersected in the human sciences in historically variable ways; that there is no a priori definition of these activities; and that, in reality, what counts as theoretical, methodological, or data analytic are often a matter of demarcation and boundary making (a struggle to uphold definition in a quest for intellectual authority) rather than an exercise in taxonomy. What this means is that recombination of the activities to which these terms refer can serve as a source of creativity. Working toward new theories, new methods, and new data is different than accepting the theoretical premises of a field and proposing methodological innovations. These are the kinds of challenges that are particularly important to foreground, as they shed light on how creativity is generated.

Creativity, I argue, emerges in the activity of building new configurations of networks of research. Affect fosters creativity because it builds trust and familiarity within a network; it provides a shared foundation on which scholars can ground their work. Therefore, affect allows scholars to recognize what kinds of arguments are possible within the network. This is not only a matter of using shared concepts that, as Abbott puts it, have an "indexical" quality. When scholars use terms like "qualitative," "quantitative," "structure," and "agency," they size each other up, quickly figuring out where they stand on the main controversies that characterize their field (Abbott 2001a, 27). But affect communicates something more general about the work a scholarly network is producing than the discipline-specific concepts Abbott refers to. It facilitates recognition, as it allows scholars to place themselves on a broader argument space; it is easier to recognize arguments for better precision, accuracy, or subversion, regardless of content, than it is to understand what is at stake in disciplinary turf wars over terms like "reflexivity" or "structuralism."

Affect is also, by extension, about focusing the attention of a scholarly community on particular aspects of a broader agenda, while taking attention away from others. Because it is attached not to specific content but to a variable combination of different kinds of moves (theoretical, methodological, analytical), affect therefore generates several potential venues for creativity.

How, then, does affect vary? Is it possible to theorize about potential patterns in the kinds of affects scholarly networks mobilize to pursue whatever innovative path they deem worth their while? Are there affinities and correspondences between these emotionally charged values, of which reasonability and simplicity are the two instances we encountered in our analysis of financial economics, and the kinds of networks in which scholars operate?

A Taxonomy of Affective Networks

Affective networks drove the conceptualization of markets as efficient, rational, and unpredictable in financial economics. But this was not because of aspects and factors specific to the discipline. Affective networks are a more general phenomenon, and in the social and human sciences, they form at the intersection of different approaches and different practices of knowledge making. Depending on what networks are coming together, affect will vary. A typology, intersecting theory, data, and method, can look something like table 6.1.

The table connects specific emotionally laden values and intellectual virtues (e.g., concreteness, reasonableness, attention to detail) to specific moves. Empirically, it posits the existence of patterns in the ways arguments are conducted independently of the specific discipline or the specific subject at hand. The table assumes that networks, unless they explicitly take up a radical agenda (as in the first row of the table), attempt to minimize conflict with positions they consider tangential to their research agenda: the crystallizing network carves out an opportunity space for innovative moves that are often backed up by traditionalist approaches. For instance, a theory-driven network may want to ally itself with noncontroversial methodological and data-analytic techniques as it focuses on

TABLE 6.1. A typology of affective networks

STRATEGY, AFFECT	EXAMPLES	INNOVATIVE FRONTS
Radical innovation: confident, courageous, distrustful, agonistic, inspired, passionate	Ethnomethodology	✓ Theory ✓ Methods ✓ Data
Recombination/Gestalt: calm, earnest, patient	Comparative-historical sociology	✓ Theory ✓ Methods (Data)
Abstraction: earnest, detached, dispassionate	Functionalism	✓ Theory (Methods) (Data)
Discovery: excited, surprised	Moving research frontier	✓ Theory (Methods) ✓ Data
Accuracy: open, attentive to detail, curious	Confirmatory science; experiments. Psychology. Behavioral economics.	(Theory) ✓ Methods ✓ Data
Technical prowess, precision: careful, exploratory, reassuring	Statistical social science	(Theory) ✓ Methods (Data)
Empirical realism: concrete, reasonable, casual	Financial economics	(Theory) (Methods) ✓ Data

theoretical innovation, and so on—an assumption we can relax later. The assumption also points to a pathway through which the initial makeup of a scholarly network in terms of the identity of its participants can reproduce itself over time: aligning one's network to the practices of allied networks has lasting effects on the development of a scholarly community.

The main point of the table is to hypothesize different constellations of emotional dispositions, attached to particular sets of values, depending on how scholarly networks come together in the production of new research—on how they recombine the theory-data-methods triad. Thus, the table predicts that a scholarly network that proposes theoretical, methodological, and evidentiary innovations all at once will flaunt its radical creativity by showcasing the courage, passion, and pugnaciousness of its members, as ethnomethodologists did in sociology in the 1970s. Fighting against the functionalist orthodoxy that dominated the discipline in that period, ethnomethodologists not only appealed to theoretical traditions in phenomenological philosophy that sociologists had never systematically considered, thereby proposing a theoretical innovation (Heritage 1984). They also focused the attention of the discipline on new kinds of data: the microdetails of conversations, captured thanks to new tape-recording technology. And they proposed new methods to represent and analyze those microdetails, in what became the conventions of conversation analysis. In line with the argument sketched in the table, ethnomethodologists were self-conscious about the radical nature of their approach, developing a technical vocabulary characterized by a distinctive rhetorical style that foregrounded the novelty and unconventional nature of their research; outsiders soon began accusing them of cultism for these very same reasons.

The table predicts that a scholarly network that makes new theoretical and methodological moves but builds on existing understandings about the nature of evidence will display a different affect. The network will strive to shift current ways of interpreting and analyzing social reality in the manner of a gestalt shift, as when existing but previously ignored features of an ambiguous drawing are highlighted so as to change one's general perception of the figure. Comparative-historical sociologists' work on social revolutions seems to be a particularly evocative example of this dynamic (Skocpol 1978). Working on the basis of existing historical work on significant cases of social revolutions, comparative-historical researchers changed sociologists' understanding of revolutions as cases of class struggle to cases of state breakdown. They paired this theoretical innovation with a new methodology—the comparative method—that allowed them to gain leverage from existing historiography so as to substantiate the new theory. As the table predicts, the emotional tone of their writing eschews strong passion. Unlike the ethnomethodologists' tendency to bracket off commonsensical understandings of reality to make them strange and unfamiliar, comparative-historical sociologists use their deep familiarity with historical cases to make new theoretical and methodological points.

The table provides further examples for other configurations, hypothesizing the presence of different affects as scholarly networks vary in the extent to which they pursue innovation across different realms. It is worth emphasizing again that there is no one-to-one connection between particular affects and particular exclusionary practices drawing from broader systems of categorical inequality: inequality, nevertheless, can emerge as networks weave alliances among themselves or engage in more oppositional stances (Tilly 1998). Rather than discussing each example at length, I pause and ask a different set of questions. The table suggests that a scholarly network will frame its contribution in, say, a language of concrete objects and reasonable moves when it considers data (and the analysis of data) as a source of intellectual creativity. Let us think at the level of individual papers and conduct a brief thought experiment to establish whether the implications of such a proposition are reasonable. Does this imply a paper written by such a scholarly network will be devoid of theory or methods? Or that such paper will only address audiences invested in data-analytic techniques? Also, does this imply that, for example, a financial economics paper calling for better use of data will in some ways be similar to a philosophical paper calling for more sustained engagement with the empirical world? Likewise, one can imagine a theoretical paper in philosophy calling for more precision in terminology. In what ways is it useful to compare its call for precision with a sociology paper introducing a new statistical technique, using precision as a way to build a common orientation for a broader network?

What the table suggests is that a paper will express commitment to concreteness and reasonability as a way to move an existing conversation (no matter how theoretical or methodological) onto empirical ground, when the author intends to preserve an existing alliance, and state of affairs, with theory- and method-oriented networks. When the paper construes that data move as theoretically innovative as well, I expect that the language will be different. And I expect that language to characterize papers making similarly constructed moves across disciplines as well. Attention to affect is meant to sensitize us to the kinds of openings a given paper is trying to make, and to invite comparisons in terms of what a paper constructs as a potential space for innovation. The point is not to make comparisons between papers across disciplines as if they were individual contributions standing on their own ground. Through affect, papers signal the following to the broader scholarly community they see as a relevant audience: what kind of innovation they are making, meaning what kind of conversation they are participating in, what family of potential objections and attacks they are prepared to defend themselves against, and what family of potential allies and fellow travelers they expect to find along the way. The empirical philosophy paper would then share with the data-driven financial economics paper a similar assessment of the scholarly networks that, within each discipline, would permit the paper to have an impact: the audience to each is a scholarly network that does not expect more abstraction or new techniques but rather thinks that concrete, systematic examples can point the way forward.

In broad strokes, the more alliances a paper relies on to move an argument forward, the less incendiary and polarizing the emotional tone of its arguments. In line with neo-Durkheimean approaches to social knowledge (see esp. Fuchs 2001), we may add, the more likely that the paper will understand its findings as if they were real and objective. Reliance on existing ways of understanding reality (whether theories, methods, data, or a combination of any of them) will mean that what one discovers cannot be the product of idiosyncrasies in research practices. It will be something about that reality (the world "out there") that calls for future discoveries. At the other end of the continuum, a paper that proposes multiple innovations will draw attention to the limitations of each of the fronts on which it innovates. And it will thus generate doubts about existing knowledge and the extent to which the available "machinery" for knowledge production needs to be updated accordingly (Knorr Cetina 2009).

Can Social Knowledge Proceed without Affect?

One of the core arguments of this book is that affect helps scholars build trust in one another. Does affect work within only certain disciplines, where a modicum of trust already exists? Is it, therefore, just a function of the cohesion of a discipline? Can we meaningfully talk about affective networks in a fragmented and large discipline such as, say, sociology? Discussions of this point abound, but for our purposes, it is useful to turn the question around: When do affective networks fragment a discipline? Precisely when affect serves as a way to avoid conflict, a discipline can indeed contain nonconflicting networks that, by virtue of their different goals and different criteria, generate centrifugal forces.

In line with this thesis, one potential explanation for the recognized lack of progress in social science is that we do not have methods that stabilize the process of discovery—we have not been able to routinize creativity. My suggestion is that this is a function of the affective dispositions we have built around methods and data, dispositions that are out of step with the structures of collaboration that sustain them. Ethnography, for instance, tends to be a solitary endeavor. This limits opportunities to conduct comparative ethnographies, and provokes end-less accusations on the part of quantitatively oriented investigators about the pitfall of subjectivity in the method (Burawoy 1998). Rather than being seen in light of existing or even innovative theoretical perspectives, ethnographies tend to be judged on methodological (and often data-analytic) principles alone.

Lack of cross collaboration means that, over time, innovative methods, or new datasets, or new theories tend to generate unsolvable conflicts that remain inter-nal to the network because the fragmentation of the discipline allows them to ex-pand without taking stock of the kinds of alliances they could forge. As the net-works turn inward, their affect becomes even less accommodating and more closed off to collaborations with other networks. Perhaps the most striking ex-ample of this instance is the rise of antiscientific anthropology: methods have be-come so reflexive that discussions of the subjectivity of the method turn into broader pronouncements about the impossibility of an objective standpoint. Field notes acquire a "mystique," they are rarely taught, and they tend to become a cen-tral component of an anthropologist's identity (Jackson, in Sanjek 1990, 3–34).

In sum, affect promotes collaboration when the push and pull of different per-spectives forces scholars to find some kind of compromise they can tolerate, and build collaborative bridges when it helps them focus on the primary contribu-tion. But in large disciplines, such pressure to accommodate and compromise with other perspectives tends to be less strong. And affect therefore tends to bring out differences rather than similarities.

The Future of Social Science

One main argument of this book is that data processing networks gave financial economics an innovative edge, and through data, the hypothesis that markets are efficient was able to gain academic prestige. As Fama once put it, the roots of fi-nancial economics are simple, and lie in the computer revolution. Computers, of course, have impacted more than just the development of this discipline. In the financial sector, the tendency to rely on increasingly depersonalized (and increas-ingly complex and opaque) algorithms for the calculation of value—most nota-bly in the realm of credit scoring—suggests that data processing networks have impacted not only academic research practices but the working of finance "in the wild" as well. The emergence of a massive technological infrastructure for the stor-age, aggregation, and analysis of financial data—both within academic finance and in the financial sector as a whole—calls for some concluding thoughts on the possibility that algorithms and big data will change the way social science is prac-ticed altogether.

Affective Networks and the Sociology of Performativity

The relationship between scholarship, especially social scientific scholarship, and the broader world such scholarship might aim to analyze or represent has been brought into question by work in the Science and Technology Studies (STS) and Social Studies of Finance traditions that foregrounds scholarship as a form of intervention or as an instance of performativity. The performativity approach, as we have seen, works from the premise that the world theorized by social science is often brought in line with theory by the very models that, allegedly, only describe it. Models act in this fashion because they help forge new networks of associations, bringing into alignment the interests of diverse constituencies through the new rationalities they embody, and the new technological tools they inform. Finance, as we have seen in previous chapters, has been a particularly productive site for this kind of analysis. Given the proliferation of new financial instruments and financial markets that has characterized the world economy, and the United States in particular, since the 1970s, it is no surprise that finance would become of interest to scholars from this research program.

Yet, two things make this approach problematic, calling, to my mind, for a rethinking of this perspective. First, real-world events do not seem to confirm the main tenet of the performative approach, namely, that models produce the world they theorize about. As a result, one of its leading proponents, MacKenzie (2011), now shies away from the language of performativity. A deeper issue is the one we have encountered throughout the book. When performativity scholars look at the development of financial markets, they tend to follow Latour's (1987, 247 and ff) path and focus on "metrology," the chain of paper-based traces of activities going on outside the laboratory that techno-science, by way of measurement and accounts, turns into information the center of calculation can process.

The problem is that scholarly networks do not always work like centers of calculation. This is especially the case in financial economics, where scholars have weaker control over the technical and scientific infrastructure that, in the natural and physical sciences, serves to stabilize scientific facts. The technology of financial markets can create more problems than it solves: the very financial instruments that were touted for their ability to increase stability and reduce risk were retrospectively found to be at the root of the 2007–2008 financial crisis. Once financial knowledge goes out "in the wild," as Callon puts it (e.g., Çalışkan and Callon 2010)—especially the broad, complex ideas (like market efficiency) that animate a scholarly agenda—it is manipulated in ways that exceed the analytical capacity of financial scholars. It is virtually impossible to keep anything constant in the economy when money itself, the fundamental unit of account, is a token in a struggle among competing interests more than a fixed unit of account (Mirowski 1990b; Polillo 2013).

The complex and nonlinear relationship between financial research and markets derives from fundamental differences between the practices that characterize each domain. Financial research is open ended, whereas markets thrive when market actors manage to develop distinctive niches within them, claiming that they can sell a product that is different from (and better than) what their competitors provide. Financial research moves forward when the networks of scholars that study a given object can find new ways to define that object; market actors, by contrast, benefit from erecting barriers around the products they sell, so that their proprietary technologies and production techniques cannot be easily imitated. Knorr Cetina thus argues that financial analysis as practiced in financial markets is irrevocably removed from scientific activity because it "cut[s] off the measurement part of representation or delegat[es] it to outside sources. . . . It is a form of research at a distance, conducted from exteriorized viewpoints. Such analysis, we might say, is what remains to be done when one of the major engines of unfolding reality and of fueling scientific change is turned off" (Knorr Cetina in Camic, Gross, and Lamont 2011, 438).

This is all to say: financial economics would not exist without financial markets, but the dynamics that power financial research are not to be found in those markets. Financial research, rather, is less about stabilizing a research outcome and black boxing it so that it can be performed, and more about maintaining an object of analysis as open and productive, so that other networks of scholars can grow around it. Given the open-ended nature of financial research, its objects of knowledge are "epistemic objects," in Knorr Cetina's useful characterization. Unlike everyday objects, epistemic objects are characterized by a "lack in completeness in being that takes away much of the wholeness, solidity, and the thing-like character they have in our everyday conception." Everyday objects are perceived as "closed boxes," whereas

> objects of knowledge appear to have the capacity to unfold indefinitely. They are more like open drawers filled with folders extending indefinitely into the depth of a dark closet. Since epistemic objects are always in the process of being materially defined, they continually acquire new properties and change the ones they have. But this also means that objects of knowledge can never be fully attained, that they are, if you wish, never quite themselves. What we encounter in the research process are representations or stand-ins for a more basic lack of object. (Knorr Cetina in Knorr Cetina, Schatzki, and von Savigny 2005, 190)

Scholarly networks organize themselves around these open objects by building relationships of trust among themselves: scholars overcome their lack of knowledge by trusting their colleagues and collaborators, placing their faith in theory, methods, data, or a combination of any of these approaches, and using particular affective dispositions to keep their focus on what sustains their collaborative efforts. Because the performativity approach looks at the broader network within which financial knowledge is mobilized and circulated, it cannot see the more complex dynamics that characterize the *production* of financial knowledge.

The Big Data of Tomorrow

The production of social knowledge, too, has experienced some drastic changes, stemming from the spread of big data. While the complex and problematic relationship between social knowledge and computers has been the focus of sociological analysis (Leahey 2005, 2008; Turner 1998), big data seems to constitute a new challenge. Specifically, what is there to stop big data from becoming as pervasive in the social sciences as they have become in financial economics, and in the broader economy as well? As a supporter of this thesis puts it, "Big Data, the phenomenon, continues unabated. Indeed, the necessity of grappling with Big Data, and the desirability of unlocking the information hidden within it, is now a key theme in all the sciences—arguably the key scientific theme of our times" (Diebold 2012, 3).

Scholars of big data are beginning to reach a consensus about the nature of this new way of producing knowledge. This consensus rests on characterizing big data in terms of both their attributes and the techniques that make the analysis of big data possible. The attributes include the volume, velocity, and variety of big data, which are said to make such data different from past datasets. The volume of big data results from its production and collection, primarily through electronic business transactions; velocity derives from the real-time quality of these activities; and variety results from the multiple sites that generate such data, as well as the increasing power of data-collecting organizations to aggregate data across platforms through tracking techniques (boyd and Crawford 2012; Laney 2001; Pasquale 2015). The analysis of big data is also understood to be different from the analysis of other datasets; with big data, algorithms replace more traditional, mostly linear techniques developed in statistics and imported to other fields. Diebold, for instance, shows how in econometrics the advent of big data caused a shift away from few variables tracked over long periods and analyzed through linear models (including autoregression), to endogenously generated constructs (factors) that track "regime switches" in the data, allowing for the detection of nonlinear, complex patterns and trends. Amoore and Piotukh (2015) similarly argue that the qualitative difference between the mass of data that all sorts of actors, from firms to states, have been gathering for the past two centuries and big data is that the latter are intimately dependent for their interpretability on what they call "little analytics": *instruments of perception* that allow for the detection of patterns in unstructured, unindexed, heterogeneous data.

The kinds of innovations we described in financial economics fall short of these three criteria—volume, speed, and variety. For instance, the CRSP—the dataset that spearheaded Fama's analysis of efficient markets and its consolidation into a dominant theory—provided historical, not real-time, observations of security prices. While the datasets generated were large, they are not considered large by today's standards. And finally, CRSP looked at only one market, the NYSE, rather than engaging in the kinds of cross-platform, algorithmic analysis that characterizes modern big data.

Yet, in spite of these differences, a big-data "thinking cap" was lurking behind the research practices of financial data analysis. The depth of observations recorded by CRSP, and their consistency over time (requiring the kinds of theoretically motivated interventions listed by Lorie) are precursors to modern-day big data. Size, as argued by Diebold, is context dependent—in a few years, the big datasets of today will seem small under new standards of the future. And while financial economics focused on one dataset, it spawned interests in other markets as well.

There is a deeper point of comparison too, and it lies somewhere else from the attributes of the data. It lies in how big-data analysts position themselves with respect to expertise, which in useful ways overlaps with the ways financial scholars positioned themselves, while differing in other, interesting ways too.

1. The most striking similarity is in the exhortation "Let the Data Speak." This is the motto of modern, big-data proponents. Though not everyone necessarily agrees with Anderson's argument that the modern "deluge of data . . . makes the scientific method obsolete" (2008, 1), more sophisticated analysts now argue that big data allow for the construction of new "ontologies," the underlying patterns in the data that make new theories about newly discovered objects possible (see Bollier 2010). Financial economists underwent a similar process: they justified data mining in terms of its ability to detect patterns that theories would not, on their own, prime the analyst to see in all their force. Thus, big-data analysts and financial economists show a deep-seated suspicion of experts exercising judgment, unless that judgment is firmly rooted in the data themselves.

2. A second, less apparent similarity lies in the strategy adopted by big-data analysts to "hide the methods" in complex and black-boxed algorithms.

Financial economists working in the EMH program never did this, but they did engage in rhetorical efforts to make their methodologies consistent with existing tools, in ways that emphasized continuity and downplayed the analytical innovations they were introducing. An ironic outcome is that, as Jovanovic and Schinckus (2013) emphasize, now financial economics is the focus of sustained efforts by physicists who aim to revolutionize how financial processes are modeled and measured, while ignoring how many of the innovations they propose are already part of the toolkit of financial economics. Financial economists were so successful at painting a facade of continuity over their methods that not even physicists seem to understand their methodological innovations!

3. Finally, and following from the points above, financial economists *differ* from modern-day big-data analysts in the degree to which they criticized received knowledge as they consolidated their discipline. Their fight against experts was a fight against practitioners, the financial "analysts" they accused of applying a nonscientific understanding to financial markets in the hope of swindling gullible investors. But financial economists did not take their fight on the turf of economics, and indeed, their analysis of efficient markets allowed for a revitalization of rationality as the key explanatory framework in other branches of economics, such as rational expectations in macroeconomics. Financial economists, in other words, did not attack expertise as such, focusing only on the kind of expertise they considered inadequate for the task of building a scientific approach to financial behavior. Big-data analysts, by contrast—and especially big-data analysts who work on questions in the traditional domain of the social sciences—have a tendency to denounce other approaches as inherently inferior. They view human interpretation as a source of bias; data, by contrast, are objective, regardless of the potential mistakes and imperfections they might contain. As Bill Stensrud of InstantEncore puts it, "One man's noise is another man's data." Furthermore, "the very point of looking to Big Data," according to Aedhmar Hynes of Text100 Public Relations, is "to identify patterns that create answers to questions you didn't even know to ask" (quoted in Bollier 2010, 14, 36). In other words, approaches that might critically interrogate the processes that produce data, or might rely on explanations that do not emerge from the data themselves, appear problematic, if not suspicious, to big-data analysts—especially when those approaches require substantive knowledge of the topic under investigation, replacing what the data say with what the expert thinks the data might say.

I raise these three comparative points to introduce a final question: Given these similarities and difference, how likely are big data to succeed in replacing other approaches to social knowledge in light of our analysis of financial economists? Our analysis of financial economists yields at least one relevant lesson for this question: social structure matters, even in fields that explicitly deny the importance of human intervention, scholarship, and expertise. For those fields, like their more expert-friendly counterparts, need to produce genealogies of scholars able to explore the deeper implications of foundational questions, and to secure a career for themselves that will allow them to do so.

Financial economists, even when they participated in remunerative consulting opportunities, or when they started their own money-management firms, ultimately built their careers as data analysts by working in small groups in academia and by specializing in nonoverlapping lines of research. They built a social structure that carried their agenda forward, one that allowed them to develop a shared and sustained focus of attention on a new set of problems, even in the face of real-world events that provided strong evidence against their theoretical approaches.

This was at once a curse and a blessing. It was a curse because the strength of the affective network built around market efficiency prevented the emergence and consolidation of alternative approaches. It was a blessing because the scholars involved in the network succeeded in building a new discipline for themselves. The way forward for big data lies here. Big-data analysis will need a social structure, one able to provide long-term career opportunities for scholars and big-data experts. And this will generate pressure toward some theoretical and methodological compromise with existing approaches. Ultimately, when big-data analysts push toward the removal of the expert, they chip away at the ground under their own feet.

Some big-data analysts see this problem, and a more cautious perspective on the need to create new bridges with existing approaches, rather than calling for radical innovations, now characterizes the work of those who, from within the academic disciplines, wish to import big data into their methodological repertoire (for an example from the sociology of culture, see Bail 2014). Understanding what collaborative structures will characterize big data in the social sciences, and whether those structures will be self-sustaining, will be spread across disciplines, or will constitute a new discipline of its own, are all issues that cannot be satisfactorily answered at the moment. But as we watch these processes unfold, hopefully the theoretical and methodological tools we developed in this book will help us make better sense of their messy reality.

Acknowledgments

This project grew out of two papers, "Wildcats in Banking Fields: The Politics of Financial Inclusion," which I published in *Theory and Society* 40, no. 4 (2011) (Springer) and "Theorizing Efficient Markets: A Sociology of Financial Ideas," published in the *European Journal of Sociology / Archives Européennes de Sociologie* 56, no. 1 (April 2015) (Cambridge University Press); chapter 4 draws from material and data discussed in these articles. I presented an early version of the latter at the June 2013 Annual Meetings of SASE in Milan, in the context of a miniconference on the economic public sphere organized by Lyn Spillman, Nina Bandelj, and Fred Wherry. After the Q&A, Dan Hirschman alerted me to Neal Caren's superb, and publicly available, Python code to extract cocitation data from bibliographic repositories like Web of Science. So in a way, this book too was born from data analysis! Thanks to Lyn, Nina, Fred, Dan, and Neal for making this project possible by putting together the initial pieces of the puzzle for me. I am also indebted to Vincent Gayon, Benjamin Lemoine, and Bruno Theret for inviting me to present my work at an international conference they organized at Paris Dauphine in 2013, to Marion Fourcade for the friendly, patient, and provocative feedback she provided after my presentation, and to Sabine Montaigne for many interesting conversations.

Audiences at Duke Sociology, UCLA, UC Irvine, and Max Planck Cologne gave me much to think about as I further developed the main arguments of the book. At Max Planck, thanks especially to Jens Beckert for the invitation, to Wolfgang Streeck for graciously hosting me, and to Mark Lutter for sharing his work on creativity. I was particularly lucky to be able to spend a sabbatical year at the UCLA Institute for Society and Genetics in 2017–2018, where I benefited from formative conversations with Hanna Landecker, Chris Kelty, Aaron Panofski, and Zach Griffen, as well as a broader group of visiting fellows in their wonderfully multidisciplinary institute. I am especially grateful to Chris and to Dominic Boyer for suggesting Cornell University Press as a publisher for my work, and to Jim Lance for being such a supportive and friendly editor. At UCLA, thanks also to Ted Porter for inviting me to present my work at the History of Science Colloquium, and to Stefania Tutino, Soraya De Chadarevian, and Amir Alexander for their incisive comments. Chapter 2 draws from my article "Market Efficiency as a Revolution in Data Analysis," published in *Economic Anthropology* 5, no. 2 (May 2018)

(Wiley). Many thanks to Aaron Pitluck, Fabio Mattioli, and Paul Langley for their wonderful comments on that project.

As the manuscript was nearing its final draft, the Sociology Department at the University of Virginia (under Jeff Olick's deft leadership as department chair) helped me organize a book workshop. Martin Ruef, Johanna Bockman, Allan Megill, Brad Pasanek, and Raf Alvarado very kindly agreed to participate. Their extensive and generous comments, carefully recorded by Colin Arnold, allowed me to see my work in a new light. At UVa, thanks also to my colleagues, especially Adam Slez, Liz Gorman, and Isaac Reed, for engaging with my work at different stages, and thanks to the Dean's Office (especially Christian McMillen) for providing financial support (including, of course, sabbatical!). I must also thank Len Seabrooke for inviting me to present my manuscript at Copenhagen Business School, and Oddný Helgadóttir, Cornel Ban, Duncan Wigan, and Eleni Tsingou for their wonderful comments and hospitality. And thanks to Gabi Abend, Randall Collins, Mauro Guillén, Jerry Jacobs, Gianfranco Poggi, Jonathan Turner, and Elliot Weininger for commenting on different parts of the projects as it was taking shape. This book would not have been possible without their help or the help of many others, but one person stands out—my friend and colleague Jen Silva, who read my work, chapter by chapter, as it went from unpolished to less unpolished draft, and unfailingly provided constructive, generous, rigorous feedback (talk about scholarly virtues!), as well as encouragement and motivation.

During the time it took me to complete this book, my extended family both grew and shrank. I dearly miss those who are no longer with us, and humbly dedicate the book to their memory. Thank you Nitya, Diya, and Jacob, for your love and support, and for your dignity in the face of great suffering. Leo and Giacomo, here's to a bright future, free of efficient markets and other neoliberal false utopias.

APPENDIX TO CHAPTER 2

Web of Science reports data on 226 articles that cite Eugene Fama's *Foundations of Finance* textbook. Figure A.1 uses cocitation data extracted from those articles to reconstruct the research clusters in which the textbook is highly cited. To produce this figure, I ran a community detection algorithm to identify distinctive research clusters and used Gephi's ForceAtlas routine to map the clusters spatially; further, to make the graph more readable, I filtered out articles with a degree smaller than fifty. The algorithm generated ten clusters; I used Neal Caren's Python script to extract the most frequent keywords in the abstracts of the papers in each cluster. To highlight higher-level similarities across clusters, I investigated the most-cited papers in each cluster and checked whether they shared themes with papers in other clusters, and whether the keywords prevalent in those clusters justified inclusion in a broader research community. As a result, I identified three such instances of broader research communities that the Fama textbook helps keep together. I labeled them "Efficient Markets and Firm Valuation," "Tests of Market Efficiency," and "Statistical Estimation," respectively. The algorithm assigns the textbook to the latter community, where the second most central citation is Harry Markowitz's foundational work on risk and return in optimal portfolios. Keywords useful to characterize this community include *optimization, parameters, mean-variance, robust,* and *estimation.* Fama's textbook gives coherence to this pioneering community by providing a wide-ranging statistical toolkit to financial analysis. The broader, multicluster community I labeled "Tests of Market Efficiency" is the densest and includes several additional contributions by Fama himself: the central focus here, as evidenced by the label,

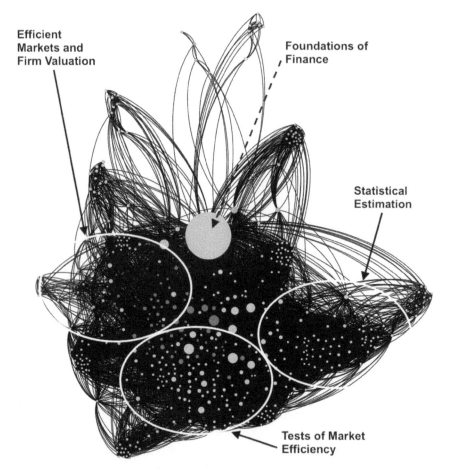

FIGURE A.1   Cocitation network, Fama's *Foundations of Finance*.

is tests of the efficient-market hypothesis. We will detail the evolution of this research community in chapter 4. The research cluster to the left, labeled "Efficient Markets and Firm Valuation," is the largest example of a literature cluster that applies the textbook's toolkit to the solution of practical problems (in this case, assessing the value of a firm; another example is the small cluster at the top that applies the efficiency framework to the problem of mergers and acquisitions). The shape of this cocitation network supports my characterization of the textbook as a document that provides both technical and substantive resources to financial economics, facilitating the growth of a multivocal research community around it.

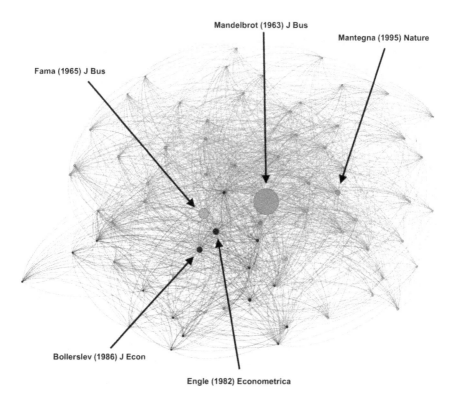

Mandelbrot (1963) J Bus

Mantegna (1995) Nature

Fama (1965) J Bus

Bollerslev (1986) J Econ

Engle (1982) Econometrica

FIGURE A.2   Cocitation network, Mandelbrot 1963.

By way of contrast, figure A.2 displays the cocitation network of Mandelbrot's 1963 classic "The Variation of Certain Speculative Prices," published in the *Journal of Business*. The number of citing papers recorded in Web of Science is much larger (2,029 articles), and this is because the paper, beyond generating a research cluster in financial economics, receives the largest number of citations from physics journals (e.g., *Physica A: Statistical Mechanics and Its Applications, Physical Review E, Journal of Statistical Physics*) and statistics. Overall, the community detection algorithm subdivides the literature into seven communities, which are too fine-grained to identify in the graph. At a higher, more visible level of classification, the area to the right is one dense research community we can label "Econophysics," the new approach to finance originating from the physical sciences. It is centered on Rosario Mantegna and Eugene Stanley's 1995 *Nature* paper titled "Scaling Behaviour in the Dynamics of an Economic Index." On the left, the lower subnetwork is centered on Tim Bollerslev's 1986 paper in the *Journal of Econometrics* titled "Generalized Autoregressive Conditional Heteroskedasticity." Slightly above and to the right, a smaller subnetwork is centered on Robert F. Engle's 1982 paper in *Econometrica* titled "Autoregressive Conditional Heteroscedasticity with Estimates of the Variance of United Kingdom Inflation"; whereas just above that, another subnetwork is centered around Eugene Fama's 1965 paper "The Behavior of Stock Market Prices," published in the *Journal of Business.* Unlike *Foundations*, Mandelbrot's work does not give rise to a cumulative research agenda; citations to it treat it as a methodological rather than a substantive contribution. And in financial economics, Mandelbrot's work is absorbed and superseded by Fama's.

METHODOLOGICAL APPENDIX TO CHAPTER 3

The unit of analysis for the statistical models presented in chapter 3 is the author-year. The sample size varies depending on the journal, ranging from 314 authors published in the *Financial Analysts Journal* to 2,212 authors published in the *Journal of Finance*. For each author, I model the probability that the author will win an award based on a number of variables, summary statistics for which are presented in table 3.1. The awards I track include the Amundi Smith Breeden Prize and the Brattle Group Prize (*Journal of Finance*); the Jensen Prize for Best Papers Published in the *Journal of Financial Economics* in the Areas of Corporate Finance and Organizations; the Fama-DFA Prizes for the Best Papers Published in the *Journal of Financial Economics* in the Areas of Capital Markets and Asset Pricing; the Michael Brennan Prize (*Review of Financial Studies*); the William F. Sharpe Award for Scholarship in Financial Research (*Journal of Financial and Quantitative Analysis*); and the Graham and Dodd Awards of Excellence (*Financial Analysts Journal*). I include second- and third-best paper awards in my count of award winners. For each year, my sample includes authors who have published in the previous one or two years (depending on the selection process for the award under consideration), in the specific area of specialization the award targets. All bibliographic data were coded from Web of Science. Because the dependent variable is dichotomous (0–1), I employ logit regression models with random effects on the author, a set of keyword dummies to control for the topical focus of the paper, and a set of variables measuring a number of theoretically relevant aspects of authors and papers.

Network Measures

To measure the degree of familiarity in collaborations experienced by each author as a function of their involvement in tight networks, I use a measure of familiarity proposed by Newman (2001) and apply it to two different networks. First, I count the number of collaborations each author accumulates in any given year, but weigh each individual collaborator to the degree each dyad of authors has collaborated in the past, and adjust the weight to the number of collaborators on each individual paper. This is a measure of dyadic intimacy, with higher values assigned to scholars who collaborate often with the same people.[1] In the case of financial economics, I draw coauthorship data from a larger sample of the top fifteen journals in the field (Kim, Morse, and Zingales 2009). Drawing from coauthorship network data only, I construct a "familiarity and prestige in collaboration" measure that weighs the familiarity measure developed above with the number of past awards won by each coauthor of the focal author. This variable tracks specifically the extent to which award-winning authors are prized for work they have done in collaboration with other award-winning authors (the Matthew effect). I develop two additional measures in order to operationalize the extent to which collaboration networks are differentiated. The first is a measure of network constraint as proposed and operationalized in Burt (1992, 2004). The second is a new measure that captures how similar the coauthorship network of each author is over time. Specifically, I construct a vector of collaborators for each author-year, sum it over three years to generate a three-year moving average (so as to capture collaborations on projects that take longer than a year), and then calculate the Pearson correlation coefficient for each pair of vectors. The cumulative score over time reflects the degree of similarity in each author's collaboration profile.

Control Variables

I include a dummy for past awards to account for potential Matthew effects operating at the level of the individual. Given the centrality of Eugene Fama's work on efficient markets to the development of the field, I count and accumulate over time the number of citations each author gives Fama's work in his or her published work. In light of Mehrling's (2005) account of the importance (but ultimate neglect) of Fischer Black's scholarship to financial economics, I include a similar measure capturing the number of citations to Fischer Black's work. Given the notorious gender skewness of the field, I also control for the gender of each scholar.

Given the weight that institutional analyses of financial economics give to the University of Chicago as a source of power and resources for financial research, I include two dummy variables coding whether the author is working at the University of Chicago, and whether the author has a PhD from Chicago. I also control for whether the author is affiliated with MIT, a center of financial analysis that historically posed an alternative to Chicago. Finally, I control for each author's length of career by including a variable in the focal journal for the time since first publication. And, to capture the extent to which authors develop their work in a conversation with mainstream economics, I count the cumulative number of citations each author gives to two flagship economics journals: *Econometrica* and the *American Economic Review*.

Notes

1. INTRODUCTION

1. The classic discussion of this concept is Harding 1976.

2. See Reed 2011 for a precise definition of this term.

3. Scholars of creativity such as Richard Swedberg have made this point with regard to theorizing: he argues that while the process of how theories are confirmed or falsified has drawn an enormous amount of scholarly interest, little has been written about the process of creative discovery, or how theories are articulated to begin with (Swedberg 2014). Similarly, I argue that the same move is necessary to better understand the role that data and methods play in the production of knowledge.

4. The classical argument by Thomas Kuhn is still very relevant in this respect. Kuhn (2011) argues that scientific discovery presupposes mastery of a tradition, through which the individual scientist develops an appreciation for the kinds of problems to which an acceptable solution is not available yet, an appreciation for the techniques necessary to tackle such problems, and an appreciation for the techniques necessary to recognize whether a solution is acceptable. Commitment to tradition focuses the attention of scientists on exactly the kinds of puzzles whose solution, Kuhn argues, moves a science forward.

2. THE RHETORIC OF MARKET EFFICIENCY

1. As Fourcade, Ollion, and Algan (2015) note, financial economics comes full circle in the early 1990s when it surpasses statistics as the discipline outside of mainstream economics that economists are most likely to cite in their journals.

2. Paul Samuelson was a renowned MIT economist who was also pioneering the formalization and mathematization of economics, and would go on to win the Nobel Prize in 1970 "for the scientific work through which he has developed static and dynamic economic theory and actively contributed to raising the level of analysis in economic science." "Paul A. Samuelson: Facts," Nobel Prize, Nobel Media AB 2014, accessed March 7, 2017, http://www.nobelprize.org/nobel_prizes/economicsciences/laureates/1970/samuelson -facts.html.

3. The "freshwater" versus "saltwater" distinction was later popularized by Paul Krugman; see especially "'Fresh Water' Economists Gain," *New York Times*, July 23, 1988.

4. See, for instance, Eugene Fama's academic webpage at the University of Chicago Booth School of Business, https://www.chicagobooth.edu/faculty/directory/f/eugene-f -fama, accessed March 7, 2017.

5. This quote is from Fama's autobiographical sketch, available in the Fama/French Forum hosted by the investment firm Dimensional, https://famafrench.dimensional.com /essays/my-life-in-finance.aspx, accessed March 7, 2017.

6. "Eugene F. Fama: Economist," Fama/French Forum, September 9, 2009, https:// famafrench.dimensional.com/videos/eugene-f-fama-economist.aspx.

7. See figures A.1 and A.2 in appendix A for cocitation networks of Fama's textbook and one of Mandelbrot's seminal articles.

8. Thus Jensen (1978) criticizes Watts's (1978) evidence of abnormal returns by arguing that those results hold only for certain years and not others, ignoring Mandelbrot's previous admonition that such findings call for new sampling methods in order to understand

whether they reflect trends undetectable with current tools: "Watts (1978) in his paper 'Systematic "Abnormal" Returns after Quarterly Earnings Announcements' finds statistically significant abnormal returns even after taking all the steps suggested by Ball. He then goes on to provide the first explicit test to determine whether those abnormal returns emanate from market inefficiency or from deficiencies in the asset pricing model. He concludes that the abnormal returns are due to market inefficiencies and not asset pricing model deficiencies. However, the inefficiencies occurred only in the period 1962–1965, and not in the period 1965–1968. Furthermore, after allowance for transactions costs, only a broker could have earned economic profits in the 1962–1965 period" (Jensen 1978, 98).

9. Moreover, Fama himself allowed for the possibility that market efficiency could be stated in a weak, semi-strong, and strong format, but that is a different issue than the underlying understanding of financial processes built into the theory.

3. COLLABORATIONS AND MARKET EFFICIENCY

1. This is a general characteristic of quantitative fields that the sociology of knowledge has also long understood. For instance, we learn from Moody (2004) that sociological research based on quantitative methods is more collaborative than qualitative or historical sociological research. Statistical methods and data analysis require skills that can be developed through rigorous training. Once acquired, however, individual expertise matters less than the collective, accumulated knowledge of the field as a whole.

2. Mike Fortun (2015) similarly argues that if we want to explain the development of a big-data field like postgenomics, it is crucial to understand how scientists came to develop a sense of wonder and surprise toward potentially boring data analysis.

3. Eugene Fama was interviewed by Richard Roll for the American Finance Association's Masters of Finance series. The interview was recorded on August 15, 2008. It is available at https://www.youtube.com/watch?v=tRSaz5TIyno.

4. I looked up the CVs of the two scholars on their academic websites. I should also note that Gruber's CV does not list his collaborators. Moreover, in both of their publicly available CVs, early papers appear to have incomplete information, which I complemented with bibliographic data from Google Scholar and Web of Science.

4. WINNERS AND LOSERS IN FINANCIAL ECONOMICS, OR FAMA VERSUS BLACK

1. In this section, I draw from Mehrling's (2005) masterly biography of Fischer Black.

2. I used Neal Caren's publicly available Python code to construct the dataset, and the open-source software GEPHI to produce the network graphs. Cocitation data are drawn from Web of Science.

3. For instance, in Stewart Myers's words: "Fischer Black's impact on corporate finance is insufficiently noticed. He did not specialize in that subject, and the fame of 'Black–Scholes' has drawn attention from his broader contributions" (in Lehmann 2004, 32). His conclusions: "What were Fischer's contributions to corporate finance? We don't know yet. He left us with too many open questions and unabsorbed ideas. It's wrong to presume to wrap up Fischer's research. So I offer no conclusions" (44). Mehrling reaches similar conclusions about Fischer Black's more general impact on the discipline: in spite of (or better, precisely because of) his steadfast belief in CAPM, "colleagues of Fischer often remark that you never could predict what his position would be on any issue under discussion" (2005, 287).

4. Of course, as we know from Merton, rewards in knowledge production fields are always stratified. Yet, disciplines and fields can still vary in terms of how individualistic or collective their research styles and reward systems are.

5. HOW FINANCIAL ECONOMICS GOT ITS SCIENCE

1. Pointing to the "peculiar combination of respect and suspicion that statistical knowledge has elicited since its institutionalization," Poovey, for instance, investigates the "tensions and contradictions inherent in statistical discourse as it was consolidated in Britain in the first decades of the nineteenth century." This allows her to make a more general point: "As a form of representation, statistics was (and remains) a mixed genre; it juxtaposed numerical, often tabular, formulations to discursive, sometimes historical or explanatory, narratives. The knowledge constituted by statistics was also mixed; it purported to record empirical, objective observations about the social system at the same time that it always embodied and often specifically recommended frankly interested conclusions about social policy and legislation" (Poovey 1993, 258–59).

2. More specifically, after a preliminary analysis, I undersampled articles appearing before 1962 and randomly sampled just over 10 percent of all articles published thereafter. Articles appearing in the early period tend to be split between those that employ no numerical displays or make limited use of tables, and those that make use of graphs. After 1962, the use of text declines and papers begin making use of equations, tables, and graphs.

6. CONCLUSION

1. Thomas Kuhn writes about the opposition between "normal science" and the accumulation of anomalies that lead to scientific revolutions, and in this respect he is echoed by Pierre Bourdieu as he opposes a cultural core to the mavericks that populate the periphery of a field. It is not that these agonistic models are uninformative in the case of financial economics: they are certainly useful in explaining how, once formed, the efficient-market hypothesis turned out to be so difficult to dislodge. But they do not adequately explain how the efficient-market hypothesis got there to begin with: how scholarly consensus emerged about what kind of evidence would be appropriate for the hypothesis to be falsified, what kind of methodology would properly connect theory and data, and what kind of theory would allow the discipline to move forward.

2. Bandelj (2009) articulates a theory of how emotions spur creative practical action in economic transactions that has deep resonance with the argument I am making here. Unlike Bandelj, however, I focus on long-term emotional crystallizations into affect rather than the improvisational effects of emotions.

3. As Sara Ahmed (2014) warns, the danger with attempts to use affect to go "beyond" emotions is the return of the Cartesian divide between body and mind that scholarship on emotions (especially feminist scholarship) had made its primary target. Massumi, for instance, famously distinguishes between emotion as "a subjective content, the sociolinguistic fixing of the quality of an experience which is from that point onward defined as personal," and affect as having "an irreducibly bodily and autonomic nature" (2002, 27). Defined by the intensity of an experience, Massumi adds, affect is "asocial, but not prosocial—it includes social elements but mixes them with elements belonging to other levels of functioning and combines them according to different logic" (28). But Ahmed counters that associating emotions with the personal is problematic as it ignores precisely their "affective" dimension: "Emotions . . . involve bodily processes of affecting and being affected, . . . emotions are a matter of how we come into contact with objects and others" (2014, 208).

4. Pixley (2004) makes a similar argument that in conditions of uncertainty, emotions are a crucial driver of solidarity. But she argues that trust itself should be understood as an emotion, whereas I think it is useful to understand trust as the result of how certain emotions are mobilized, not as an emotion of its own.

APPENDIX B

1. More specifically, the familiarity score for each researcher r is a sum of past collaborations ($\delta = 1$ for each collaboration), weighted by the number of coauthors n_c on each paper τ up to and including present papers. Formally: $\sum_{\tau=1}^{t} \frac{1}{n_{c_\tau}} \sum_{I(r)} \frac{\delta_{ij}^{c_\tau}}{n_{c_\tau} - 1}$. For more technical details, see Lutter 2014.

References

Abbott, Andrew. 2001a. *Chaos of Disciplines*. Chicago: University of Chicago Press.
——. 2001b. *Time Matters*. Chicago: University of Chicago Press.
Abend, Gabriel. 2008. "The Meaning of 'Theory.'" *Sociological Theory* 26 (2): 173–99.
Ahmed, Sara. 2014. *The Cultural Politics of Emotion*. 2nd ed. Edinburgh: Edinburgh University Press.
Alexander, Jennifer Karns. 2008. *The Mantra of Efficiency: From Waterwheel to Social Control*. Baltimore: Johns Hopkins University Press.
Alexander, Sidney. 1961. "Price Movements in Speculative Markets: Trends or Random Walks." *Industrial Management Review* 2: 7–26.
Amabile, Teresa M., and Julianna Pillemer. 2012. "Perspectives on the Social Psychology of Creativity." *Journal of Creative Behavior* 46 (1): 3–15.
Amoore, Louise, and Volha Piotukh. 2015. "Life beyond Big Data: Governing with Little Analytics." *Economy and Society* 44 (3): 341–66.
Anderson, Chris. 2008. "The End of Theory: The Data Deluge Makes the Scientific Method Obsolete." *Wired*, June 23. https://www.wired.com/2008/06/pb-theory/.
Bail, Christopher A. 2014. "The Cultural Environment: Measuring Culture with Big Data." *Theory and Society* 43 (3–4): 465–82.
Bailey, Roy E. 2005. *The Economics of Financial Markets*. New York: Cambridge University Press.
Ball, Ray. 1978. "Anomalies in Relationships between Securities' Yields and Yield-Surrogates." *Journal of Financial Economics* 6 (2–3):103–26.
Bandelj, Nina. 2009. "Emotions in Economic Action and Interaction." *Theory and Society* 38 (4): 347–66.
Banz, Rolf W. 1981. "The Relationship between Return and Market Value of Common Stocks." *Journal of Financial Economics* 9 (1): 3–18.
Barnes, Barry. 1986. "On Authority and Its Relationship to Power." In *Power, Action and Belief: A New Sociology of Knowledge, Sociological Review Monograph*, edited by J. Law, 180–95. London: Routledge & Kegan Paul.
Barnwell, Ashley. 2017. "Durkheim as Affect Theorist." *Journal of Classical Sociology* 18 (1): 21–35.
Bastide, Françoise. 1990. "The Iconography of Scientific Texts: Principles of Analysis." In *Representation in Scientific Practice*, edited by M. Lynch and S. Woolgar, 187–229. Cambridge, MA: MIT Press.
Bazerman, Charles. 1988. *Shaping Written Knowledge: The Genre and Activity of the Experimental Article in Science*. Vol. 356. Madison: University of Wisconsin Press.
Berk, Jonathan, P. DeMarzo, and J. Harford. 2011. *Fundamentals of Corporate Finance*. 2nd ed. Boston: Prentice Hall.
Bernstein, Peter L. 1992. *Capital Ideas: The Improbable Origins of Modern Wall Street*. New York: Free Press.
Bicksler, J. L. 1972. "The State of the Finance Field: A Further Comment." *Journal of Finance* 27 (4): 917.
Black, Fischer. 1982. "The Trouble with Econometric Models." *Financial Analysts Journal* 38 (2): 29–37.

———. 1998. "Beta and Return." In *Streetwise: The Best of the Journal of Portfolio Management*, edited by Peter L. Bernstein and Frank J. Fabozzi, 74–84. Princeton, NJ: Princeton University Press.

Black, Fischer, and Myron Scholes. 1973. "The Pricing of Options and Corporate Liabilities." *Journal of Political Economy* 81 (3): 637–54.

Blackburn, R. 2008. "The Subprime Mortgage Crisis." *New Left Review* 50: 63–106.

Block, Fred, and Margaret R. Somers. 2016. *The Power of Market Fundamentalism: Karl Polanyi's Critique*. Cambridge, MA: Harvard University Press.

Bloor, David. 1991. *Knowledge and Social Imagery*. Chicago: University of Chicago Press.

Bodie, Zvi, Alex Kane, and Alan J. Marcus. 2008. *Investments*. New York: McGraw-Hill/ Irwin.

Bollier, David. 2010. *The Promises and Perils of Big Data*. Aspen: Aspen Institute.

Bourdieu, Pierre. 1993. *The Field of Cultural Production*. New York: Columbia University Press.

boyd, danah, and Kate Crawford. 2012. "Critical Questions for Big Data." *Information, Communication & Society* 15 (5): 662–79.

Brav, Alon, J. B. Heaton, and Alexander Rosenberg. 2004. "The Rational-Behavioral Debate in Financial Economics." *Journal of Economic Methodology* 11 (4): 393–409.

Brayne, Sarah. 2017. "Big Data Surveillance: The Case of Policing." *American Sociological Review* 82 (5): 977–1008.

Brealey, Richard A., and Stewart C. Myers. 2003. *Principles of Corporate Finance*. New York: McGraw-Hill/Irwin.

Breit, William, and Barry T. Hirsch. 2004. *Lives of the Laureates, Fourth Edition: Eighteen Nobel Economists*. 4th ed. Cambridge, MA: MIT Press.

Breslau, Daniel. 1997. "The Political Power of Research Methods: Knowledge Regimes in US Labor-Market Policy." *Theory and Society* 26 (6): 869–902.

Breslau, Daniel, and Yuval Yonay. 1999. "Beyond Metaphor: Mathematical Models in Economics as Empirical Research." *Science in Context* 12 (2): 317–32.

Burawoy, Michael. 1998. "The Extended Case Method." *Sociological Theory* 16 (1): 4–33.

Burt, Ronald S. 1992. *Structural Holes*. Cambridge, MA: Harvard University Press.

———. 2004. "Structural Holes and Good Ideas." *American Journal of Sociology* 110 (2): 349–99.

Çalışkan, Koray, and Michel Callon. 2009. "Economization, Part 1: Shifting Attention from the Economy towards Processes of Economization." *Economy and Society* 38 (3): 369–98.

———. 2010. "Economization, Part 2: A Research Programme for the Study of Markets." *Economy and Society* 39 (1): 1–32.

Callon, Michel. 1998. *Laws of the Markets*. Oxford: Blackwell.

Camic, Charles, Neil Gross, and Michelle Lamont, eds. 2011. *Social Knowledge in the Making*. Chicago: University of Chicago Press.

Camic, Charles, and Yu Xie. 1994. "The Statistical Turn in American Social Science: Columbia University, 1890 to 1915." *American Sociological Review* 59 (5): 773–805.

Campbell, John Y., Andrew W. Lo, A. Craig MacKinlay, and Andrew Y. Lo. 1996. *The Econometrics of Financial Markets*. Princeton, NJ: Princeton University Press.

Cattani, Gino, and Simone Ferriani. 2008. "A Core/Periphery Perspective on Individual Creative Performance: Social Networks and Cinematic Achievements in the Hollywood Film Industry." *Organization Science* 19 (6): 824–44.

Cattani, Gino, Simone Ferriani, and Paul D. Allison. 2014. "Insiders, Outsiders, and the Struggle for Consecration in Cultural Fields: A Core-Periphery Perspective." *American Sociological Review* 79 (2): 258–81.

Chua, Wai Fong. 1995. "Experts, Networks and Inscriptions in the Fabrication of Account-ing Images: A Story of the Representation of Three Public Hospitals." *Accounting, Organizations and Society* 20 (2): 111–45.

Cleveland, William S. 1984. "Graphs in Scientific Publications." *American Statistician* 38 (4): 261–69.

Cole, Stephen. 1983. "The Hierarchy of the Sciences?" *American Journal of Sociology* 89 (1): 111–39.

———. 1992. *Making Science: Between Nature and Society.* Cambridge, MA: Harvard University Press.

Collins, Harry M. 1998. "The Meaning of Data: Open and Closed Evidential Cultures in the Search for Gravitational Waves." *American Journal of Sociology* 104 (2): 293–338.

Collins, Randall. 1984. "Statistics versus Words." *Sociological Theory* 2: 329–62.

———. 1998. *The Sociology of Philosophies.* Cambridge, MA: Harvard University Press.

———. 2004. *Interaction Ritual Chains.* Princeton, NJ: Princeton University Press.

Collins, Randall, and Mauro F. Guillén. 2012. "Mutual Halo Effects in Cultural Produc-tion: The Case of Modernist Architecture." *Theory and Society* 41 (6): 527–56.

Constantinides, George, Milton Harris, and René M. Stulz. 2003. *Handbook of the Econom-ics of Finance: Financial Markets and Asset Pricing.* Amsterdam: Elsevier.

Coopmans, Catelijne, Janet Vertesi, Michael E. Lynch, and Steve Woolgar. 2014. *Repre-sentation in Scientific Practice Revisited.* Cambridge, MA: MIT Press.

Cootner, Paul H. 1964a. "Comments on the Variation of Certain Speculative Prices." In *The Random Character of Stock Market Prices,* edited by P. Cootner, 333–37. Cam-bridge, MA: MIT Press.

———. 1964b. *The Random Character of Stock Market Prices.* Cambridge, MA: MIT Press.

———. 1977. "The Theorems of Modern Finance in a General Equilibrium Setting: Para-doxes Resolved." *Journal of Financial and Quantitative Analysis* 12 (4): 553–62.

Copeland, Thomas E., and John Fred Weston. 1988. *Financial Theory and Corporate Policy.* Vol. 3. Boston: Addison-Wesley.

Cowles, Alfred. 1960. "A Revision of Previous Conclusions Regarding Stock Price Behavior." *Econometrica* 28 (4): 909–15.

Cozzens, Susan E. 1985. "Comparing the Sciences: Citation Context Analysis of Papers from Neuropharmacology and the Sociology of Science." *Social Studies of Science* 15 (1): 127–53.

Crane, Diana. 1969. "Social Structure in a Group of Scientists: A Test of the 'Invisible College' Hypothesis." *American Sociological Review* 34 (3): 335–52.

Daston, Lorraine. 1992. "Objectivity and the Escape from Perspective." *Social Studies of Science* 22 (4): 597–618.

———. 1995. "The Moral Economy of Science." *Osiris* 10 (1): 2–24.

Davis, Gerald F. 2009. *Managed by the Markets.* New York: Oxford University Press.

Dempsey, Mike. 2013. "The Capital Asset Pricing Model (CAPM): The History of a Failed Revolutionary Idea in Finance?" *Abacus* 49: 7–23.

Derman, Emanuel. 2007. *My Life as a Quant: Reflections on Physics and Finance.* Hobo-ken, NJ: John Wiley and Sons.

Diebold, Francis X. 2012. "On the Origin(s) and Development of the Term 'Big Data.'" PIER Working Paper No. 12-037. September 21. https://ssrn.com/abstract=2152421.

Dimson, Elroy, and Massoud Mussavian. 1998. "A Brief History of Market Efficiency." *Euro-pean Financial Management* 4 (1): 91–103.

Durand, David. 1968. "State of the Finance Field: Further Comment." *Journal of Finance* 23 (5): 848–52.

Durkheim, Émile. 1995. *The Elementary Forms of Religious Life.* New York: Free Press.

Eckbo, B. Espen. 2008. *Handbook of Empirical Corporate Finance*. Vols. 1–2. Amsterdam: Elsevier.

Edwards, Franklin R. 1976. "Review of *Interest Rates on Savings Deposits* by Mryon B. Slovin and Marie E. Sushka." *Journal of Finance* 31 (5): 1523–25.

Elton, Edwin J., and Martin J. Gruber. 1972. "Earnings Estimates and the Accuracy of Expectational Data." *Management Science* 18 (8): B409–24.

Elton, Edwin J., Martin J. Gruber, Stephen J. Brown, and William N. Goetzmann. 2006. *Modern Portfolio Theory and Investment Analysis*. 7th ed. Hoboken, NJ: Wiley.

Elton, Edwin J., Martin J. Gruber, and Manfred W. Padberg. 1976. "Simple Criteria for Optimal Portfolio Selection." *Journal of Finance* 31 (5): 1341–57.

Espeland, Wendy Nelson, and Mitchell L. Stevens. 1998. "Commensuration as a Social Process." *Annual Review of Sociology* 24: 313–43.

Fama, Eugene F. 1963. "Mandelbrot and the Stable Paretian Hypothesis." *Journal of Business* 36 (4): 420–29.

——. 1965. "Random Walks in Stock Market Prices." *Financial Analysts Journal* 21 (5): 55–59.

——. 1970. "Efficient Capital Markets: A Review of Theory and Empirical Work." *Journal of Finance* 25 (2): 383–417.

——. 1976a. "Efficient Capital Markets: Reply." *Journal of Finance* 31 (1). 143–45.

——. 1976b. *Foundations of Finance: Portfolio Decisions and Securities Prices*. New York: Basic Books.

——. 1991. "Efficient Capital Markets: II." *Journal of Finance* 46 (5): 1575–617.

Fama, Eugene F., and Kenneth R. French. 1992. "The Cross-Section of Expected Stock Returns." *Journal of Finance* 47 (2): 427–65.

——. 1993. "Common Risk Factors in the Returns on Stocks and Bonds." *Journal of Financial Economics* 33 (1): 3–56.

Fama, Eugene F., and Michael C. Jensen. 1983. "Separation of Ownership and Control." *Journal of Law and Economics* 26 (2): 301–25.

Fama, Eugene F., and James D. MacBeth. 1973. "Risk, Return, and Equilibrium: Empirical Tests." *Journal of Political Economy* 81 (3): 607–36.

Farrell, Michael P. 2003. *Collaborative Circles: Friendship Dynamics and Creative Work*. Chicago: University of Chicago Press.

Fisher, Lawrence, and James H. Lorie. 1964. "Rates of Return on Investments in Common Stocks." *Journal of Business* 37 (1): 1–21.

——. 1968. "Rates of Return on Investments in Common Stock: The Year-by-Year Record, 1926–65." *Journal of Business* 41 (3): 291–316.

Fortun, Mike. 2015. "What Toll Pursuit: Affective Assemblages in Genomics and Postgenomics." In *Postgenomics: Perspectives on Biology after the Genome*, edited by S. S. Richardson and H. Stevens, 32–55. Durham, NC: Duke University Press.

Foster, Jacob G., Andrey Rzhetsky, and James A. Evans. 2015. "Tradition and Innovation in Scientists' Research Strategies." *American Sociological Review* 80 (5): 875–908.

Fourcade, Marion. 2009. *Economists and Societies: Discipline and Profession in the United States, Britain, and France, 1890s to 1990s*. Princeton, NJ: Princeton University Press.

Fourcade, Marion, and Kieran Healy. 2016. "Seeing Like a Market." *Socio-Economic Review* 15 (1): 9–29.

Fourcade, Marion, and Rakesh Khurana. 2013. "From Social Control to Financial Economics: The Linked Ecologies of Economics and Business in Twentieth Century America." *Theory and Society* 42 (2): 121–59.

Fourcade, Marion, Etienne Ollion, and Yann Algan. 2015. "The Superiority of Economists." *Journal of Economic Perspectives* 29 (1): 89–114.

Fox, Justin. 2011. *The Myth of the Rational Market: A History of Risk, Reward, and Delusion on Wall Street*. Reprint ed. New York: HarperBusiness.

French, Craig. 2003. "The Treynor Capital Asset Pricing Model." *Journal of Investment Management* 1 (2): 60–72.

Frickel, Scott, and Neil Gross. 2005. "A General Theory of Scientific/Intellectual Movements." *American Sociological Review* 70 (2): 204–32.

Friedman, Milton. 1953. "The Methodology of Positive Economics." In *Essays in Positive Economics*, 3–43. Chicago: University of Chicago Press.

Fuchs, Stephan. 2001. *Against Essentialism: A Theory of Culture and Society*. Cambridge, MA: Harvard University Press.

Fullbrook, Edward. 2004. *A Guide to What's Wrong with Economics*. New York: Anthem Press.

Galison, Peter. 1988. "History, Philosophy, and the Central Metaphor." *Science in Context* 2 (1): 197–212.

Galison, Peter, and Caroline A. Jones. 2014. *Picturing Science, Producing Art*. London: Routledge.

Garber, Marjorie. 2002. "Our Genius Problem." *The Atlantic*, December.

Garfinkel, Harold. 1960. "The Rational Properties of Scientific and Common Sense Activities." *Behavioral Science* 5 (1): 72–83.

——. 1988. "Evidence for Locally Produced, Naturally Accountable Phenomena of Order, Logic, Reason, Meaning, Method, etc. in and as of the Essential Quiddity of Immortal Ordinary Society (I of IV): An Announcement of Studies." *Sociological Theory* 6 (1): 103–9.

Gelman, Andrew, Cristian Pasarica, and Rahul Dodhia. 2002. "Let's Practice What We Preach: Turning Tables into Graphs." *American Statistician* 56 (2): 121–30.

Giddens, Anthony. 1990. *The Consequences of Modernity*. Vol. 18. Cambridge: Polity Press.

Gieryn, Thomas F. 1983. "Boundary-Work and the Demarcation of Science from Non-Science: Strains and Interests in Professional Ideologies of Scientists." *American Sociological Review* 48 (6): 781–95.

Gitelman, Lisa. 2013. *Raw Data Is an Oxymoron*. Cambridge, MA: MIT Press.

Gmür, Markus. 2003. "Co-citation Analysis and the Search for Invisible Colleges: A Methodological Evaluation." *Scientometrics* 57 (1): 27–57.

Goede, Marieke de. 2005. *Virtue, Fortune, and Faith: A Genealogy of Finance*. Minneapolis: University of Minnesota Press.

Goffman, Erving. 1983. "The Interaction Order: American Sociological Association, 1982 Presidential Address." *American Sociological Review* 48 (1):1–17.

Gooday, Graeme. 2004. *The Morals of Measurement: Accuracy, Irony, and Trust in Late Victorian Electrical Practice*. Cambridge: Cambridge University Press.

Hacking, Ian. 1983. *Representing and Intervening: Introductory Topics in the Philosophy of Natural Science*. Cambridge: Cambridge University Press.

——. 1984. *The Emergence of Probability: A Philosophical Study of Early Ideas about Probability, Induction and Statistical Inference*. Cambridge: Cambridge University Press.

Hammond, Daniel. 1990. "McCloskey's Modernism and Friedman's Methodology: A Case Study with New Evidence." *Review of Social Economy* 48 (2):158–71.

——. 1992. "An Interview with Milton Friedman on Methodology." *Philosophy and Methodology of Economics* 1: 216–38.

Hands, D. Wade. 2003. "Did Milton Friedman's Methodology License the Formalist Revolution?" *Journal of Economic Methodology* 10 (4): 507–20.

Hardin, Russell. 2002. *Trust and Trustworthiness*. New York: Russell Sage Foundation Publications.

Harding, Sandra. 1976. *Can Theories Be Refuted? Essays on the Duhem-Quine Thesis.* Boston: D. Reidel.

Hargens, Lowell L. 2000. "Using the Literature: Reference Networks, Reference Contexts, and the Social Structure of Scholarship." *American Sociological Review* 65 (6): 846–65.

Heck, Jean Louis, and Philip L. Cooley. 1988. "Most Frequent Contributors to the Finance Literature." *Financial Management* 17 (3): 100–108.

Heritage, John. 1984. *Garfinkel and Ethnomethodology.* Cambridge: Polity Press.

Houthakker, Hendrik, and Peter J. Williamson. 1996. *The Economics of Financial Markets.* New York: Oxford University Press.

Huang, Chi-fu, and Robert H. Litzenberger. 1988. *Foundations for Financial Economics.* Amsterdam: North-Holland.

Hudson, John. 1996. "Trends in Multi-authored Papers in Economics." *Journal of Economic Perspectives* 10 (3): 153–58.

Hull, John C. 2005. *Options, Futures and Other Derivatives.* 6th ed. Boston: Prentice Hall.

Jasanoff, Sheila. 2004. *States of Knowledge: The Co-production of Science and the Social Order.* London: Routledge.

Jensen, Michael C. 1978. "Some Anomalous Evidence Regarding Market Efficiency." *Journal of Financial Economics* 6 (2–3): 95–101.

Jovanovic, Franck. 2008. "The Construction of the Canonical History of Financial Economics." *History of Political Economy* 40 (2): 213–42.

Jovanovic, Franck, and Christophe Schinckus. 2013. "Econophysics: A New Challenge for Financial Economics?" *Journal of the History of Economic Thought* 35 (3): 319–52.

——. 2016. *Econophysics and Financial Economics: An Emerging Dialogue.* New York: Oxford University Press.

Kettell, Brian. 2001. *Economics for Financial Markets.* Oxford: Butterworth-Heinemann.

Keys, Phyllis, and Pamela A. Turner. 2006. "Women as Finance Academics: Role Models and Researchers." *Journal of Financial Education* 32: 1–19.

Kim, E. Han, Adair Morse, and Luigi Zingales. 2009. "Are Elite Universities Losing Their Competitive Edge?" *Journal of Financial Economics* 93 (3): 353–81.

Knorr Cetina, Karin. 2009. *Epistemic Cultures: How the Sciences Make Knowledge.* Cambridge, MA: Harvard University Press.

Knorr Cetina, Karin, and Urs Bruegger. 2002. "Global Microstructures: The Virtual Societies of Financial Markets." *American Journal of Sociology* 107 (4): 905–50.

Knorr Cetina, Karin, Theodore R. Schatzki, and Eike von Savigny. 2005. *The Practice Turn in Contemporary Theory.* New York: Routledge.

Kohler, Robert E. 1994. *Lords of the Fly: Drosophila Genetics and the Experimental Life.* Chicago: University of Chicago Press.

Kuhn, Thomas S. 2011. *The Essential Tension: Selected Studies in Scientific Tradition and Change.* Chicago: University of Chicago Press.

Laney, Doug. 2001. *3D Data Management: Controlling Data Volume, Velocity, and Variety.* META Group, February 6. http://blogs.gartner.com/doug-laney/files/2012/01/ad949 -3D-Data-Management-Controlling-Data-Volume-Velocity-and-Variety.pdf.

Lang, Gladys Engel, and Kurt Lang. 1988. "Recognition and Renown: The Survival of Artistic Reputation." *American Journal of Sociology* 94 (1): 79–109.

Latour, Bruno. 1986. "Visualization and Cognition: Drawing Things Together." In *Knowledge and Society: Studies in the Sociology of Culture Past and Present,* vol. 6, edited by H. Kuklick, 1–40. London: JAI Press.

——. 1987. *Science in Action: How to Follow Scientists and Engineers through Society.* Cambridge, MA: Harvard University Press.

Latour, Bruno, and Steve Woolgar. 1986. *Laboratory Life: The Construction of Scientific Facts.* Princeton, NJ: Princeton University Press.

Leahey, Erin. 2005. "Alphas and Asterisks: The Development of Statistical Significance Testing Standards in Sociology." *Social Forces* 84 (1): 1–24.

——. 2008. "Methodological Memes and Mores: Toward a Sociology of Social Research." *Annual Review of Sociology* 34 (1): 33–53.

Leamer, Edward E. 1983. "Let's Take the Con out of Econometrics." *American Economic Review* 73 (1): 31–43.

Lehmann, Bruce. 2004. *The Legacy of Fischer Black*. New York: Oxford University Press.

LeRoy, Stephen F. 1976. "Efficient Capital Markets: Comment." *Journal of Finance* 31 (1): 139–41.

Lo, Andrew W., and A. Craig MacKinlay. 2002. *A Non-random Walk down Wall Street*. Princeton, NJ: Princeton University Press.

Lorie, James H. 1965. *Current Controversies on the Stock Market*. Vol. 20. Chicago: University of Chicago, Selected Papers, Graduate School of Business.

——. 1966. "Some Comments on Recent Quantitative and Formal Research on the Stock Market." *Journal of Business* 39 (1): 107–10.

Lutter, Mark. 2014. "Creative Success and Network Embeddedness: Explaining Critical Recognition of Film Directors in Hollywood, 1900–2010." Max Planck Institute for the Study of Societies (MPIfG) Discussion Paper 14 (11). July 9. https://ssrn.com/abstract=2464150.

Lynch, Michael. 1988. "The Externalized Retina: Selection and Mathematization in the Visual Documentation of Objects in the Life Sciences." *Human Studies* 11 (2/3): 201–34.

MacKenzie, Donald. 2003. "Long-Term Capital Management and the Sociology of Arbitrage." *Economy and Society* 32 (3): 349.

——. 2006. *An Engine, Not a Camera*. Cambridge, MA: MIT Press.

——. 2011. "The Credit Crisis as a Problem in the Sociology of Knowledge." *American Journal of Sociology* 116 (6): 1778–841.

MacKenzie, Donald, and Yuval Millo. 2003. "Constructing a Market, Performing Theory: The Historical Sociology of a Financial Derivatives Exchange." *American Journal of Sociology* 109 (1): 107–45.

MacKenzie, Donald, Fabian Muniesa, and Lucia Siu, eds. 2007. *Do Economists Make Markets? On the Performativity of Economics*. Princeton, NJ: Princeton University Press.

Mandelbrot, Benoit. 1967. "The Variation of Some Other Speculative Prices." *Journal of Business* 40 (4): 393–413.

——. 1969. "Long-Run Linearity, Locally Gaussian Process, H-Spectra and Infinite Variances." *International Economic Review* 10 (1): 82–111.

Massumi, Brian. 2002. *Parables for the Virtual: Movement, Affect, Sensation*. Durham, NC: Duke University Press.

Mayers, David, and Edward M. Rice. 1979. "Measuring Portfolio Performance and the Empirical Content of Asset Pricing Models." *Journal of Financial Economics* 7 (1): 3–28.

McCloskey, Deirdre N. 1998. *The Rhetoric of Economics*. Madison: University of Wisconsin Press.

Megill, Allan. 1994. *Rethinking Objectivity*. Durham, NC: Duke University Press.

Mehrling, Perry. 2005. *Fischer Black and the Revolutionary Idea of Finance*. Hoboken, NJ: John Wiley and Sons.

Merton, Robert K. 1973. *The Sociology of Science: Theoretical and Empirical Investigations*. Chicago: University of Chicago Press.

Meulbroek, Lisa K. 1992. "An Empirical Analysis of Illegal Insider Trading." *Journal of Finance* 47 (5): 1661–99.

Meyer, Joachim, Marcia Kuskin Shamo, and Daniel Gopher. 1999. "Information Structure and the Relative Efficacy of Tables and Graphs." *Human Factors* 41 (4): 570–87.

Mirowski, Philip. 1990a. "From Mandelbrot to Chaos in Economic Theory." *Southern Economic Journal* 57 (2): 289–307.

——. 1990b. "Learning the Meaning of a Dollar: Conservation Principles and the Social Theory of Value in Economic Theory." *Social Research* 57 (3): 689–717.

——. 1991. *More Heat Than Light: Economics as Social Physics, Physics as Nature's Economics.* Cambridge: Cambridge University Press.

——. 1995. "Three Ways to Think about Testing in Econometrics." *Journal of Econometrics* 67 (1): 25–46.

——. 2001. *Machine Dreams: Economics Becomes a Cyborg Science.* Cambridge: Cambridge University Press.

Mirowski, Philip, and Dieter Plehwe, eds. 2009. *The Road from Mont Pelerin: The Making of the Neoliberal Thought Collective.* Cambridge, MA: Harvard University Press.

Modigliani, Franco, and Merton H. Miller. 1958. "The Cost of Capital, Corporation Finance and the Theory of Investment." *American Economic Review* 48 (3): 261–97.

Moody, James. 2004. "The Structure of a Social Science Collaboration Network: Disciplinary Cohesion from 1963 to 1999." *American Sociological Review* 69 (2): 213–38.

Mullins, Nicholas C. 1972. "The Development of a Scientific Specialty: The Phage Group and the Origins of Molecular Biology." *Minerva* 10 (1): 51–82.

Mullins, Nicholas C., Lowell L. Hargens, Pamela K. Hecht, and Edward L. Kick. 1977. "The Group Structure of Cocitation Clusters: A Comparative Study." *American Sociological Review* 42 (4): 552–62.

Newman, M. E. J. 2001. "Scientific Collaboration Networks. Ii. Shortest Paths, Weighted Networks, and Centrality." *Physical Review E* 64 (1): 016132.

NobelPrize.org. 2013. "Eugene F. Fama: Facts." Accessed October 20, 2019. https://www.nobelprize.org/prizes/economic-sciences/2013/fama/facts/.

Overtveldt, Johan Van. 2009. *The Chicago School: How the University of Chicago Assembled the Thinkers Who Revolutionized Economics and Business.* Evanston, IL: Agate B2.

Panofsky, Aaron. 2014. *Misbehaving Science: Controversy and the Development of Behavior Genetics.* Chicago: University of Chicago Press.

Parker, John N., and Edward J. Hackett. 2012. "Hot Spots and Hot Moments in Scientific Collaborations and Social Movements." *American Sociological Review* 77 (1): 21–44.

Pasquale, Frank. 2015. *The Black Box Society: The Secret Algorithms That Control Money and Information.* Cambridge, MA: Harvard University Press.

Peterson, David. 2015. "All That Is Solid: Bench-Building at the Frontiers of Two Experimental Sciences." *American Sociological Review* 80 (6): 1201–25.

Pinch, Trevor J., and Richard Swedberg. 2008. *Living in a Material World: Economic Sociology Meets Science and Technology Studies.* Cambridge, MA: MIT Press.

Pixley, Jocelyn. 2004. *Emotions in Finance: Distrust and Uncertainty in Global Markets.* Cambridge: Cambridge University Press.

Poitras, Geoffrey, and Franck Jovanovic. 2010. "Pioneers of Financial Economics: Das Adam Smith Irrelevanzproblem?" *History of Economics Review* Winter (51): 43–64.

Polillo, Simone. 2013. *Conservatives versus Wildcats: A Sociology of Financial Conflict.* Stanford, CA: Stanford University Press.

Polonchek, John A., Myron B. Slovin, and Marie E. Sushka. 1986. "Tender-Offer Premia as a Management Signal." *Managerial and Decision Economics* 7 (1): 69–76.

Poovey, Mary. 1993. "Figures of Arithmetic, Figures of Speech: The Discourse of Statistics in the 1830s." *Critical Inquiry* 19 (2): 256–76.

——. 1998. *A History of the Modern Fact: Problems of Knowledge in the Sciences of Wealth and Society.* Chicago: University of Chicago Press.

Porter, Theodore. 1995. *Trust in Numbers: The Pursuit of Objectivity in Science and Public Life.* Princeton, NJ: Princeton University Press.

Preda, Alex. 2002. "Financial Knowledge, Documents, and the Structures of Financial Activities." *Journal of Contemporary Ethnography* 31 (2): 207–39.

———. 2009. *Framing Finance: The Boundaries of Markets and Modern Capitalism*. Chicago: University of Chicago Press.

Pye, Gordon. 1968. "State of the Finance Field: Reply." *Journal of Finance* 23 (5): 853–56.

Read, Colin. 2013. *The Efficient Market Hypothesists: Bachelier, Samuelson, Fama, Ross, Tobin and Shiller*. Basingstoke, UK: Palgrave Macmillan.

Reay, Michael J. 2012. "The Flexible Unity of Economics." *American Journal of Sociology* 118 (1): 45–87.

Reed, Isaac Ariail. 2011. *Interpretation and Social Knowledge*. Chicago: Chicago University Press.

Renfro, Charles G. 2009. *The Practice of Econometric Theory: An Examination of the Characteristics of Econometric Computation*. Berlin: Springer-Verlag.

Roll, Richard. 1977. "A Critique of the Asset Pricing Theory's Tests Part I: On Past and Potential Testability of the Theory." *Journal of Financial Economics* 4 (2): 129–76.

———. 1979. "A Reply to Mayers and Rice (1979)." *Journal of Financial Economics* 7 (4): 391–400.

Ross, S. A., R. W. Westerfield, and J. Jaffe. 2008. *Corporate Finance*. New York: McGraw Hill/Irwin.

Rossman, Gabriel, Nicole Esparza, and Phillip Bonacich. 2010. "I'd Like to Thank the Academy, Team Spillovers, and Network Centrality." *American Sociological Review* 75 (1): 31–51.

Ruef, Martin, Howard Aldrich, and Nancy M. Carter. 2003. "The Structure of Founding Teams: Homophily, Strong Ties, and Isolation among U.S. Entrepreneurs." *American Sociological Review* 68 (2): 195–222.

Samuels, Warren J., Jeff E. Biddle, and Ross B. Emmett. 2008. *Research in the History of Economic Thought and Methodology*. West Yorkshire, UK: Emerald Group.

Sanjek, Roger. 1990. *Fieldnotes: The Makings of Anthropology*. Ithaca, NY: Cornell University Press.

Sauvain, Harry. 1967. "The State of the Finance Field: Comment." *Journal of Finance* 22 (4): 541–42.

Sawyer, R. Keith. 2012. *Explaining Creativity: The Science of Human Innovation*. New York: Oxford University Press.

Scheff, T. J. 1994. *Microsociology: Discourse, Emotion, and Social Structure*. Chicago: University of Chicago Press.

Scott, James C. 1990. *Domination and the Arts of Resistance: Hidden Transcripts*. New Haven, CT: Yale University Press.

Shapin, Steven. 1989. "The Invisible Technician." *American Scientist* 77 (6): 554–63.

———. 1994. *A Social History of Truth: Civility and Science in Seventeenth-Century England*. Chicago: University of Chicago Press.

Shwed, Uri, and Peter S. Bearman. 2010. "The Temporal Structure of Scientific Consensus Formation." *American Sociological Review* 75 (6): 817–40.

Simonton, Dean Keith. 2004. "Psychology's Status as a Scientific Discipline: Its Empirical Placement within an Implicit Hierarchy of the Sciences." *Review of General Psychology* 8 (1): 59–67.

Skocpol, Theda. 1978. *State and Social Revolutions*. Cambridge: Cambridge University Press.

Slobodian, Quinn. 2018. *Globalists: The End of Empire and the Birth of Neoliberalism*. Cambridge, MA: Harvard University Press.

Slovin, Myron B., and Marie E. Sushka. 1993. "Ownership Concentration, Corporate Control Activity, and Firm Value: Evidence from the Death of Inside Blockholders." *Journal of Finance* 48 (4): 1293–321.

Smith, Laurence D., Lisa A. Best, D. Alan Stubbs, Andrea Bastiani Archibald, and Roxann Roberson-Nay. 2002. "Constructing Knowledge: The Role of Graphs and Tables in Hard and Soft Psychology." *American Psychologist* 57 (10): 749–61.

Smith, Laurence D., Lisa A. Best, D. Alan Stubbs, John Johnston, and Andrea Bastiani Archibald. 2000. "Scientific Graphs and the Hierarchy of the Sciences: A Latourian Survey of Inscription Practices." *Social Studies of Science* 30 (1): 73–94.

Smith, Tom, and Kathleen Walsh. 2013. "Why the CAPM Is Half-Right and Everything Else Is Wrong." *Abacus* 49: 73–78.

Spigelman, Joseph H. 1969. "The Data Service Industry." *Financial Analysts Journal* 25 (3): 88–99.

Steinmetz, George. 2005. *The Politics of Method in the Human Sciences: Positivism and Its Epistemological Others.* Durham, NC: Duke University Press.

Summers, Lawrence H. 1985. "On Economics and Finance." *Journal of Finance* 40 (3): 633–35.

Summers-Effler, Erika. 2010. *Laughing Saints and Righteous Heroes: Emotional Rhythms in Social Movement Groups.* Chicago: University of Chicago Press.

Swedberg, Richard. 2014. *Theorizing in Social Science: The Context of Discovery.* Stanford, CA: Stanford University Press.

Thorsten, Hens, IV, and Klaus Reiner Schenk-Hoppe, eds. 2009. *Handbook of Financial Markets: Dynamics and Evolution.* Amsterdam: North Holland.

Tilly, Charles. 1998. *Durable Inequality.* Berkeley: University of California Press.

Traweek, Sharon. 2009. *Beamtimes and Lifetimes.* Cambridge, MA: Harvard University Press.

Treynor, Jack L. 1987. "Market Efficiency and the Bean Jar Experiment." *Financial Analysts Journal* 43 (3): 50–53.

Turner, Stephen. 1998. "Did Funding Matter to the Development of Research Methods in Sociology?" *Minerva* 36: 69–79.

Uzzi, Brian, and Jarrett Spiro. 2005. "Collaboration and Creativity: The Small World Problem." *American Journal of Sociology* 111 (2): 447–504.

Vedres, Balázs, and David Stark. 2010. "Structural Folds: Generative Disruption in Overlapping Groups." *American Journal of Sociology* 115 (4): 1150–90.

Vernimmen, Pierre, and Pascal Quiry. 2009. *Corporate Finance: Theory and Practice.* Malden, MA: John Wiley & Sons.

Watts, Ross L. 1978. "Systematic 'Abnormal' Returns after Quarterly Earnings Announcements." *Journal of Financial Economics* 6 (2): 127–50.

Weininger, Elliot B., Annette Lareau, and Omar Lizardo, eds. 2018. *Ritual, Emotion, Violence: Studies on the Micro-Sociology of Randall Collins.* New York: Routledge.

Weston, J. Fred. 1967. "The State of the Finance Field." *Journal of Finance* 22 (4): 539–40.

——. 1974. "New Themes in Finance." *Journal of Finance* 29 (1): 237–43.

Whitley, Richard. 1986a. "The Rise of Modern Financial Theory." *Research in the History of Economic Thought and Methodology* 4: 148–78.

——. 1986b. "The Transformation of Business Finance into Financial Economics: The Roles of Academic Expansion and Changes in U.S. Capital Markets." *Accounting, Organizations and Society* 11 (2): 171–92.

——. 2000. *The Intellectual and Social Organization of the Sciences.* Oxford: Oxford University Press.

Yonay, Yuval P. 1998. *The Struggle over the Soul of Economics: Institutionalist and Neoclassical Economists in America between the Wars.* Princeton, NJ: Princeton University Press.

Zald, Mayer N. 1995. "Progress and Cumulation in the Human Sciences after the Fall." *Sociological Forum* 10: 455–79.

Index

Page numbers in *italics* indicate illustrations.

Lightning Source UK Ltd.
Milton Keynes UK
UKHW040251040720
366021UK00002B/180/J